C000161410

Prince of the Ring

Prince of the Ring

The Naseem Hamed Story

Gavin Evans

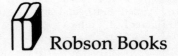 Robson Books

To Tessa, Caitlin and Pat

First published in Great Britain in 1996 by Robson Books Ltd, Bolsover House, 5–6 Clipstone Street, London W1P 8LE

Copyright © 1996 Gavin Evans

The right of Gavin Evans to be identified as author of this work has been asserted by him in accordance with the Copyright, Designs and Patents Act 1988

British Library Cataloguing in Publication Data
A catalogue record for this title is available from the British Library

ISBN 1 86105 021 6

Photoset in North Wales by Derek Doyle & Associates, Mold, Clwyd. Printed and bound in Great Britain by Butler & Tanner Ltd, Frome.

Contents

Acknowledgements

I would particularly like to thank the following people and organisations for their assistance: John Perlman, Brendan Ingle, John Ingle, Graham Hicking and the libraries of Sheffield Newspapers Limited, the *Yorkshire Post* and *Boxing News*.

A total of 87 interviews were conducted for this book, in addition to numerous informal discussions, press conferences and written submissions.

Reference books and publications which proved particularly useful for cross checking background information included: *British Boxing Records* (compiled by Bob Mee), 1995 and 1996 editions; *Ringside with the Amateurs*, by David Prior, 1995; *Computer Boxing Update* (Ralph Citro Inc, 1993 and 1995 editions); *The Ring Boxing Encyclopedia and Record Book*, 1974 edition; *Boxing News* (1987–1996); *Boxing Monthly* (1993–1996); the *Sheffield Star* (1986–1996).

Newspaper and magazine stories by the author included: 'The artist currently known as Prince', *Men's Health*, January/February 1996; 'The Prince who would be King', *SA Sports Illustrated*, November 1995; 'Hamed warns Bungu: "Three rounds and you're gone!",' *Boxing World*, September 1995; 'I can't wait to sort Naz out, boasts Bungu', *Boxing News*, 18 August 1995; 'Face to Face with Robbo', *Boxing News*, 22/29

December 1995; 'Prince Naseem: the artist currently known as', *Arena*, December 1995; 'Why Naz flipped over Ryan', *Boxing News*, 2 February 1996. Others were interviewed for the author's London Diary column in *Boxing World* magazine and for *Ikon* Magazine, which was closed by its publishers prior to publication of the story.

Introduction

When I was growing up my father told me the greatest fighter who ever set foot on this earth was Sugar Ray Robinson.

Sugar Ray – the original, forties and fifties master – could do it all: dance and slug, knock you out going backwards, take trip-hammer blows without breaking *and* he was smart and pretty to boot. Watching those old black-and-white re-runs of his battles as a child, I was inspired to box, and kept at it, on and off, for over a decade, finally 'retiring' at the age of twenty-two, after which I preferred to write about other men taking their shots, rather than absorbing any more myself (though, like so many other boxing writers, I once made the painful mistake of trying my luck with a world-rated professional).

Of course it had not taken me very long to realize that the only time I could ever be a Sugar Ray Robinson was in my shadow-boxing dreams, but then I thought there never could be another Sugar Ray – not even the superb Ray Leonard could quite match the brilliance of the original master. On that score, I knew, for once, my father was right: until I saw Naseem Hamed in action.

Well, all right, that may be overstating things a little. It probably sounds somewhat ludicrous to suggest a valid comparison between a novice, then still not out of his teens, and

1

the finest fighter the world has ever seen. Rather, it was a case of seeing the astonishing talent this young man had, and realizing that it was possible that in his little body and head lay potential of the kind that Britain and perhaps the world had never seen. Later, watching Hamed cruelly humiliating the world class Vincenzo Belcastro, and then destroying other highly rated fighters like Freddy Cruz and Sergio Liendo, it seemed to me the future had, indeed, arrived.

I remember watching from ringside in Shepton Mallet when, in a display of stunning flair and power, Hamed destroyed the tough Mexican fringe contender Enrique Angeles, and thinking that I had never, in twenty-five years of following this strange sport, seen anyone with this level of natural ability. I had been in the United States in 1978 to watch the young Sugar Ray Leonard and in 1986 to see the budding Mike Tyson, but neither of them compared, at least not in terms of capacity for future greatness.

Soon after, Hamed's manager/trainer Brendan Ingle told me how Naseem used to imagine he was Muhammad Ali, Sugar Ray Leonard and, yes, Sugar Ray Robinson, when he was shadow-boxing. But he didn't stop there. The Alis and Sugar Rays were not confined to his dreams – he was living these dreams out and going several steps further. Ingle, in fact, honestly believed he was already there with the gods – and this from a man in his late middle age who worships both Robinson and Ali.

After watching Hamed knocking the socks off men twice his size in sparring, discovering that the legends about him beating up heavyweights were true, and seeing more of his astonishing acrobatic grace, middleweight power, almost psychic reflexes, hand-eye coordination, time-distance perception and instinct for the kill, it seemed this young man's predictions that he would win world titles at three, four or five weights were unduly modest.

I was rattling on in this manner at a dinner party, after watching Hamed despatch yet another world class fighter, Juan Polo Perez, when a friend and fellow sportswriter, John Perlman, suggested that if what I had to say was remotely close to the mark, then it was not too early to write a book on him.

At first the idea seemed far-fetched: Hamed was, after all, only twenty-one and had not yet won a world title of any description. But at the same time, even at this stage, he seemed to have transcended his sport, attracting advertising contracts by the dozen, constantly being featured on television chat shows and in glossy magazines, drawing younger, trendier punters to the sport and building a reputation for himself as a kind of fashion icon, a music fundi, a snooker whizz, a nightclub regular, and also managing to establish a multi-faceted identity that included being British, Yemeni, Arab, Muslim, black and a son of Sheffield. And I knew from having interviewed him in depth for magazines as varied as *Arena* and *Boxing World*, that he had a very good story to tell.

Part of his allure was the non-stop tattoo of over-the-top verbiage, the impish humour, occasionally hinting at self-parody, the marvellously kitsch displays of style he would come up with and the superb promotional job his people were doing for him. But featherweights don't draw flies in Britain, let alone ten million viewers for a minor fight, unless they can do the business, and it was hard to escape the impression that the boxer still known as Prince could do the business better than any I had ever seen.

After returning from Cardiff where I'd watched him degrade and then crush Steve Robinson, I interviewed him again for various magazines and my last residues of doubt disappeared. By then I had heard the best and the worst about him, but from everything I had seen in the ring and in the gym, and from all he and those around him had told me, it seemed almost inconceivable that he would not deliver in something close to the terms he had set out – barring a chance collision with an 18 wheeler in his new Porsche (and even then I'm not sure I'd bet on the lorry).

Eventually, the book was begun. It has to be said that the boxer would have preferred to leave more time to posterity (and to allow his profile and selling power to grow even bigger) before becoming a biographical subject. This book is therefore not an official biography, but after eighty-six interviews with sixty people, other than those with Naseem himself, the picture of his life has become a good deal clearer.

Boxing, as Brendan Ingle puts it, can be a 'filthy, rotten game'. It is also an extremely brutal game which rewards and honours one thing above all others: the ability to fight. The best fighters are not often the best people, though they are not necessarily the worst either. At the human level, his sport has produced its share of villains and a few heroes too, and so far Naseem Hamed is neither. What counts is that he is one helluva boxer, and that he can put bums on sofas.

What these two qualities bring are the things that count most for the Prince himself. His aims are to be the greatest boxer who ever lived – better than Ali, better than Sugar Ray, to win a clutch of world titles, to earn £40 million (or maybe £400 million), and to retire, undefeated, with his bucks and his marbles still intact. After that, he talks vaguely of a future in religion, or perhaps a career in show business.

It's all an extremely tall order in this sport where young men grow old very quickly, often without realizing it.

Naseem believes he is different – that he has learnt from the mistakes of boxing's past and, perhaps, that he doesn't really need to learn. He has a will to succeed in his own, immodest terms, which is extraordinary to witness, and has an absolute faith in his destiny. This all helps to make him completely fearless when climbing through the ropes. He is, genuinely, very different from any other boxer I have ever interviewed, spoken to or watched, and this is what makes him such an interesting subject.

It is a bit early to tell whether what is written for him is to be a legend, as he puts it, but the journey will definitely be worth watching.

1

Champion of the Known World

Try to imagine what it was like being inside Naseem Hamed's 21-year-old skin just before the ring steward said it was time to walk down the aisle to fight the world champion.

Ever since you first laced on a pair of sparring mitts in a sweaty church hall 14 years earlier you've known with absolute certainty that you have been chosen for greatness; that you are someone very special; that God has given you this immeasurable talent and that your destiny is to be the greatest fighter ever to walk this earth. It's not something you thought *may* be or that you've gradually come to appreciate; from the start you've just known it and nothing that has happened since has given you the slightest moment of doubt.

Now the laughing and joking and dancing in the dressing room is over and it's time to focus, to shut out the distractions and taste the next hour. And it feels good. A few minutes more

to wait and then, at last, after a year of frustration, it will be time
to deliver and time to collect.

You'll strut your stuff, perform, jive to your song and smile at
his, somersault over those ropes. They'll boo and hiss, spit and
throw things and then, when the bell rings, you'll make those
bastards eat dirt. You'll compel the doubters to pay homage.
You'll force stubborn Steve Robinson to submit to your will.
You'll make him miss and make him pay and then finish him in
four. You'll prove to the world that you are Allah's own fighter –
the finest on the planet. And when it's done, your month of
abstinence will be over and you'll hit the highway and then
dance the night away.

For Naseem Hamed boxing is all about exhilaration. Yes, of
course, there are also the dimensions of achievement, competition, domination, vindication, the glorification of self and God,
money, status, power, sex and a whole lot more, but most of all
it's a thing of pure pleasure. Like no other boxer since
Muhammad Ali in his prime, here is young man who just adores
the thrill of the ride. It's 'The Prince's' idea of fun – vindictive,
cruel fun, but fun nevertheless – and this is a major dimension of
what makes him such a compelling figure.

Before every fight, but particularly the big ones, he carries
within him a mixture of the anticipation of a long-withheld
present – like a child who has had to wait almost a year for his
birthday to arrive and wishes those last days would hurry up –
and a spot of irritation with those who've been trying to get in
the way of destiny. Naseem holds glittery baubles like world title
belts in inordinately high regard, but before the Robinson fight
he'd had a frustrating time trying to get one – being given the
run around by the champions in his weight class – his people
finally having to pull strings to get a shot at a bigger champion
from a lesser international control body, who just happened to
be from the same promotional group.

For a long time Hamed knew he would one day do business
with Steve Robinson, and though he would have preferred to
pick up a couple other titles first, it was a prospect he always
relished. 'I basically knew he was there to be taken,' he says. 'I
watched him box five times and I saw through his style and knew

he was perfect – he was made for me.'

And he showed no compunction about letting Robinson know this as part of a long psychological battle he waged against this potential rival. He views the war of wits in the run-up to a fight as being of crucial importance to breaking down an opponent's confidence – but more pertinently, it's just his way. Anyone who emerges as a potential rival is an object fit for derision.

His opening jab at Robinson came after he had won every round against Vincenzo Belcastro for the European bantamweight title seventeen months earlier. Robinson praised his effort and Naseem cheekily retorted he too would one day be getting the treatment, and after that he never lost an opportunity to denigrate his potential rival calling him 'boring', 'ordinary', a 'fourth division fighter' and the like. When Naseem had last fought in Cardiff, ten months previously, he was booed and jeered and the crowd called him a faggot. And whenever he went back to cause mischief at Robinson's fights, he got more of the same, and revelled in it. It made the whole thing more personal, more of a vendetta, more fun.

Robinson and his people countered weakly that Steve was the strongest nine stoner in the world – far too big, powerful and experienced, too manly, for this irritating upstart. For goodness' sake, he'd whipped three former world champions; who the hell had Hamed fought? A bunch of undersized hasbeens, that's who.

But their words lacked the resonance of Naseem's insults and achieved no more than to provide the challenger with an excuse to further humiliate the champion – to feed his lust for vengeance and his sense that he had something to prove.

When the Team Naseem van arrived at the final pre-fight 'head-to-head' press conference Brendan and Naz were already playing out their battle plan. They kept the press and the champion waiting by arriving over twenty minutes late at the Cardiff International Arena (which the locals call the CIA with straight faces). Naseem positioned his leopard-spotted, wraparound, oval-shaped shades, and as soon as he saw the cameras he gave them the walk and the look that makes everyone aware that even though he may be the smallest fellow in the house, he

owns the place. Then he unzipped his tracksuit jacket and
revealed the logo on his black Joe Bloggs T-shirt: '*PRINCE*
Naseem Hamed WORLD CHAMPION'.

Watching the taut, irritated countenances in the WBO
champion's camp and the red-faced resentment of some in the
Cardiff press contingent as they read it, you could see what some
of them were thinking. Here is nice old Stevo, the Cinderella
man who took his chances, grabbed a world title and outgutted
some of the finest featherweights in the world. It's bad enough
he's been messed around by his English promoter – forced into
this fight at short notice and short change – but then in comes
this arrogant, cocky, conceited man-child and compounds it all,
taking over, with the London lackey press in his wake, treating
this proud son of Cardiff like garbage.

Next thing for Naz was to give them all a sucker punch – draw
them with a conciliatory feint and then swat 'em, just like he was
planning for fight night. He started with a backhanded
compliment, patronizing the champion gently: 'You are
obviously the best boxer I will have fought because I haven't met
a world champion before . . . You've always been a polite kind
of guy and you've got a lot of pride.' He told them that all the
braggadocio of the past months was really no more than a touch
of garnish for the ticket sales. 'Fights have to be built up. You
can't have two guys being nice to each other. There's got to be a
bit of a grudge, a bit of controversy.'

Just when everyone thought they were getting a rare taste of a
hype-free, Naz-lite, he came in with the old one-two. 'If a fighter
doesn't know how to build up a fight he might as well step down
and leave it to a 21-year-old who is a prince destined to be the
king.' He pointed to the logo on his T-shirt then glared at
Robinson. 'When you are flash and can back it up, no problem.
You can wear what you want and say what you like. I'm flash
because I can back it up. I'm just so glad you are going to turn up
for me to take this title.' He raised his head haughtily, back-
pedalled for a second by telling Steve he was not underestimating
him, and then closed in: 'That doesn't mean I'm not going to kick
your backside and take you out in four rounds.'

As he said this his lip curled and his eyes flared – his contempt
for the opposition shining through. 'I can take a man out with

one shot. I can move. I can switch from southpaw to orthodox. I have hand-speed and accuracy. I'm the complete package,' he chanted, jabbing his finger at his chest. 'You will enter the ring a champion but you'll be an ex-champ when you leave.' And on and on, and all Robinson could do was look stoic and dignified and try his best to sound convincing. By the end the entire Welsh press contingent and assorted hangers-on had broken any pretence of impartiality and were cheering for their countryman – and Naz was loving it.

But not everyone in the challenger's camp saw things from quite the same angle. Promoter Frank Warren was concerned that his little earner was getting too far up the noses of the locals. After all, Frank was supposed to represent the promotional interests of both men, and he may just want to do business in Cardiff again. So he announced that Naz had agreed to donate £1000 of his purse to a fund to build a statue of the 'legendary Jim Driscoll' who died of pneumonia in Cardiff seventy years earlier. This offer came across as a sop to the locals, though Warren later told me that winning over the Welsh was far from his mind – they were too far gone.

You could see from Naz's expression that he couldn't quite recall making any such commitment, and who the hell was Jim Driscoll anyway? Then he remembered: a useful Welsh featherweight called Driscoll was the only man to knock Robinson down and go on to fight for the WBO title. Problem was he was thinking of a fellow called *Tim* Driscoll not *Jim* Driscoll – peerless Jim – the master pugilist who was the finest British featherweight of them all. But it was too late: a local reporter sensed his confusion and asked him what he knew of Driscoll. 'I hear he's a real good fighter,' Naseem hesitantly replied. Those who caught it, chuckled smugly and put it in their columns the next day. Brendan and Frank winced. Naz seemed oblivious to the dimensions of his mistake. Jim Driscoll, Tim Driscoll, what's the difference? Could beat 'em both in the same night. And though Frank Warren, who has on his office wall an 85-year-old canvas poster advertising a Driscoll fight, wouldn't say it in this company, he agreed. 'Naseem's reflexes, his handspeed, his unorthodoxness, his strength – I can't see any featherweight beating him. Not even Jim Driscoll,' he said later.

*

The Driscoll *faux pas* was one for Robinson to take home in his black woolly cap after his sustained verbal battering, but it was small consolation for an extremely likeable twenty-six-year-old who had not had things his own way for a while. First, his previous promoter, Barry Hearn, had sued him for breach of contract to the tune of £170,000, then he was forced into a mandatory defence against Hamed – a fighter who had never before even ventured into the featherweight division but who had mysteriously been granted the WBO's number one ranking. This meant that despite the best attempts of his lawyers, Robinson had no option but to take the fight at a month's notice and at a gross purse of just under £200,000, his highest ever, yet far lower than if he'd been in a position to play hardball for a while and, even more significantly, considerably less than the half a million-plus Naseem was getting.

Frank Warren will tell you there is no injustice here – that it was Hamed and Ingle's decision to make the challenge and the WBO's to accept it. He'll also give you the figures to prove that under his Sports Network promotions, Robinson had become by far the highest paid featherweight in the world. 'I was the guy who made sure Steve had all his defences in Cardiff, including the Hamed fight,' he says indignantly. 'Eight world title defences in his home town. Never had to travel. I never lost a purse bid and he didn't have a mandatory challenge for eighteen months.'

He happily acknowledges that Hamed received significantly more money. Fighters are products who get paid according to their market rate and their relative bargaining power. 'Of course – Naz is the attraction,' Warren says in an irritated tone. 'Steve's two fights prior to this we struggled with. Wherever Naz boxed we sold out, and when he boxed on ITV he drew ratings of ten million, and not in world title fights. Robinson's last couple of world title fights on ITV delivered just over three million.'

Despite these hard facts, it is worth stressing that Steve Robinson is a fighting man of considerable skills and enormous resolve, whose career had followed a remarkable trajectory for which the cliche 'fairy tale' seems, for once, almost apt – almost, if only nasty little Naseem hadn't entered the plot.

When Robinson turned professional in 1989 he was marked with the unfortunate epithet 'journeyman' – just another willing Welshman at a time when Welsh boxing was going nowhere. Whenever a fight was close the decision went against him and by early 1993 his record showed 13 wins and nine losses, even though several of the negatives should have been positives. However, under the tutelage of the canny Trinidadian trainer, Ronnie Rush, he had acquired a dedication and resolve that had been absent earlier in his career. He gave up his £52-a-week day-job as a storeman, increased his training regime, and things suddenly turned around.

When the WBO featherweight champion Ruben Palacio tested HIV positive and was stripped of his crown, Robinson, who was already in training, was called in, with only 48 hours' notice, as a replacement against England's John Davison for the now-vacant throne. He fought his heart out and not only took the title but held it for two and a half years. Several times he started out the underdog and prevailed. He outworked and outpunched the quick, slick former WBO champion Colin McMillan to win a clear decision. Then it was the turn of the hard-hitting Merseysider, Paul Hodkinson, the former WBC kingpin, who was outboxed, outmuscled and then knocked out in the final round. Next the former three weight world champion Duke McKenzie was stopped with a sickening hook to the body in the ninth round.

Robinson had developed into a formidable world class featherweight with an impressive winning streak, carrying with him an increasingly refined and varied arsenal: tremendous strength, a tight defence and firm chin, an impressive array of hard punches, superb conditioning and a high workrate, as well as the dedication and determination to prevail against the odds. He played the leading role in the revival of professional boxing in Wales, was enjoying a growing international reputation, and was determined to unify the world title.

The problem faced by the Robinson camp was that while their man was a well respected champion, he was up against a sporting and promotional phenomenon of an altogether different order.

Right from the start of Naseem's amateur career, Brendan Ingle regarded him as a future champion and ensured that he was given the exposure his talents deserved. Before he was eight years old he was sparring and hanging out with the pros. His amateur debut was highlighted by the Sheffield Press. By the age of fifteen he was making headlines in the sport's leading newspaper, *Boxing News*, for his acrobatic antics and flamboyant demeanour as much as for his skills. When he signed his professional contract on his eighteenth birthday in February 1992 he did it in the House of Commons.

Anyone doubting the ability of this 5-foot-3, nine-stone youth, need only watch him in training – pounding the likes of British middleweight champion Neville Brown and holding his own with the 6-foot-3, 14-stone Johnny Nelson – to appreciate his amazing prowess. He destroys opponents with reputations as survivors, spoilers, toughies, cuties and contenders and seldom takes anything in return. He is ambidexterous, possessed with a contortionist's flexibility and blessed with an antenna from God which allows him to evaporate in the face of an onslaught and pump home his own rapid-fire combinations from impossible angles or land perfectly placed bombs while gazing at the other unfortunate's feet. He surrounds his opponents, always a step or two ahead of them, being everywhere and nowhere at the same time, moving with such grace and speed that he seems to be operating to different laws of motion.

When Naz was still twenty years old Ingle was displaying the far reaches of self-restraint by placing him only on a par with the finest fighters in the history of this strange profession and saying he could win titles all the way up to middleweight if he wanted to. 'Let me just say this to you: the best fighter I'd ever seen was Ali,' he told me then. 'At the moment Naseem's as good as Ali. People ask me, "How can you say that?" Ali could only box orthodox. This fella can box southpaw, orthodox, he can switch. Ali could shuffle, he can shuffle, but he can also knock you out with either hand from any angle you want and you can't touch him. I've watched all the great featherweights – the Henry Armstrongs, the Willie Peps, the Alexis Arguellos, and Naz is the best I've ever seen. In truth I've never seen anything like him.'

Brendan Ingle has always been a master of hyperbole – an

Irishman who knows how to talk up a product – but when it came to 'The Prince', the sport's journalistic hardmen, the punters whose bums go on seats and, most of all, the armchair fans whose viewing habits determine commercial viability, were prepared to take him at his word. In comparison, Robinson was a good, solid, workaday champion with a sound reputation and a proven regional base, but never one to attract the higher superlatives.

Despite this glaring disparity in drawing power, it was hard to convince a Robinson fan that Warren was doing anything other than sacrificing one fighter he was supposed to be promoting for the good of another, and for the good of his own pocket. As Warren now acknowledges: 'There was no way I was going to win them over. They were all pissed off because there was a campaign down there in the newspapers.'

Both fighters put in four weeks' training for this one, which, for Robinson was four weeks less than normal and for Hamed, two weeks less than his maximum. Steve stayed at home with his new wife, Angela, and their children and worked quietly and determinedly in and around Cardiff. His sparring (principally with the Commonwealth super bantamweight champion Neil Swain, a southpaw like Hamed) was done in his manager Dai Gardiner's new gym in Cwmcarn (Gardiner's Fleur-de-Lys gym was burnt to cinders a month earlier), while the padwork and ground work and their strategizing took place in Ronnie Rush's living room in Ely, not far from Steve's own home.

Long after it was over, Steve told me there were problems a-plenty he had to cope with. 'I was training, sure,' he explained, 'but I just wasn't a hundred per cent. Things weren't right for the fight and I kept asking questions about the money and the court cases and the problems with Frank Warren, and it was in the back of my mind. I wasn't psychologically right and I didn't have long enough to prepare so my stamina wasn't right.'

Before the fight, however, he chanted a different mantra: 'I'm feeling very good, very strong, just fine. I've been training solidly for four weeks, so no problems. My conditioning is excellent and my mind is so focused on the fight that I won't let any of the problems get in the way. There are things about this build-up which have angered me and I'm ready to explode. I've just got to make sure it's a controlled explosion.'

His mum, Yvonne, confirmed this self-diagnosis. 'Steven said to me: "Mam, I'll fight him for nothing in the gutter." I've never seen him so determined. Steven's not a rude boy, he'd never put anyone down. He's very quiet. But he came in the other day and said: "Mam, I'm frightened, frightened that I'm going to really hurt him, because he's getting me so mad. You haven't seen the best of me yet," he said.'[1]

As usual, Naseem's training sessions took place in the St Thomas's Boys' Club hall in Wincobank, Sheffield. There were whispers about a dissipation in his energies, with some of his gym mates saying he started serious training too late. Some added that he missed the odd training session and that discipline and routine had become 'a bit of a problem'. Brendan Ingle acknowledged that he was not training quite as hard as he had for his European title fight against Vincenzo Belcastro in 1994. But assistant trainer John Ingle, Brendan's son, and one of Naz's closest confidants, gave a slightly different perspective. 'I think Naz is still training as hard as ever,' he said. 'He hasn't really slackened off. The nightclubs are nothing new – when he was younger he used to go to a snooker place out of time until 2 a.m. Sure, he doesn't sleep much at night and then gets up at 11 a.m., but it's always been like that. He doesn't drink, smoke or do drugs and he's always in shape.'

What is apparent to an outsider is that whenever Naseem does train – and usually that's two or three times a day (regularly after midnight) – it is fast and frenetic and extraordinarily impressive in a madcap way. He defies several of the shibboleths of boxing conditioning: he goes to bed well after midnight and sometimes as late as 4 a.m. and rises whenever it suits him; he never does roadwork (though now and then he does short sprints and swims); he seldom skips and never uses weights. He may do some flexibility exercises, ground work, pull-ups and work on the heavybag, speedball and pearball, but his gym sessions are usually framed around intensive sparring sessions, as well as padwork with John Ingle and shadow boxing.

Naseem explains his unorthodox regime in terms of what is

necessary for him to excel. 'My training is all based around sparring, and I train excessively hard. That's where I get my fitness and my strength and my strong mind from. I spar with heavy opponents and I push them back, and I get stronger and stronger.'

He gets on to a pet topic – debunking the conventional wisdom about fight preparation. 'Some people in boxing say you must get early nights and get up at five in the morning to go for a run, but if you're not like that, don't do it. It's rubbish. I'm not the kind of guy to get up in the morning to go running. Running is for runners and I like to stay in my bed in the morning, but I can spar two hours with any boxer from flyweight to heavy-weight and I train any time I get the urge. I do what is necessary to win and when I step into that ring I'm fit enough to do twelve rounds, easily, and then twelve more.'

What he may also tell you is that he has absorbed every aspect of this sport and then revolutionized it with his own style. 'I have sparred with all the different kinds of fighters, including champions – different styles and weights – since I was seven. I've gone through every move and manouevre, every way of boxing and surviving and punching.'

Sparring in Ingle's gym has to be seen to be appreciated. There are three signs on the wall above the ring, one warning boxers to wear their headgear and never to spar without supervision and two others stating: 'Boxing can damage your health'. It is with this in mind that Ingle insists that most sparring sessions involve body work only, though in the last weeks before a fight occasional, well-supervised head sparring', is permitted. Underneath the ring canvas is an extra half inch of padding to slow the boxers down – that way, says Ingle, 'when they get into a fight they just glide around the ring.' The emphasis is on defence – on slipping, ducking, parrying, riding punches, moving out of the way, confusing the opposition, switching stance and developing speed, rather than on hurting the sparring partner.

With Naseem, however, things have always been a little different. Whoever he's in the ring with, flyweight or heavyweight, he goes all out. He seems incapable of holding back, or at least unwilling to try. Brendan explains this in terms of his innate competitive instinct, but always stresses that he is a completely different person outside the ring. What is clear is that inside the ring he is ruthless and cruel once the bell rings and this applies even if he's sparring with his younger brother, Ali (which he has since stopped doing), or close friends. Even Brendan, whose own professional career ended in the middleweight division in the early 1970s, has taken the pain on a few occasions. 'Before our last sparring session he said to me, "Old man you're going to get hurt." It was just body sparring and I'll tell ya, me body ached for days.'

Johnny Nelson, who is a former British, European and Commonwealth cruiserweight champion and twice came within a whisker of winning world titles, puts it like this: 'When I spar with him I've got to go full out. I've got to. There were a lot of guys who came down here and wanted to join the gym and when they got in with Naz he ridiculed and destroyed them. It's very hard because he is so fast and you've got to wait twenty rounds before he gets a little tired.'

Another regular sparmate is the former British welterweight champion Chris Saunders. 'I weigh nearly eleven stone and he weighs less than nine, but that doesn't mean a thing because he punches as hard as just about any welterweight. I'd say he punches as hard as Del Bryan but he's a lot quicker than Bryan,' Saunders says, in reference to the British champion whose title he lifted. 'Me and Naz we'd go full out against each other, and not just body sparring – we did some head sparring as well – and we really had a go at each other. Even when he was eighteen he would give me a run for my money and he's helped me a great deal because it's sharpened me up and made me a lot quicker and taught me new moves. I tell you, he's phenomenal.'

Also helping in his preparations for Robinson was Ryan Rhodes, the unbeaten middleweight prospect who has been working out with him since they were both little children. 'We spar together all the time and we have *really* good spars,' he says. 'I can hold my own with him – we're fairly evenly matched, but he's quicker in everything.'

The two men honoured to be Hamed's chief sparring partners for Robinson were Kevin Adamson, a slick, fast Walthamstow light middleweight and Jonathan Thaxton, a tough, hard-hitting

21-year-old light welterweight and former British and European kick boxing champion, both rated within the top twelve in their divisions in Britain. Adamson once challenged Lloyd Honeyghan for the Commonwealth title, Thaxton went on to flatten Paul Ryan, the British, Commonwealth and WBO intercontinental champion, in the first round a few months later.

When Naz enters the gym, always late, everyone turns to have a look, to give and maybe get a nod of acknowledgement. He makes sure *his* music is playing – rap, techno and jungle – and warns everyone not to touch it (not that anyone would dare to), says a few conciliatory words to his chopping block sparmate and then gets to work on Jon Thaxton's ten-stone body. Sometimes Naz plays and dances but mostly he's ripping in the punches without any hint of mercy. Several times Ingle calls his charge off, telling the former kick-boxer he can do eight rounds rather than 10, but Thaxton bravely stays the distance. Naseem is simply too quick, too elusive and hits too hard for the bigger man and he is hurting him. After nine rounds the tape stops and Naz orders a bystander to turn it over. One round later Thaxton's day is mercifully over, but Naseem continues to pound away at the pads, worn, as usual, by John Ingle.

'I'm telling you now, he hits like a middleweight,' says Thaxton later. 'I've sparred with Saunders, Adamson, and his power matches them, no problem. You think of two cars: if they're moving together at ten miles per hour they're not gonna do too much damage, but if they're going at a hundred miles per hour, different story. The thing with Naz is, he punches so fast and accurate and hard. He's a strong, strong fella. And I've only done body sparring with him, and that was bad enough. What it would be like with open sparring, I wouldn't like to find out.'

Thaxton, who travelled from Norwich to Sheffield twice a week for three weeks to spar with the Prince, reckons every one of those 48 rounds he did with Hamed for the Robinson fight was an honour and an education, and when it was over he couldn't stop singing the praises of his tormenter. 'I rate him with Roy Jones as one of the two best fighters, pound-for-pound, in the world at this moment,' he gushes. 'Yea, Naz, Roy Jones, they're two of a kind. He thinks he'll beat anyone and in my opinion, he will. He's a once-in-a-lifetime fighter. Once in a lifetime.'

Adamson also has a rough time, despite a height advantage of 10 inches and over two stone in weight. He's a fleet-footed, jab-and-move man, but he struggles to keep away from the little fellow in front of him. Unlike Thaxton, he does the occasional full sparring round, as well as the usual bodywork.

'The power he has is phenomonal for his weight,' Adamson acknowledges. 'He hits like a strong light welterweight, easy, and he's very strong for his size. He throws some beautiful body shots and they really hurt. For full sparring he is a lot more tricky on his feet and if you make a mistake he can drop you, no matter about the weight. You have to be one hundred per cent aware and your punches have to keep flowing to keep him off, and with him I wouldn't hold back one bit because when he's coming on full-strong, full-speed I can't afford to. If I hold back I just get an onslaught of punches.'

Watching this made you wonder how the hell Robinson could survive. The fact that the tautly muscled WBO featherweight champion had a walk-around weight of close to 10 stone (meaning he was naturally 12 pounds heavier than his challenger, as well as being 4½ inches taller), and had the benefit of three extra years of professional experience and eight world title fights, did not count for much. He was up against Naseem Hamed. Enough said.

The weigh-in, 28 hours before the fight, was a mad, chaotic, theatrical occasion. Supposedly for the fighters, press, camp attendants and selected guests only, somehow over a hundred Robinson followers managed to worm their way into an already cramped room at the CIA. Robinson's late arrival was greeted with cheers and whoops and peels of raucous laughter to laddish barks of 'Bring on the princess' and 'Send back the boy'. Then Mike Goodall, the announcer, announced: 'Will you please welcome to the scales, Prince . . . ', but he was beaten to the punch by a joker who got in the syllable 'cess', prompting a general round of hilarity, and a chant of 'Prin*cess*, Prin*cess*', followed by: 'Send him back to Yemenese.'

Had the champion been white, one might have suspected that racism, rather than jingoism, was at work, but not one of Robinson's minions I spoke to mentioned either fighter's colour.

This is a Cardiff crowd and Steve is one of their true-born sons, and the little fellow from Sheffield, or 'Yemenese' or whatever, is just an infuriating impostor to be insulted. Naz seemed completely unfazed by all this, and later says he didn't even hear all these comments. 'Even if I did I would just think they were being childish. They don't know the score. For mature men to come out with silly stuff like that, well, it doesn't cross your mind to get angry.'

The Prince's tactic was rather to make Robinson angry. For a couple of minutes he chatted quietly but provocatively to the champion – telling him, in effect: you say you will win; you're unhappy that I'm getting paid much more than you; how about a winner-takes-all deal? Steve was unsettled, and muttered something about leaving this to his manager. 'Hamed was going on at me about the purse money – that he was getting more than me,' he said later. 'It was getting to me at the back of my mind, and I was so angry, which I shouldn't have been.'

For Naz, Robinson's mumbled response was yet another sign that he had his man beat, and when the boxers stepped on to the scales Robinson lost another psychological battle. Hamed made the weight first time with three-quarters of a pound to spare and then took a drink from his water bottle. By fight time his weight had risen by only two pounds. Robinson was four ounces over the limit and had to wait for his little drink. Fifteen minutes later, after a brief workout, he returned to make it by a quarter of a pound.

Immediately after the weigh in, he made light of this little embarrassment, insisting everything was just fine. 'I had no problems making the weight, really. I mean, what's four ounces? I just took off some clothes and made it easy the second time.' Two months later, however, he admitted it wasn't that easy. 'I'm a natural featherweight, but they usually give me eight weeks to train for a fight, and I am down to the weight about three or four days before the fight. This time I had four weeks and I only made the weight on the day of the weigh-in, and the last few days were a bit hard. I made it all right in the end, but it could have made me a bit sluggish.'

Steve Robinson had one more humiliation to endure. With scores of his diehard followers begging for tickets he asked

Warren's pressman, Andy Ayling, for his twenty ringside passes, and was extremely peeved when he only got ten. A lengthy altercation followed, but Ayling held his ground truculently, telling Steve in an offhand tone that he was promised ten and that's all he's getting. 'That definitely irritated me,' Robinson later acknowledged. 'They only gave me half what they promised. It was all psychological.'

When I caught up with him in the passages of the CIA after the weigh-in, Robinson did his best to sound upbeat and recited all the advantages Ronnie Rush had been stressing over the past month. 'I'll be too big for him, too strong and hit too hard. I've improved with every fight. I'm definitely hitting harder and I'm actually getting bigger – just look at my shoulders,' he said, tapping his pecs. 'He's never fought anyone in my league but I've beaten the best – McMillan, McKenzie, Hodkinson – everyone predicted I'd lose to them and I whipped them easily. Can he take my power? I don't think so. And I'm not worried about his style. I've been sparring with southpaws and guys who fight like him and I know just what to do. I might stop him, but I don't like to make predictions – I'll just say I'm very confident of still being world champion tomorrow night.'

Hamed, however, had a faith of a different order – absolute self-belief and total conviction that he could not lose. 'There is no way I would look into his eyes and say to myself, "Can I beat him?",' he said later. 'I had it in my mind that he's gonna get beat and beat well, and there was nothing he had that made me think, "I'm gonna struggle here." There was never any doubt in my mind. To tell you the truth, I've never, ever sat down and said to myself, "What if you lose? What if you do actually get beat? What if you get beaten by a better fighter?" because my mind is so positive that I can't get beat. I've got so much self-belief in what God has given me, so I know, definitely, that I am blessed with a gift and I know, basically, that when I enter that ring God is on my side.'[2]

The day of a fight is a killer for many boxers. It is often when the real fear starts to kick in: fear of defeat, fear of the financial implications of losing, fear of humiliation, fear of failure, fear of looking bad, fear of pain. Invariably, these fears mesh into one general sense of foreboding, which comes out in an irritability with everyone around. You won't find many fighters focusing too specifically on, for example, the pain of body blows in their quiet moments, but if the task ahead seems too formidable, if the fighter has been unsettled in the pre-fight shenanigans, if his hidden aches and minor injuries from training are niggling too much, if he's still shaking off the effects of that cold or bout of flu, if his bowels aren't working right, and if he dwells too long on these anxieties, a mood of defeatism can creep in and the fight is often lost well before he's made his way to the ring. But if that fear is channelled, the adrenalin it helps to prompt, along with the focused mental approach that goes with it, can be a major factor in victory.

It is one of the old truisms of the game that every fighter feels some fear, and those who say they don't are liars or in a state of self-denial. But Naseem appears to be a genuine exception. When you watch him during the countdown before a fight it is clear that fear, at least as the word is generally understood, is not part of his condition. Certainly, he experiences the thrill of anticipating the ride to come – and there's a good deal of adrenalin production in that – but such is his absolute assuredness in his own abilities that defeat, pain and looking bad do not seem to enter even his sub-conscious mental processes.

What he feels in the hour by hour countdown before a fight is an overwhelming desire to start performing. 'I love boxing,' he says. 'It's in me, it's part of me and I think about it all the time, and I rise to every occasion. I just treat every fight the same as any other and I'm raring to go. A lot of boxers say they have fear but I don't. I've never been frightened before a fight – totally the opposite.' His priority is to find things to do around the hotel which keep his low boredom threshold at bay. In the ten hours before facing up to Steve Robinson, Naseem and his entourage ate, used the swimming pool, joked and played around, watched videos and listened and danced to hours and hours of music (an esoteric mixture of rap, jungle, ragga, hip hop, house and garage), and he tried to get in an afternoon sleep.

They laughed a lot, told weak jokes, teased Adamson about being the token southerner in a northern party and, now and then, someone would imitate Thaxton's Norwich vowels. To

Naseem's sparring partners, who expected a tenser mood for such a major league occasion, it all had a tinge of unreality about it. 'I wouldn't say I'm the most relaxed person when it's time for me to box,' says Adamson, 'but Naz is different. He likes people around him and his music on, so he can get the same sort of atmosphere from the gym. But for the Robinson fight he was *unbelievably* relaxed. All seven of us in that changing room are just dancing, having a laugh and enjoying ourselves, and you think the guy is about to have his first world title fight at a weight above what he boxes at. I just couldn't believe it.'

'Yeah, I've never seen anything like it in my life,' Thaxton agrees. 'I know what I'm like in the changing rooms, but he's dancing and singing and he's got no worries, and outside there's 16,000 people disliking him a *lot*, and he's just loving it.'

Naseem's entire entourage were with him in his dressing-room before the fight, including his two older brothers Riath and Nabeel, with his father Sal popping in to wish him luck (in contrast to Steve's mum, Yvonne, who stayed at home with her cigarettes and a glass of vodka to babysit for her grandchildren, and listened on the radio because she does not have a Sky dish). The mood was one you would expect at an after-party. Naseem's prayers had been said earlier in the evening and his copy of the Koran was in his kitbag, but now it was time to get the adrenalin flowing. Music pumped out of a portable sound system.

Behind the laughter, however, was serious intent. Everybody had to be sure of their tasks. Naseem assembled his fighting gear. Brendan and John did the bandages and the taping, making sure every detail was in order: his boots correctly laced, his groin protector fastened just right, his body oiled up. How are you feeling? Have you been to the toilet? Does that feel comfortable? Naz finally pulled on his short white towelling gown and climbed into his new, heavy-looking, Joe Bloggs-designed leopardskin tassled 'skort' trunks (with 'Prince' on the front of the waistband, and 'King' on the back). They feel *good*! Wicked! He was the only one in the room who seemed completely at ease.

Once gloved up and ready, he began shadow boxing with Brendan, then left the dressing-room and shadow boxed in the inside parking section of the stadium, loving every minute of it. In the past, before his fights, he's imagined he's one of the sport's 'legends' (he likes that word) doing his thing: Sugar Ray Leonard finessing Marvin Hagler or humiliating Roberto Duran, Muhammad Ali crucifying Ernie Terrell or annihilating Cleveland Williams. But this time he was Prince Naseem Hamed, legend to be, with the taunts, feints and punches in his head all aimed at Steve Robinson.

Outside, under the arclights, it was pouring with rain. The last time I had been in Cardiff, exactly two years before, was to watch Lennox Lewis come from behind to take out Frank Bruno on another cold, drizzly night at Cardiff Arms Park. The weight of the ring caused such damage to the pitch that it is now out of bounds for boxing promoters, so they settled instead for the adjacent Cardiff Rugby Football Club stadium, which seats 16,000. Despite the weather the predicted sell-out was easily achieved. It was not quite as cold as in 1993, but the rain was harder and more persistent. In the main prelim fight, local favourite Nicky Piper lifted the well-sodden and in many cases, well-oiled Welsh spirits when he came from behind to knock out Noel Magee for the Commonwealth light heavyweight title – but it was to be their last bit of comfort for the night.

The chants of 'Stevo, Stevo, Stevo', started at 7.30 p.m. and never stopped. Finally, after two hours of this, it was time for the big one and the Welsh voices really came into their own. 'Oleee, Ole, Ole, Ole, Stevooo, Stevo, Stevo, Stevo', and 'Ha-*med*, Ha-*med*, who the fuck is Hamed?', over and over again. Then there was a burst of techno music followed by the display of the Welsh flag and a particularly defiant rendition of the Welsh national anthem – the only anthem played as the promoters wisely opted not to chance the embarrassment of 'God Save the Queen' being hissed, heckled and booed. At this point a section of the crowd started to get out of hand, surging forward, climbing over the barriers and blocking the entrances. An anxious and irritated Frank Warren stepped into the ring to tell them there would be no fight until they moved.

Finally, with calm restored, Naseem was given the signal that his time has arrived. 'As soon as they tell me, "Television's ready – you're on," that's it. I become a different person,' he says. 'All the guys get around me and I just blank out everything else. I'm ready to walk out there to my music and do the business. I feel so calm, cool and collected, and I just can't wait to get into that ring and start fighting.'

From the back of the stadium a silhouette of a caped, dancing figure appeared, striking what might be mistaken for an outrageously camp pose. It's the sort of high-kitsch display that makes old salties like Henry Cooper despair for the fight game, but which helps deliver the ratings that keep the promoter's Roller running. A falsetto voice chanted: 'I am ready, I am ready,' and exploded into a rapid beat rendering, at ear-numbing decibles, of 'I Believe' – a change from his usual number, 'Here Comes the Hot Stepper'. Naz later explained: ' "I Believe" is a really good garage-housy track which I picked because I believed I was going to win the world title. The music is very important 'cos it's got to give me a buzz. It's got to hit me that it's the right time to fight, that the energy and adrenalin are there.'

Surrounded by the eight security guards hired by the promoters, his cornermen and sparring partners, Naz danced his way towards the ring, but from outside that huddle all you could see were his canary-coloured gloves occasionally reaching for the stars. A large section of the crowd was booing and shouting obscenities. Some were jostling the minders and throwing things. Moments before Naseem reached the ring a coin hit him. He stopped for a moment and picked it up – a memento. Finally, he mounted the steps, placed his hands on the middle of the top rope and did the trademark frontflip, which he nicked from Ryan Rhodes a couple of years earlier. Hamed's leopardskin trunks follow gravity, prompting a few pressmen to ask whether he'd left his knickers at home. He landed neatly, brushing his white towelling gown top off his face, stood to attention and glared at the crowd defiantly.

Soon the entire Hamed vanguard had joined Naz in the ring: Riath hoisting the WBC International super bantamweight title belt above his head (much to the chagrin of the WBO officials who asked him to remove it), Nabeel holding the Yemenese flag, Johnny Nelson the Union Jack and Brendan Ingle and the other cornermen bustling around in their leopardskin uniforms.

Another burst of pyrotechnics and our 'Enry sinks further in his ringside chair. The outline of a red Welsh dragon appeared in neon, followed by a roar and a cloud of smoke which covered the stadium and had the asthma sufferers reaching for their inhalers. Robinson had chosen a reggae number, 'Natural Mystic Blowing', and as he approached the ring the crowd erupted. More ululating as Steve, Ronnie Rush and Dai Gardiner made their understated entrance. Wearing his usual red trunks with 'Stevo' on the front, the champion held aloft the WBO title belt and his challenger gave him a look of pure disdain. Naz was still dancing and smiling and clearly having a wonderful time. 'When have you seen a guy of the age of twenty-one, fighting for his first world title, coming down the aisle dancing to his music, getting into it, doing a flip into the ring, still dancing, and then dancing to his opponent's music?' he asked me later. 'I didn't expect to enjoy Steve's music, but I did. That's how confident I was. I knew I was going to win that world title and it showed in that smile on my face.'

By the time the introductions were over it was 9.45 p.m. and the rain was driving into the ring. For a few seconds while they sized each other up during the pre-fight instructions, Robinson looked like a winner – an image enhanced when Naseem's corner remove his top and the boxers touch gloves. From the waist up Steve looked several divisions bigger. Not only is he half a head taller, but he has broader shoulders, a far tighter and more defined musculature and a bigger head. His body is a taut, powerful-looking 5-foot-7½, and he was 134 pounds by fight time. Hamed, at 5-foot-3 and at fight time 127 pounds, has a carriage which is harder to define. Once he gets moving it is clear everything is in perfect proportion, but from below he seems to have a body which belongs, simultaneously, in three divisions: the head of a straw weight, upper body of a bantam and legs of a middleweight – almost elephantine in comparison with Steve's spindly featherweight pins.

With most boxers in the lighter weights a low centre of gravity and heavy legs are seen as a drawback – the idea being that height is an absolute advantage and that weight is most usefully situated in the upper body. With Hamed, however, this does not apply. His entire platform is based on that solid undercarriage – his strength, his speed, balance, flexibility and ability to take a punch. But far more than his legs, it's his eyes which tell the story of what is to come. This is supposed to be the moment of truth, when the heart is pumping overtime, the adrenalin is flowing, and the head is feverishly anticipating the opening moves. Robinson's eyes were glistening with pride, indignation and intense concentration, but Naseem's were unnervingly calm – completely focused, brimming with sneering contempt, but still calm. It's a look of absolute self-confidence.

Round One

At the bell, Naseem, from the southpaw stance, moved straight into attack mode. Steve plodded forward cautiously, his head tucked behind his arms and gloves. Naz opened with a body punch while Steve misseed twice with rights, one of them brushing Naz's cheek, prompting a skinhead contingent in the crowd to let loose with a 'Hamed, Hamed, who the fuck is Hamed?' Hamed let them know by landing a right uppercut after switching to orthodox. Halfway through the round he paused to glance at the press rows and gave a withering look to one Welsh journalist, as if to say, 'Told you so, arsehole', before sticking his chin out and smirking, dropping his hands to his sides, Ali-style, trying to draw the champion out of fortress Robinson and into his own web, and saying, 'Come on, hit me.' He let Steve lead and tried counterpunching, making the Welshman miss but seldom connecting with anything more promising than Steve's liver.

From the start Hamed's extraordinary elasticity was apparent. At times he bent so far backwards to avoid the oncoming traffic that he gave the appearance of double-jointedness, yet his feet were always squarely planted and he was never off-balance. Naz ended with a right hook which landed solidly. It was a sparse round in terms of scoring punches, but one where the challenger had already asserted his superiority. Robinson was unable to find a way of coping with Hamed's combination of speed, switch-hitting and elusiveness. When Naz returned to his corner, he asked Brendan: 'Did I do all right?' to which his second father, trainer and nose wiper replied, 'You did great, marvellous.'

Round Two

Hamed opened with a crisp three-punch combination, but soon began clowning again – trying to draw the champion out of his shell. He made Robinson miss by disconcertingly wide margins – on one occasion executing a neat sidestep and waving him past as his momentum carried him forward. During a brief Robinson-instigated clinch at the halfway mark Naz tossed Steve to the canvas as if he were a tiny, leg-rutting pooch – earning a caution, but making a point. It became clear that Hamed had no problem pushing Robinson around, and to the surprise of many, that he was the stronger of the two. The champion's strength was one of his aces, and now it seemed to have been taken away from him. Naseem was quick to capitalize, reminding Steve with curled lips and contemptuous eyes: 'You told me you were the strongest.'

Later he explained the significance of that moment: 'Before the fight he and everyone else was telling me he was the strongest featherweight in the world. I said I was stronger. They said I was crazy. I was only twenty-one. I was not strong enough, not mature enough. I proved a lot of people wrong. I threw him around, broke him down mentally and took him out.' Steve also admits to being taken by surprise. 'He was stronger than I thought – really quite strong, and he's elusive at the same time, but I still don't think he's as strong as me.'

After this Naz momentarily shook Steve with a wonderfully timed right uppercut, giving a little bum-wiggle and an underhand wave to mark the harmless passing of yet another Robinson punch. He stood square on, his hands again at his sides, challenging the champion to take a potshot at his chin, but Steve kept his own poker-set features tucked behind those yellow mitts, and did not respond. The champion showed great reluctance to move out of his tight crab-like defence and while this might have presented problems for Hamed's offence, it also meant that the champion's chances of roughing up his challenger were reduced.

Eventually Hamed connected with a long left to the face,

which somehow found a way through the burglar bars. Robinson responded with a charge but Naz ducked low and squirmed out of the way, firing off solid counters in retreat. With 40 seconds to go Hamed connected with a peach of a right uppercut which slithered through a crack in Robinson's defences. His legs stuttered momentarily and this prompted another Naz hip-shake and a grim smile from the champion just before the bell.

Round Three

Hamed came out fighting from the orthodox stance this time, as he did in most of the remaining rounds, and Robinson tried to take advantage of this change by leading with a big right, which missed by a millimetre. The crowd in the bleachers whooped and cheered, thinking their man had finally registered. This illusory moment of respite was extremely brief, however. After 30 seconds Naseem opened up with a tattoo of crisp blows, raising a swelling around Steve's right eye, though the champion did manage to reply with a solid right to the head. Naz grinned contemptuously, did yet another bum-shake and made the Welshman miss with five unanswered punches. Taunting some more, Naz then snapped in a single right uppercut. Robinson, already looking down-hearted, continued to press forward doggedly and had another rare moment of success when he made Naz miss with a huge right uppercut. They exchanged blows after the bell and once again the yahoos chanted: 'Hamed, Hamed, who the fuck is Hamed?'

For anyone other than the security guards, with their eyes glued to the crowd, it was another very clear Hamed round. Anyone, that is, except the American ringside judge Walter Calavieri who somehow decided that Robinson's single connecting punch was worth more then 30-odd Hamed punches. The other two judges, Paul Thomas and Samuel Vermet scored it for Naz.

Round Four

For months before the fight, this was the round Naseem said he would use to end it and he came out more purposefully, with the express intention of fulfilling his prediction. For a while he dropped his clowning routine and went hunting. But Robinson, an extremely capable defensive boxer, made Hamed miss with four consecutive punches, though soon after he took a vicious left-right combination to his body and then a right-hook-left combination to the head when cornered. Halfway through the round Hamed began taunting his man again – 'Go on, try to hit me' – and even made a showy point of smoothing down his own tightly cropped hair. Doing his version of the Ali shuffle, he then poked out a series of light, probing punches.

Robinson grabbed Naseem and tried to pull him in, but the youngster wriggled loose and made the champion miss again. Steve pressed forward and briefly trapped Hamed, but again the challenger's strength, flexibility and speed were in evidence as he moved into the open water once again. At the bell Naz raised his arms and laughed in Robinson's increasingly puffy face. He had failed to fulfil his prediction and had limited success in getting through with much more than single, hard punches, but he showed no sign of concern.

Later he paid tribute to Steve for this achievement. 'Full credit to him. Great champion. He went over the round I said I was going to do him in, so the credit's there. I went for the fourth round, but he wasn't there to be took out. He was strong, he stood his ground. I don't think I could have stopped him earlier.'

From where I was sitting, within arm's reach and earshot of Naseem's corner, I heard Brendan Ingle telling him to step it up a bit and use the jab more, to which Naz answered: 'Shut up and let me do the fighting.' The Irishman gave his stock reply: 'Marvellous.'

Round Five

As Robinson rose it was clear that the swelling around his right eye had spread, and Hamed immediately attempted to exacerbate the damage. He invited Steve to have a go at his body – 'Come on, try to hit me there' – but missed with his own one-two combination. Moving moves in a rhythmic, Tai Chi-like slow motion, probing with feeler punches, he beckoned his opponent in. Then he stepped in, boxing orthodox, switching effortlessly to southpaw and once again offering a target. He fired a right hook to the body and at that moment Robinson countered with his best punch of the fight, a fast, solid left hook which landed square and hard on Hamed's jaw, and then he connected again. The first hook was a blow which would have dropped many featherweights but Hamed showed no sign of being hurt and did an exaggerated little booty wiggle, again with a smirk on his face.

Later Robinson said of this moment: 'I don't think I caught him clean. It was more of a glancing blow. He took it and pulled a face but I think I hurt him – he admitted that after the fight, and if I had caught him with a few more shots then, I would have had him.' Hamed sees things very differently: 'I took a good left hook against Robinson and I took it very well and people have found out I have a great chin to go with all the ability. They now know I haven't got a glass jaw and that I can take a punch from a real, strong featherweight. He caught me with some good shots, but he didn't hurt me.'

After this Naseem taunted Steve some more, pointing again to his own body – 'Go on, try to hit me' – before countering with single, hard right jabs and a left which knocked Robinson back. Then, with a sneer on his face, Hamed came in to land a scintillating four-punch combination – a long left hook to the chin, right hook half-blocked by Steve's gloves, left jab to the face and a fast, solid right uppercut which landed flush under the champion's chin. Robinson dropped heavily, his legs flailing in the air, going down for only the second time in his professional career. He clambered up at the count of four and returned to his defensive shell.

Hamed fired off a torrent of big time blows, pinning Robinson to the ropes, but the champion showed great pride and courage in fighting back, before clasping the challenger in a vice-like clinch. Naz simply threw him to the floor again, and got a warning from referee Ismael 'Wiso' Fernandez. He then came in with a three uppercut combination, followed by a right cross, and again pinned the champion to the ropes. As the bell rang Robinson's legs still appeared wobbly and he looked exhausted. Hamed also looked a bit puffed from his efforts but returned to his corner with a wide grin on his face as his ecstatic father, Sal, rose from his ringside seat, shouting and waving in delight.

In the champion's corner there was a flurry of feverish activity and advice. 'He caught you with a good shot, OK,' said Ronnie Rush. 'Now listen to me: you're packing up, you're packing up. You gotta start unloading shots when you get close. You hear?' He took stock for a second. 'Take your time,' he said, and the bell tolled.

Round Six

Naz went straight back to where he left off, landing big with both fists, and at times making Robinson miss by over a foot on the rare occasions he attempted anything. Steve covered up even tighter than before, fighting out of a pronounced crouch. While he looked so much bigger before the first bell, by now he seemed to have shrunk, both literally and figuratively and Hamed looked like the fighter with the perfect physique – the advanced model, built for speed, agility, power and comfort.

Steve shuffled forward mechanically, but without purpose, doing his best to cover up in the face of the onslaught. The crowd tried to lift his flagging spirits: 'Robinson, Robinson, Robinson,' they chanted, but Naz spoiled his moment by joining in the chorus, mouthing the words with the added indignity of going through this ritual with his head a few tantalizing inches from the champion's. It was an extraordinary moment which perhaps more than any other revealed both the level of Naseem's superiority and the extent of his arrogance and disdain for his opponent. At times boxing is as much a mind game as it is a body

game, but with this gesture Naseem took the art of mindfucking
to new levels.

Afterwards Naseem came in for plenty of press and Control
Board criticism for his taunting tactics, but he insists it is an
effective psychological ploy. 'Obviously there's method behind
it. You watch Muhammad Ali doing it, you watch Sugar Ray
Leonard doing it – the credit they got was phenomenal, but they
were in America. When you get a British fighter doing it, they
just don't like it.' While this claim is not entirely correct – the 15
rounds of verbal and physical torture Ali subjected Ernie Terrell
to certainly came in for months of sustained and vociferous
public criticism – he has a point when it comes to psychological
effectiveness, as Robinson later admited. 'He was putting me off
by pulling faces and stuff, and he upset my concentration. My
mind wasn't a hundered per cent. If it had been right I would
have ignored his making fun and got on with the job like I
usually do, but on the night I just switched off. He's the type of
fighter who gets to you.'

Halfway through the round, during a lull in Hamed's
offensive, Steve had another flash of success, landing a decent
right cross to Hamed's chin, but the Sheffield lad showed no sign
of being deterred. He dropped his hands again, and suddenly
launched an attack, bashing Robinson from post to post and
landing 19 hard punches without reply. This was clearly the
correct moment for referee Fernandez to step in, but he seemed
transfixed and, inexplicably, took no action.

Hamed, grinning and smirking, was loving every second,
completely relaxed and loose. Robinson, meanwhile, was
sucking in air, wounded and exhausted, the blood spraying from
his mouth with each solid blow that came his way. A proud and
stubborn champion, he had nothing left.

Round Seven

Naseem opened with a cracking left hook from the orthodox
stance, and went strutting slowly in, completely contemptuous
of the champion, and continually making him miss by margins
that would usually be embarrassing, except that Steve was now

way past that point. Forty seconds into the round Robinson threw a purposeful-looking combination in the direction of Hamed's body and the boy wonder simply raised his arms theatrically, bringing them down again to parry the blows, and then landed a hefty left hook to the body. Soon after he sidestepped Steve's desperate lunge so that the champion flew into the ropes. A minute into the round Robinson pressed forward with a token attack, but Hamed slipped effortlessly out of range, talking to him some more, ridiculing his efforts: 'Steve, Steve, this is me, this is me. I told you I was the champion, Steve.' This ritual of humiliation, arguably a defensible tactic earlier in the fight, became just another dimension of the cruel and unusual punishment Naseem was dishing out.

Hamed was working at a slower pace now, conserving his strength and taking a breather. Robinson stoically pumped out a combination, which fell short, and Hamed imitated his best effort with a look of disdain. Though tired, he was landing at will, smiling and talking continually. He ended the round with a crunching left hook followed by a combination. For the first time in the fight Hamed was panting heavily in his corner between rounds, but Ingle realized that the turkey was tender enough for the knife. 'He's ready now,' he told Naseem.

Round Eight

Amazingly, as the bell rang, the yobs were still at it: 'Hamed, Hamed, who the fuck is Hamed?' They should have known by then. Robinson, his right eye almost shut, was having trouble getting Hamed in focus, not that this would have helped much. The crowd gave him one more song to spur him on to the impossible, but there was absolutely nothing he could do about this jackhammering phantom in front of him. His tormentor was landing from seemingly impossible angles, gliding around the canvas, slipping and blocking everything that came his way, bending and twisting and then firing unexpectedly.

With his hands by his knees and in the southpaw stance, Naseem followed the retreating Robinson around the ring, had a little stretch, jabbed, jabbed again, changed stance and probed with a left jab. The champion momentarily dropped his tight guard to try something, and Hamed unleashed a perfectly timed left hook. It connected flush on the chin and Steve's legs did a little involuntary jig before he collapsed backwards, hitting the deck and then falling forwards on to his face in Naz's corner. He clambered bravely to his knees, but, at last, Wiso Fernandez decided he'd seen enough. At 1 minute 48 seconds of the eighth round it was all over and Naseem Hamed was champion.

The Sheffield lad raised his gloves in triumph, then shouted and gave what looked like an obscene gesticulation at one of the Welsh reporters. The adrenalin subsiding he ambled over to embrace the stricken former champion, saying: 'Steve, you was a great champion. You was stronger than I thought and you really did well. I didn't think you was going to last how you did, but you did great.' Robinson's only words of reply were: 'You're a very hard puncher.' Naseem raised Steve's hand and paraded him around the ring, a move which brought a muted cheer from the crowd. The former champion clearly appreciated Hamed's gesture and later told me: 'He's very arrogant, but after the fight he wasn't too bad, like he said, "good fight" and everything. I don't hate him. I don't love the guy, but I don't hate him. He's all right.'

Of the finalé Naz had this to say: 'I was breaking him up mentally, and physically it was happening at the same time, and he just fell to pieces at the end. I caught him with a brilliant left hook. He fell for it. He dropped his hands and BAM! I caught him, and the shot was so perfectly timed that his legs just gave away. I picked the exact right time and it was the perfect ending.' Robinson was more reluctant to acknowledge the beauty of his own execution. 'He's quite a hard puncher but I took his best shots, but I just took too many and when it went to the later rounds I couldn't take it any more.'

From his ringside seat, Naz's father, Sal, his eyes glistening with tears of joy, stepped through the ropes and hugged his son, followed by the rest of Hamed's camp. In the Yemen and the entire Arab world, where MBC television claim that 'up to' 100 million have watched Naseem's coronation, there was an eruption of spontaneous jubilation. In Sana'a, people poured out of their houses and into the markets and streets, fired their guns in the air and partied all night. In Lindholme prison, near Doncaster, where Naseem has been doing boxing exhibitions for years, every single one of the 600 inmates and half the screws were among the millions of Sky viewers who watched the spectacle. For several minutes they jumped up and down, high-fiving each other and roaring with delight in celebration of the fact that their homeboy had done what he said he would. At home in her living room in Ely, Cardiff, Yvonne Robinson switched off her radio and went to bed.

After the fighters went back to their dressing-rooms, a woman from the crowd climbed over the perimeter fence screaming: 'Warren! Warren! How does it feel to stitch one of your boxers up? It's a disgrace! Three weeks' training!' This prompted the yahoos to get going once again. 'You're just a fuckin wanker, just a fuckin' wanker,' and 'Warren is a wanker, Warren is a wanker.'

Meanwhile, Brendan Ingle, grinning and shaking his head as he slowly made his way back, his worries over for now, told me, 'Naz coulda beaten anyone tonight. I've been saying since he was a little kid that he was somethin' special, that he would be great. I've always said Ali and Sugar Ray Robinson were the greatest but this kid can go on to be better. He was having his first fight at the weight and he outclassed an outstanding world champion – didn't lose a single round. It was an awesome display. His level of skill is unbelievable. What can I say? He did great, marvellous, but that Steve Robinson has a heart as big as you get. His corner should've pulled him out earlier, but I tell ya, he's got a heart. Typical Welsh do-or-die effort. All power to him.'

At 11.30 p.m. Naz arrived for his first press conference as world champion, freshly laundered and not a mark on his face. Robinson was too hurt and upset to make it. 'It feels good! It feels good!' Nassem began, bubbling over with superlatives about his own performance, and a few about Robinson's resilience, spiced up with barbed digs at the Welsh press for giving Robinson a chance and some well-coached compliments for the WBO. Colin Hart of the *Sun* – one of the event's sponsors – asked why he goaded Robinson, to which Naz, showing that the fight had not quite left him, replied, 'Aaah, don't say I taunted him or I ridiculed him. At the end of the day that's *your* opinon, Colin Hart. You can say what you *want*! At the end of the day it was *psychological* what I did in that ring. What I had to do to win, I did!'

But he was quickly back in bubbly mode, praising himself, Robinson, the referee, the WBO again, his sparring partners, Sheffield, the Arab world, and himself some more. When asked whether he could continue to leap divisions he said he could rise another four weights, and could not resist a put-down for Britain's world-rated lightweight Billy Schwer. 'Billy will probably be looking at the fight and thinking, "I hope he doesn't come up to my weight." Tell Billy, he's all right, I'm not coming up just yet.'

Shortly before midnight Steve Robinson left Cardiff Arms Park on foot with a clutch of family members and friends to comfort him. Minutes later, Naz departed from the opposite entrance in his spanking new, £98,000 blue V12 Mercedes sports car, his girl of the moment by his side. As he roared off into the night, still beaming with self-satisfaction, it seemed impossible to contemplate a scenario where he would leave as anything other than an emphatic victor. In eight rounds of boxing in his maiden world title fight he had dished out a merciless beating and had taken only four solid blows for his trouble. It was hard to think of anyone in featherweight history – not even Peerless Jim Driscoll – who could have lived with him in that rainswept Cardiff ring, and the impertinent thought occurred that Naseem Hamed might, already, be the finest fighter of them all.

2

Roots

Brendan Ingle is an Irishman in England who appreciates the significance of heritage. He understands it not only for what it is worth to an individual – and he places considerable store in that – but also as a marketing tool. In a game where fighters are products or they are nothing, Brendan has an instinctive feel for the market that few can touch – an adman's gift for images and phrases which amuse, tease and titillate the punter. Sometimes he will milk the irony in national identity – big, black English boxers with leprechaun names was a favourite. Fidel Castro Smith was too bland a name for his future British super middleweight champion, he decided, so he rechristened him Slugger O'Toole. Paddy Reilly from Ballyjamesduff had more of ring about it for a 17 stone English heavyweight, than boring old Clifton Mitchell.

He may also play on the reversal of accepted images (giving the fancy dan ducker and diver Herol Graham the nom de plume 'Bomber') or he'll use a minor advantage as a major marketing tool (dressing the heavyweight Pele Reid in the Brazilian

colours to highlight his name). But when the moment demands
he can also play the game with his tongue a little further from his
cheek, as with Naseem Hamed's early identity as the 'Arabian
Knight' – milking the notion of Middle Eastern mystique
through the use of ceremonial head-dresses, daggers and the
like. So when Brendan talks in these terms about his finest-ever
fighter, his remarks have to be taken with so many pinches of
salt.

One point he likes to make is that Naseem's gifts, his fighting
style, and certainly his mental approach, are all drawn from his
Yemeni heritage, from his Arab genes even. He makes this link
in particular when discussing his two tours of Yemen with his
young fighter, in late 1993 and early 1995. 'We went to the
village where his father comes from, outside Sana'a,' he says in a
compelling tone of quiet wonderment. 'Marvellous people, but
they all carry guns out there and they shoot and the concentration and the accuracy and the determination to succeed – it's
terrific, and Naz has got that too. I drove around there, and you
could see the way the men there drive, and Naz boxes like that,
with the same recklessness.'

He warms to his theme, extending it beyond its natural limits,
and inevitably gets on to his favourite roots vignette: 'You know,
in that part of Yemen where his people come from, they can be
totally vicious if they have to. You have to shoot 'em to lick 'em,
and I tell you, this fella is like that too. If you break his hands
he'll kick you. If you break his legs he'll bite you. If you pull his
teeth he'll nut you. He has that will to win and the ruthlessness
to go with it, and he's so accurate and strong that people can't
understand it. He carries his own referee in both hands so no
matter what angle they move, he can counter them.'

Quite why this martial spirit and talent settled on little Naz –
the smallest of the nine Hamed children – and not say on his
gentle, intellectually inclined oldest brother, Riath, or podgy,
wheeler-dealer youngest brother Murad, is something Brendan
doesn't venture to explain, because metaphors like his are only
supposed to be taken so far.

The broader point, though, is certainly a valid one. Naseem
Hamed is very much a product of this rich heritage, and it is
something he himself frequently acknowledges. His own

perspective though is that his roots are rather more diverse than Brendan's tales of Arabian Knights might sometimes suggest. His identity is a multi-layered one, with each aspect having been absorbed with obvious pride and without prejudice against the others.

The Arab world, Yemen, Britain, Sheffield and Britain's black communities, each have their place in his own self-image. As he puts it: 'I see myself as a British Arab – born and bred in Britain and I am proud to be British, I'm proud to be Arab, I'm proud to be black and I'm proud to be from Sheffield. I think Britain is one of the best countries in the world to live and I'd never live anywhere else – not even for tax purposes – so obviously I feel more comfortable in Britain than I would in the Middle East.'

The security and direction he gains from his belief in God and an afterlife is another key aspect to his identity. Coming from a relatively liberal Islamic community and family, he is never bombastic about his religious belief and seldom allows it to act as a barrier to his access to the secular world. In fact he prefers to keep quiet on the details rather than to proselytize, but he always makes it clear Islam is a major source of strength and direction for him. 'It's very important for me to be religious and to believe in God,' he says. 'It's one of the biggest parts of my life because at the end of the day what are you living for? Why are you on earth, on this planet? I think it's all a test, which is why it is very important that I keep my life so clean. A lot of people ask me what's the secret of my success and I can honestly say I think I've been given this gift from God and I use it to the best of my ability.'

Another major element of who he is and how he sees himself is generational – as a young man whose teen years covered the late eighties and early nineties, and who, in a typically eclectic way, has consciously absorbed some of the tastes and attitudes of his youth generation in Britain. This is apparent in his fashion statements – the mix he enjoys of street style and designer labels – and perhaps even more so in his musical interests. 'That's a great inspiration in my life – music. I like all kinds of music. I like a lot of soul bands. I've always been into swing and soul and reggae, and now jungle and hip hop. It depends on the mood I'm

in, like if you catch me right before a fight I wouldn't be
listening to soul. It would probably be jungle or ragga, but not
aggressive kind of music. I like a lot of garage – pumping music
with a great beat to get the adrenalin going.'

The more intimate units of identity – as a member of
Sheffield's Yemeni community, its broader black community,
his local mosque, his family and Brendan Ingle's gym and
extended family – are perhaps even more significant. Certainly
when he speaks of his own family it is always with a warmth and
respect which few other subjects inspire. 'We're a large and very
stable family and I am very close to them,' he says. 'I love my
family and my family loves me. My family is great.'

He also has tremendous respect and love for his 'second'
family, the Ingles. Ever since he was seven years old he has been
a feature of their household – eating and sometimes sleeping at
their house, travelling around the country with Brendan and
receiving daily lectures on morality and life skills. 'It was like
father and son basically, in a different sort of way,' says Naseem.
'I learnt more from Brendan than I did in my whole school
career, and without him I don't know where I would have been.
He's like a second father really, and his son, John, is great too.
They're there for me and I'm there for them, so it clicks in as a
very good relationship.'

There are no signs of contradiction or discord in the way any
of these elements have been absorbed. The overwhelming
impression is that they have each added to his sense of self and
his general security as an individual. He wishes he had grown
to more than 5' 3'', but in most respects he seems like a young
man at ease with himself. Despite all the strutting braggadocio,
Naseem is certainly no chip-on-the-shoulder Linford Christie, or
insecure man-child Mike Tyson exuding inner turmoil and pain.

Beyond the ring lights and television cameras the arrogance is
definitely never far from the surface, but there is also an
endearing calmness about him, and a sense of humour that
occasionally allows for an element of self-parody, though even in
the private domain there are hints of the egotistical swagger and
occasional petulance that are so much part of his public persona
and which his current success, fame and wealth have, if
anything, encouraged. He probably over-emphasizes the

distinction when he says: 'I'm a totally different person outside the ring – not arrogant, not bombastic, nothing to prove – just an ordinary, totally down to earth rich guy.'

His upbringing was safe, settled, secure, comfortable and free from conflict by the standards of most of those in his profession. It is clear that his will to succeed has not been a response to deprivation – either material or emotional – as it is with so many great fighters. Despite his playground scraps and occasional street fights, he certainly did not emerge from an environment where fighting was a matter of life and death or where other human beings were regarded as physical obstacles to survival.

The canon of boxing history is full of these: Don Jordan, the world welterweight champion of the late fifties – a child assassin who murdered over thirty men before he'd reached the age of twelve, he learnt to box in the reformatory. Sonny Liston, perhaps the most underrated heavyweight champion of them all, had nineteen criminal arrests for everything from armed robbery to smashing a policeman's kneecap, and was taught the art of self-defence, as if he needed it, in the slammer, but never broke free from the mob. Mike Tyson, who was packing a gun and mugging old ladies before his teens, received his first boxing lesson behind bars.

Even the kind of moderately 'respectable' blue collar working class upbringing, which when combined with huge doses of ingenuity, talent and determination helped mould the likes of Gene Tunney, Muhammad Ali or Julio Cesar Chavez, does not quite fit the bill where Naseem was concerned, though it is closer to the mark than any of the others. In the strictest sense, coming from a family of shopkeepers, he was not even working class, but more to the point, his extraordinary, religiously inspired sense of destiny outstripped even the young Cassius Clay's rapidly burgeoning self-belief, and transcended the traditional motivational categories.

In so many ways, from his family, class, religious and cultural background, to his character and personality, to the physical and mental qualities he brought with him to the ring, Naseem Hamed stands out as unique in the annals of his sport. He was and is very much a one-off phenomenon.

★

That Naz ever laced on a boxing glove is something most people
would put down to luck and fortune, and he puts down to the
design of Allah.

In the late 1950s, Aden (later to become communist South
Yemen and since May 1989 part of the unified Republic of
Yemen) was still a British colony and this status facilitated its use
as a source of cheap labour for Britain, particularly in Sheffield's
steel industry which was undergoing a period of rapid expansion
at a time of industrial boom. A labour supply for the steel
foundries was opened up, particularly from the south but also
from what is now the north of the country where Suleiman
Hamed grew up. Yemen has long been a country of extreme
wealth and extreme poverty, as well as one of chronic political
and social instability. For many young men at the time,
emigration to Britain represented the hope of regular
employment and a better life, even if the jobs they were going to
in the Sheffield steel mills were hard, dangerous and extremely
unhealthy – so much so that local men were reluctant to accept
them under the conditions offered. The Yemenis were a godsend
for the fretful steel bosses at the time and the trickle of
immigration which started in the late forties, slowly turned into
a flow.

Sal, as Naseem's dad likes to be called, was one of these young
men. Having grown up in the village of Malah Rada, 120 miles
from North Yemen's capital, Sana'a, he decided in 1958 to seek
work in Sheffield, and travelled by boat through the Suez Canal
to England for the first time. Like most Yemenis he sent all he
could back to his wife, Caria, at home, until, four years later, she
joined him, and by 1967 they had formally emigrated.

They were among the first Yemenis to move into the working
class suburb of Wincobank, within walking distance of
Hatfield's Steel Works and the other foundries and mills in the
valley below. Both being people with plenty of drive and
ambition, they worked extremely hard, scrimped and scraped
and saved whatever they could to create the best possible life for
their rapidly expanding family.

Their first daughter, Mona, was born in 1965, three years

after Caria's arrival. She was followed two years later by a second daughter, Noel, and then in quick succession their first son Riath and their second son Nabeel, after which Sal and Caria used their savings to buy a small general dealer's store in Newman Road – the same long street where the Ingles and the St Thomas's Boys' Club gym are found. Being the only store in the area for several years, theirs was always busy and the Hameds earned a reasonable living. Before Naseem was born his parents were already starting to occupy a position of some importance in the surrounding neighbourhoods, despite being one of the first 'ethnic' families in a community which, at that stage, was still rather insular.

There was a gap of three years before the third daughter, Phosia, who now runs the shop, was born, followed by the boy who was to be the smallest of their children, Naseem Salem Ali, born at Sheffield's Northern General Hospital on 12 February 1974. Naseem (which, in Arabic, means 'gentle breeze') remained the baby of the family for the next three and a half years. Almost from the start he proved to be extremely confident, outgoing, physically adventurous and a born show-off.

They lived in cramped conditions above the shop, where Sal and Caria worked extremely long hours, but as Naseem grew older, conditions gradually improved, to the point where they were able to buy the adjacent house and join the two premises. This was when Naseem was four years old, soon after his third brother, Ali, was born. Ali was followed by Murad and finally the fourth sister, Saba.

The environment the Hamed children was raised in was loving, warm and not overly strict. With the parents working all day, the older siblings tended to look after the younger ones, with Riath, as the oldest boy, taking particular responsibility for his younger brothers. Naseem has great admiration for the sacrifices his parents made and for their struggle to make a better life for their family. 'It's a real achievement travelling seven thousand miles from Arabia to get over here, to work as hard as they did, to get established, to earn so much money, to get off their feet and eventually have a good standard of living,' he says. 'I think this achievement of the goals they had – the way they worked so hard all their lives and with such determination – has been an influence on me in the way I devote myself to my sport.'

Sal is a deeply religious man who has long played a central role in the affairs of their small local mosque – a converted house in Rothay Street, about a half a mile from their home. His children were raised with a strong emphasis on the tenets of Islam – a faith in a single omnipotent God, and in Mohammed as his last and greatest prophet, chosen to deliver God's final message to mankind. All his children were taught that whatever else they did, they should make sure they marry fellow Muslims, say their daily prayers on their prayer mats five times a day, and fast at Ramadan. From an early age they were required to study the Koran and later to learn Arabic – the language of the Koran (as well as being, in a modern form, the Yemeni lingua franca) through classes at the Yemeni Community Centre, for two hours an evening, five days a week.

This religious and ethical framework provided the basis for Naseem's single-minded sense of destiny. His reluctance to discuss the details publicly appears to be partly a consequence of public prejudices and ignorance about a religion, which, in British minds, is more commonly associated with Iranian *fatwahs*, holy wars and the severing of hands, than with its central tenets which to anyone from outside a monotheistic tradition would seem to have a great deal in common with both Judaism and Christianity. As he puts it: 'I am deeply religious but I prefer to keep my religion to myself in the sense that to me it is a personal and private thing, and you don't like to get people upset.'

What he frequently discusses is his view that his success is a gift from God, and that his self discipline in preparing for fights has been largely a product of his Islamic upbringing. 'It's very important for me that religion has kept my life so clean. It's just great for boxing and for all sport,' he says. 'You can't drink alchohol, or smoke or do any drugs whatsoever, or anything that can twist your mind to a different angle. That's why I'm such a clean-living guy.'

When Naseem was two years old the family travelled to the Yemen, returning after he turned four. He remembers very little of these years, and it certainly had more impact on his older siblings. But while the Yemen itself remained a vague memory until he was to visit the country again for a fortnight shortly before his twentieth birthday, Sheffield's 3000-strong Yemeni community was integral to his life from the start.

Throughout the fifties and the sixties the Yemeni community was treated almost as a foreign pocket of *Gastarbeiters*, and despite its increasing social and health problems, particularly in terms of industrial disease, it received minimal outside support. In the late sixties the community began to organize itself and to find its voice. Sal, a strong and resourceful man, was part of a group of activists and elders who formed the Yemeni Community Association with the aim of catering for the cultural, political and economic needs of the community and of providing assistance to its young people and its poor. From the start he was a member of its management committee and is currently its chairman, while Naseem's oldest brother, Riath, has managed its cultural centre as well as Naseem's own business interests.

At the time of its formation most of its membership was working class, Arabic-speaking, Muslim, and broadly socialist in orientation, with many of them coming from communist South Yemen. The association included a strong core of younger activists who ensured it was tightly organized and that its mission extended beyond the community's own parameters. It received support from both the Labour Party and Communist Party and made common cause with the trade union movement and with other black political and cultural organizations in Sheffield and attempted to develop a sense of identification between the Yemeni community and the broader black community, helping to found the city's Black Community Forum.

Dr Abdul Shaif, another of the Yemeni Community Association's founder members and its current spokesman, says the sense of community and direction it has provided was central to Naseem's development. 'Its origins go back before Naseem was born, so he came into the association from birth, as a member of the Yemeni community,' he says. 'One of our aims is to look for talents and to try and harness them, and to give people support and encouragement and help them to develop a sense of confidence and I think Naseem owes a lot to the Yemeni community for that.'

Naseem's identification with the black community seems to have come partly from his own, fairly limited, experience of overt racism, but rather more so from the influence of his family and peers – from his brothers, the community association and his gym mates.

As for his self-assurance, Naseem says it comes from both parents, and he has no sense of bashfulness about being fulsome in his public devotion to them. 'I praise my mum and dad so much for the way they raised me,' he says. 'I really had the very best upbringing possible.' He will talk at length about his father's determination and drive, and has always particularly admired his status in the organization and the community more generally.

When he discusses his mother, he emphasizes her positive spirit and devotion to the family. He loves talking about how she spoils him with her attention and her wonderful cooking (no one can compete with her Yemini fried chicken, rice, chutney and salad) and how he can now treat her by buying her anything she wants, from a new kitchen to a new house. He'll tell you, tongue in cheek, that she is the only woman in his life and, more seriously, that she is one of his prime sources of direction. 'My mum is a very confident woman, and that's where I get it from. We Hameds are all confident,' he says.

Abdul Shaif, who has known Naseem from birth, says the assertiveness, and sense of direction, as well as the overt pride and swagger, were part of the package from the moment Naseem could string a sentence together. 'He was always cheeky. He had the arrogance when he was very young, but to me personally he has always been very respectful,' he recalls. 'He always stopped and shook my hand from when he was very little. He was always a nice and gentle young boy, very caring about his family and friends, and about the community, but always with the arrogance and the talents which would develop as he grew up.'

In June 1978, not long after the family returned from their two year visit to North Yemen, Naseem began his formal education at the Wincobank Nursery and Infant School. While he eventually settled in and was accepted, it was not an entirely happy period of his life. Being Muslim and Arab and brown-skinned made him different at an age when difference can easily become a reason for exclusion. He was, for instance, the target of occasional name-calling with a racial edge, being dubbed 'chocolate drop' and occasionally 'Paki' by some of his peers, though as he became accepted it was replaced by the more affectionate 'Nabby' and later 'Naz'. Brendan Ingle says that one of the reasons Riath, Nabeel and Naseem began boxing was their father's concern about this kind of racist name-calling. Naseem, however, believes stories of his experiences of racism have sometimes been overstated and says it was seldom a major issue for him, though this does not detract from his awareness of racism in British society, his self-identification as a black man and his willingness to take a public stand on the issue. 'But personally, I've never had *major* problems with racism and racist remarks. Maybe at infant school, yes, but then I got a reputation for myself and I never got no trouble, and no racial problems and basically I got on with everybody.'

Despite his lack of interest in his school work, Naseem created strong impressions during his four years at Wincobank Infants School. Brenda Barley, the school secretary, came to know all the Hamed children, as well as their parents, and says her memories of Naseem are particularly vivid. 'He was a lovely kid – very impish and mischievous, but you couldn't help but love him,' she recalls. 'He was a real little scamp but not really naughty and never in real trouble. In fact they were all great kids. They were a very close-knit family and you could see they loved each other very much, though the children used to fight with each other a bit.'

Dorothy Clark, who gave Naseem library instruction when he was seven and eight years old, saw him in a slightly different light. 'I remember him as being fairly quiet, or at least quite shy with me, so he was difficult to get through to, but he definitely wasn't one of the problem children,' she recalls. 'I don't remember him being one of those who got into many fights, but I used to watch him in the playground and he loved games and was always very quick on his feet, very fast, very agile.'

Great legends tend to follow great fighters, thinkers and doers. Often they are discovered or are invented as a way of explaining their genius or of providing moral-laden lessons on how they made their start on the path to immortality. Alfred the Great had his burnt cakes, Isaac Newton his falling apple, George Washington his admission to felling the cherry tree.

In boxing, a sport more taken with mythology than any other, we know that Muhammad Ali made his start as a 12-year-old who tearfully turned to a police boxing trainer after his new bicycle was stolen and the young 'fairy boy' Mike Tyson had his first taste of his destiny when he could no longer contain his anger after a larger local bully pulled off the head of one of his pigeons. Both of these incidents probably owe more to fact than to fiction. This distinction mattered rather more in those days than it does today. In the media-wise late twentieth century, where the lines between image and reality, truth and fantasy are more blurred than ever, myths and legends are as much the stuff of star-making as they were in King Alfred's days, particularly when Brendan Ingle happens to be around.

So we come to the story of Naseem Hamed's start on the path to glory. It has been told scores of times, in several versions, but this is the way Brendan gave it to me: 'I'm travelling on the bus up Newman Road towards my house, sitting on the top deck, and it stops at the bus stop outside the local school. I just happen look outside and I see this young lad who I thought was Pakistani – looked about six years old – fighting off these three bigger white kids, and I had to laugh because he was darting in and out and dashing around and they couldn't touch him and he was hitting them. This tiny fella was too fast for them. I was very impressed, and I thought to meself, This fella has the makings of a great boxer in him – he can really move. Well, a week later I passed his father's shop and got talking. Then I see this little kid who comes up to say hello, and straight away I recognize him from the fight outside the school. It is definitely the same kid, and then I realize he's Riath and Nabeel's younger brother, so I ask him to come down to the gym and that's how he gets started.'

One of the most commonly told additions to this version of the tale is that the three bullies were shouting racist abuse at Naseem – calling him a 'Paki'. Another variation is that it's Sal who approached Brendan to take his boys to the gym. As Brendan put it: 'Naz's father says, "Brendan, can I have a word with you," and I says, "Sure, Sal," and he says, "My boys are at school and they are getting called names and I want to bring them down to the boxing club." So I says, "No problem." So he brought the three of them out – Riath, Nabeel and the little fella who was the fella I saw in the school yard.'[1]

And this is how Naseem told the story to a local newspaper shortly after his thirteenth birthday: 'He saw me fighting three boys who had called me names. I was skipping and moving to keep out of their way. Brendan got off the bus and spoke to my dad. Then he went home and told his wife: "I've just seen a champion." Next day I went to his club and I've wanted to be become a boxer ever since.'[2]

However it is told, the central tenet of the story is the same: even the untrained Naz was a little warrior with the natural speed, agility and elusiveness to beat off more than one bigger lad.

But, according to Naseem, the actual incident never happened. Today, this is what he says about the legend: 'Basically, I think it's a load of rubbish. I never had major racist problems and I've never got bullied at all in my life. Never. The story was a good publicity stunt and created a lot of interest at the time – people wanted to hear it and it worked and gave my career a big amount of interest, and now everybody's familiar with it, but to tell you the truth I can't remember that incident at all. I think it was made up. I can't remember fighting three guys in the schoolyard – I don't know where that came from, but that's Brendan's story and Brendan will stick to it. What he saw, he saw, but I can't remember doing it. What I do remember is that just down the road from our house was Brendan's gym and there was a lot of success coming from there, so I went there, went in the gym and got started. Riath had boxed there but didn't have it in his heart and drifted from the game. Nabeel had it in his heart, but drifted too, but I went there to the gym and looked at it at a different level and I kept it up because that was what I wanted to do.'

Brendan, however, is adamant that the incident happened and that there was no exaggeration. And his son, John, insists that his father had no cause to make it up. 'Naz was the only Arab or Pakistani boy his age in the school at the time, and my father definitely recognized him because he told us about it when it happened. I think Naz has just forgotten,' he said.

★

Whatever the truth, all that really matters is that Naseem had his first boxing lesson early in 1981, at the age of seven, at the St Thomas's Boys' Club under Brendan Ingle's tutelage. He walked into this large, dark converted church hall with its boxing ring in the far corner, its collection of heavy bags, the pearball, the speedball, the pull-up bars, and the odour of decades of sweat absorbed into the splintered floor and chipped walls with the paint peeling off, covered with posters and glory days clippings from a game where time passes very quickly and the participants age even quicker.

There he found a kind of ordered informality that is a feature of most boxing gyms, but more so in Brendan's, and this immediately appealed. There was no tight arsed martial-arts-type regimentation, but instead about forty boys and men engaged in a variety of activities related to the sport – sparring, hitting the bags, punching the pads, shadow-boxing, practising moves, doing ground exercises and the like – while now and then Ingle shouted instructions to keep the flow going, or approached one of the fighters to provide some individual tuition or to make a point about some aspect of life and living.

But under Brendan's benign rule there was far more to it than that. Go to the gym today and you'll see things you won't find in any other in the world. For a start, the methods of tuition are very different. The boxers learn unusual combinations and unorthodox punches, like the bolo, from an early age. You'll see Brendan calling a group of young boxers together for an exercise where they shadow-box round and round circles painted on the floor, moving their feet back and forth, in and out. It's a strange ritual and one that seems to contradict the traditional iron rule of never going off balance by crossing your feet, but for Ingle there is simple logic in this paradox: the exercise is all about remaining in balance whatever position you're in. 'It's about footwork, flexibility, movement and posture,' he explains, not entirely helpfully, though the evidence can be seen in the balance and ability to switch effortlessly from orthodox to southpaw, to square on and back, which most of his better protégés share – Herol Graham, Johnny Nelson, Paul 'Silky' Jones, Naseem

Hamed, Ryan Rhodes and many others.

There are other unusual exercises too: the better boxers have to go round after round with their sparring partners firing on both cylinders and all they're allowed to do is avoid the punches. They are seldom warned to keep their hands up, and tend to dangle them comfortably at waist level when outside the fray. They practice hitting and catching the ceiling ball for hours to improve hand-eye coordination, and they are all encouraged to learn acrobatic manoeuvres – backflips, rope leaps, somersaults and the like – for agility, self-confidence and marketability.

Like most boxing trainers, Ingle takes the constant threat of brain damage from boxing very seriously. Unlike most, he has a practical solution to minimize the damage. As he puts it, 'punishment in the ring is cumulative. If water drips long enough on a rock, it will crack.' And where most of the drips land is in the gym, which is why 'open' sparring is a rarity in his domain and why defensive excellence is such a prized commodity there. He even teaches them ten different ways to avoid being caught by a jab.

He explains to each batch of novices why body sparring is generally preferable to head hunting: 'Ya see here, lads, it's better off learning that way, than having wars. All the damage is done through open sparring. You can have a bit of controlled open sparring, but you get in there and start bashing each other up, and you're not going to learn anything, and if you damage me, I'm going to try and damage you, and I damage you, you're going to try and damage him, and it just goes on.'

He looks at them one by one with his intense, quizzical, wise eyes. 'You *got* to learn the skill and what I'm going to try and do over the next couple of days is just make you see that there's an easier way of doing it than finishing up getting bashed up. If my nose is bashed up, I'm not going to want to spar tomorrow, or if I'm sparring to the body and you hit me accidentally on purpose in the face, what chance is there I'm not going to hit you back? You got me?'

That stare again, demanding affirmation, and this time the novices nod as his eyes pass over them, before he seals the point, changing a discussion point to a rule. 'That's the way it goes,' he says emphatically, and then takes a verbal step back to round off the day's lesson. 'Being in here thirty-odd years, I've completely changed the whole lot. You get a workout and you don't what?' – he pauses for the answer that never comes – 'Beat up. Understand? And you learn the skills. Consequently, when you get to box you enjoy it better and, please God, you don't get hurt.'

Ingle fervently believes his methods, refined and built up over the last three and a half decades, are, as he puts it, 'taking this sport through to the twenty-first century'. Just as boxing evolved from the fencing-derived, lean-back, one-punch-at-a-time, post-bare-knuckle style of the end of the last century, to the lean-forward, combination-punching, ducking, weaving and slipping style which took root after the 1920s, so he believes the unusual, though generally entertaining, style he teaches will become *de rigueur* over the next few decades, and that its success will revolutionize the sport. Other trainers will be compelled to follow or will find themselves at a disadvantage.

But his tuition goes way beyond the art of self-defence. Within the gym there are frequently tensions and fights over a wide range of other issues – from theft of property to 'theft' of girlfriends – but Brendan Ingle has made sure that racism or religious bigotry have never been allowed to surface. Black and white, Catholics, Protestants, Hindus and Muslims mix very easily, as they do in most boxing gyms. His one trick is to make a bit of a joke about it – referring to himself as a 'stupid Mick' or 'dumb Paddy' for example – and in this way get them all immunized to the common racist terms of insult. But just to make sure, when boxers join the gym they are told emphatically that 'religion and politics is personal and private' and should be left at the door.

Most of these boys are from the toughest and poorest sections of Wincobank, with backgrounds far more deprived than anything the Hameds had experienced. Some are from children's homes, others are young criminals on probation, many come from the flats in the Flower Estate, where the local council once placed what it considered to be its real welfare hard cases, only to discover that this wasn't such a smart idea, with consequences in crime and problems for the local schools which seemed impossible to cope with. With the rise in unemployment following the closure of the steel mills, in some sections crime became one of the major pasttimes of the menfolk, and in this male-oriented community, the sins of the fathers tend to be carried over to the sons. When all else fails, the sons are sent to Brendan Ingle's door. 'If anyone's got a shot at putting the lad straight, it'll be Brendan,' they say, so the bad boys come to box.

Brendan doesn't try to put them straight with 'tough love' or an iron-fisted regime, but rather with a mixture of humour, reason, team building and plenty of patience. When the boys are caught stealing – and they nick everything from handwrap bandages and jockstraps to shoes, money and equipment there – they are not kicked out. They have to return what they have stolen, stand in the ring, announce their crime, and apologize. And they all seem to do it, with the result that no one has been expelled yet.

With each boxing lesson he mixes in a sermon on what he calls life skills – social skills, communication skills and how to interact and treat people. Each would-be world champion gets his chance to climb in the ring, announce his name, tell everyone about his last fight, do a frontflip or some other antic, and then sing a song (most of the younger tearaways choose 'I Can Sing a Rainbow'). They're not allowed to mumble, they have to say Please, Thank you, and Sorry, and they're taught to be proud of who they are, to be tolerant of other races and religions, and to believe that Britain is the best place in the world (and this is coming from an Irishman who tells you he once hated the English, but eventually learnt to admire them, even though he still hates what they did to his country). They're told not to steal or lie or mix boxing with too much sex, or to hang out with the 'wrong crowd', and even not to swear in the gym. He repeats these lessons over and over again, believing that repetition is the key to learning. Most are ignored, but a little gets through.

Some of the boys come to learn how to defend themselves against bullies, and, if they stick at it, seldom go away disappointed. Others, probably most, arrive in the gym as lads with an aptitude for fighting and an inclination to use their fists to settle a dispute, and Ingle places great stress on avoiding extra-mural battling and particularly bullying. 'They almost all have had fights outside the gym at one time or another,' Ingle says. 'Naz also had a few scuffles when he was a kid – he always fancied fighting – but the emphasis, the pressure, is on disciplining themselves and learning control – to learn that "sticks and stones will break your bones but words won't hurt you", and to learn to walk away. Of course they get guys having a go at them – Naz will have had that growing up – but the point is that if you can fight, people respect you and they will leave you alone.'

When Naseem first arrived there, these are the lessons he was immediately confronted with, and he took to the whole experience instantly. From then on he could not keep away. As he remembers it, the whole ethos impressed him enormously but he was there to box, and was particularly transfixed by the sparring – not just the punching but the skill in avoiding punches. 'I remember that first time well,' he recalls. 'I went into the gym and I thought it looked like a great sport, a great art, a great craft – where a fighter could hit another fighter and not get hit back. So I thought, If you can be like that – get good with your hands and good on your feet – you're not hardly going to be hit, and then obviously you can have a long career and you're going to be successful. So it was a great feeling that first time and I got into it from the start. I thought, This is the sport for me, and very soon I gathered I was a natural – a natural fighter, natural mover, with natural speed and agility and the attitude for the game, so I knew I was going to go far, and right from the beginning I knew I was going to be a professional boxer and a world champion. That's when the dream started.'

He was not universally popular, and in fact not everyone took to the little youngster instantly. 'From day one, when he first came here, he's always said: "I'm going to be world champion", and he was always as brash and cocky as he is now and he hasn't changed at all,' Nelson recalls with a big, affectionate, admiring grin. 'The only thing is, that when he arrived here he had nothing to back it up with, and people scorned him and looked down at him because of what he was saying, because they found it all to be a bit presumptuous.'

Graham, the hero of the gym for many years, fondly remembers Naseem as an extremely self-assured child, who had no compunction about assuming his friendship, and making demands on it: 'I lived just down the road from him and he used to come to my house, knock on the door, and say, "Come on, we're going training", and I would go. Even then, he was so sure of himself, very forward, he knew what he wanted, he ruled, and that was that.'

With anyone other than Ingle, it is possible that Naseem would have drifted away like his two older brothers. But the relationship between this tiny seven year old Muslim shop owners' son and the 41-year-old Catholic socialist was set in stone from day one. They took to each other in a big way. Naz just loved 'Old Irish', and Ingle just couldn't stop singing the praises of this precocious little lad he was nurturing. There are many boxers in the past who have fallen out with Ingle, who encountered his darker side when he believed they'd crossed him, or who failed to understand his often convoluted logic, the riddles and conundrums and stories that seemed to have no point unless you listen all the way through to the bite at the end, but Naseem was never one of them. He always knew there were no greener pastures than those he was grazing on, and that for his character and talents he had the best cultivator in the business.

The path that led Brendan Ingle to Newman Road was similar to the one followed by Sal Hamed. Raised in Dublin as one of fifteen children of a working class family, he left school when he was fourteen, and tried his hand at every little job he could find – van delivery boy, casual gardener, decorator's assistant, errand runner and general dogsbody for anyone with some heavy work needing attention and a few pence to spare. He also learnt to fight from an early age, having to defend himself against the taunts of his peers because his surname was inherited from an English Protestant grandfather (who had converted to Catholicism). 'I would have to fight and they would say to me, "Your grandfather's English and a turncoat", and I would have to fight, and then they'd say, "Ah, you think you're tough just because all your brothers box", and I would say, "No, I fight my own fights," and then we'd start fighting again.' He chuckles a little ruefully and adds: 'So I've had it from all sides every time I've opened my mouth, and the same over here because I was Irish.'

He left Ireland at the age of eighteen in 1958 (the same year
Sal Hamed left the Yemen), because his prospects of a regular
job in Ireland seemed negligible. His brother, a professional
boxer, had settled in Sheffield and one day returned to Dublin
waving £300 and with three new suits in his bag. He told
Brendan the city of steel was thriving, and that was that.
Brendan took a job on a building site in Sheffield, and found a
room in the Manor – the poorest section of the city, which at the
time was covered by layers of soot and smoke which seemed to
leave everyone with a permanent cough.

But after one brief visit back to Ireland, he decided Sheffield
was the place for him. 'It was the best thing I ever done. I love
Ireland and when I left I used to think the English were the
biggest bastards on two legs – tricky, cunning, crafty, devious,
but when I came here I joined the library and now I know
they're the cleverest race. What the English done in Ireland was
terrible, but now I realize that was the situation at the time, and
if it had been the Spaniards or French it would still have been
terrible,' he says shaking his head and then smiling like someone
who has found a universal truth. 'Now I'm British by choice,
and I am so glad I came here because I have learnt so much about
people, but I'm still Irish.'

Ingle's speech and methods are full of such paradoxes. Once a
firm supporter of communism, and still an ardent, union-
supporting, welfare-backing socialist, he also strongly admires
Margaret Thatcher and some of her policies and strongly
opposes nationalization. He's an Irish nationalist who opposes
armed struggle and is not convinced by the wisdom of
unification; a crypto-pacifist whose hero is Nelson Mandela; a
fighting man who passionately abhors violence; a rich 'miser'
known for his generosity and community spirit; a 'slow learner'
at school who is now a self-made intellectual, always eager to
discuss world history, politics, literature or current affairs; a
boxing trainer who alternately describes his sport as a 'filthy,
rotten game' and as being 'so pure there's nothing quite like it'.

In 1961, when his girlfriend, Alma, was the St Thomas's
Church secretary, he was asked by the vicar, the Revd Fred
Herrington, to start a youth club in the church hall. Having
boxed on and off as an amateur since the age of eight, and having

followed the sport fanatically since he was three, he certainly knew the ropes, and as he didn't know much else, the youth club became a boxing club. He bought some equipment with his own money, but it was not long before most of this was stolen or destroyed. Gradually, however, he developed a core of loyal lads and the club took off. In 1963 he married Alma, and they're still together and in love, and boxing has ruled their lives ever since.

Two years later, when the money from Brendan's job as a steelworker was short and the family was growing, he turned professional. He was already twenty-five – a bit old to start a boxing career – but he won his first fight against a gypsy called Dick Griffiths (for a princely purse of £11, after deductions). He stuck at it for the next eight years, having over thirty outings at welterweight and middleweight, winning two thirds of them but retiring at the end of 1973, when he was nearly thirty-four, after a trio of losses in Dublin, London and Copenhagen. As the veteran boxing agent and cutman Paddy Byrne recalls, 'He came from a fighting family. His father was an amateur champion and his brother was very good. Brendan was a fair professional – better than average – very tricky and awkward, but not a big puncher.'

After retiring he began to build up his own stable of professionals as well as continuing to work with the amateurs, something that was technically forbidden by the stuffy amateur establishment, though they tended to turn a blind eye to the practice. He found the amateur game was full of rivalries, petty jealousies and festering little resentments. Not only were some of the amateur authorities unhappy with the mix of pros and amateurs in Ingle's gym, but some did not like his training methods, his lack of deference to their authority, his Irish identity and the fact that he was receiving sponsorship which they felt should have gone into other coffers. There was particular resentment about a large grant the club received from the Sports Council for its work among underprivileged youth.

In June 1978, soon after his finest boxer, Herol Graham, won the senior ABA middleweight title, it all came to the fore and his club was disqualified by the English ABA, primarily on the grounds that amateurs and professionals were being trained in the same gym. Ingle was beside himself with fury and there were some who feared his dark side would emerge with unfortunate consequences. Even today, he remains bitter about the experience and retains a high degree of suspicion, some would say paranoia, about the amateur authorities. 'Up and down the country – all over England – amateurs trained with the pros, without them blinking an eye. I thought if they can do it, then I can do it, but you see, I was a trouble causer, an *Irish* trouble causer, and some of them felt humiliated by the success of my methods, so they told lies about me and used the excuse of the professional thing, and of the Sports Council grant to disqualify me.'

After a few days of blind rage, Alma sat him down, quoted the Bible to him, and Brendan's unusual logic got to work: he came to the conclusion that what he needed was to give up tea drinking to prove his self-discipline. 'I used to drink gallons of it and then in 1978, when they disaffiliated the club and they told all those lies, I didn't want it to get me down, so I thought if I can discipline meself to stop drinking tea, I can discipline meself to do anything,' and he has never touched tea since. Asked about the incident, current ABA secretary Colin Brown, who was not involved at the time, confirmed that the main issue of dispute was professionalism: 'There was a big inquiry and they were suspended. All the tension that led to this conclusion was about amateurs being trained by professionals. People will say that there is bias, and that's what he may think, but don't ask me why. He's a professional trainer and he shouldn't have been involved with amateurs.'

Eventually they found their way back – the amateurs boxing under the banner of the Unity Amateur Boxing Club in ABA tournaments, but retaining the St Thomas's identity in club tournaments, and the pros getting on with their business and continuing to train and spar with their unpaid counterparts (though officially Brendan's work was, from then on, restricted to the pros). Ingle's success in the amateurs was marred by the tensions with the ABA, but he was starting to have impressive results with his growing 'mercenary' contingent, rapidly surpassing anything that had previously been achieved in Sheffield.

In the hundred years of professional boxing before Ingle arrived on the scene, Sheffield had produced just three British champions. Over the past fifteen years, Ingle has produced a steady stream of fighters who won British, Commonwealth, European, international and world titles, including Herol Graham, Brian Anderson, Fidel Castro Smith, Neville Brown, Chris Saunders, Naseem Hamed and Paul 'Silky' Jones.

It is true that some of Ingle's best boxers over the years have left him – some after acrimonious splits over everything from money, to his managerial methods, to complaints of being ignored; others because of rival offers or desires to go it alone. Silky Jones, Fidel Castro Smith, Neville Brown, Clifton Mitchell, and, most sadly, near the end of his career, Herol Graham, all did this. Some of them are not on speaking terms with him any more, though others, like Brown and Mitchell, returned to the fold. But these are things that happen to most trainers and managers. Overall, Ingle's has been a record which few trainers in Britain can compare with and the reason for this relates both to his methods and to his personality and character.

St Thomas's gym has never had any kind of formalized hier-archy. With most of the boxers, amateurs and pros, boys and men, novices and veterans, are all in it together and they mix easily, share jokes and insults and trade punches. But those who have made a name for themselves tend to get placed a little higher in the informal pecking order. When Naseem first arrived in 1981, the undisputed star of the gym was Herol Graham, who may well have been the best British fighter since Jim Driscoll never to win a world title, and was probably Britain's finest middleweight and light middleweight of the past two or three decades – better, at 160 pounds, than subsequent world champions Nigel Benn, Chris Pyatt, Steve Collins and Chris Eubank.

There is a strong sense in Sheffield, which Graham certainly shares, that he would have been given far better breaks if he had been backed by the southern English 'establishment', though Ingle feels he would not have achieved as much as he did if he had been enticed to the more distracting environment of London. He had been a professional for over a decade and had won 41 out of 42 fights before he was given his first world title shot, only to lose by a majority decision as a result of a deducted point, against one of the all-time greats of the middleweight division, Mike McCallum.

The top London managers did their best to keep their
budding stars away from the 'Bomber'. Eubank avoided him
after being outclassed in several sparring sessions.'[3] Benn wasn't
interested either. 'The word got around – keep away from
Bomber Graham,' Herol recalls, 'and Naz is the same – not a lot
of people want to box him because he has the ability to move,
dance around them and dictate the fight.' The difference,
Graham argues, is that Ingle now understands the power politics
of the game far better than he did in the early eighties (though
Ingle insists he was well versed in that aspect of the game by the
time Graham made his mark). 'At the time I started, Brendan
didn't know a lot about that, really. He's learnt it through
having me, and is now making sure the same things don't
happen to Naz, but it's a shame he didn't know it then, when I
was around, because I've missed out on a lot, but there you go,
you live your life and make it as merry as you can.'

Today, several years after the 'Bomber's' retirement and his
fall-out with Ingle, Naseem still doffs his cap to his first pugilisic
hero and the two of them still get together now and then. 'Herol
Graham was a great boxer. I learnt a lot from him,' says Naz,
which is about as effusive as he gets about any other fighter, with
the exception of Muhammad Ali. But the relationship did not
involve a one-sided hero worship. While Ingle would frequently
take Naseem to Graham's fights around Britain, and later to
Europe as well, Graham for his part was a regular cheerleader at
Naseem's amateur fights, encouraging him and teaching him
various tricks of the trade along the way.

Johnny Nelson, who was a gangling fourteen-year-old at the
time, believes Graham was one of the prime formative influences
on Hamed's progress. 'If you look at Naseem's style, he's got a
little bit of everybody and some of himself, but you can see he
really learnt from Herol. He was fortunate he was in a good gym
with a good trainer and mentor, with good people to look up to.'

The way it worked, throughout their time together, was that
Naz would chase Graham around the ring and Herol would
block and duck but never fire back. 'People sometimes ask me,
"Why does Naz fight like you?" and I say, "Well, we used to
spar together all the time, and I mean *all* the time," ' Graham
says. 'He was only a little midget, so I used to do the running

around. He got to know all my movements, and would try to nullify them. He would just chase me around and that's how he learnt.' Unlike Graham, however, Naz developed into an attacking knockout artist as well as a defensive wizard. He was also fortunate to have been blessed with rhythm, reflexes, metabolism, innate physical strength, hand-eye and time-distance coordination, as well as the ability to focus, which all come under the heading 'natural ability'.

Some boxers get to the top without it. Primo Carnera in the 1930s became world heavyweight champion because he was huge and most of his major fights were fixed. Frank Bruno eventually became WBC heavyweight champion because his strength, extreme dedication and marketability made up for his deficiencies in the talent department. But from day one it was apparent that in addition to dedication and excellent tuition, Naseem Hamed arrived with trememdous natural gifts in terms of physical potential.

It is perhaps worth pointing out that Naseem is natually left handed (with a propensity towards ambidexterity), a condition which has long fascinated geneticists and other specialists because of what it might reveal about the human brain. Current statistical data suggests left-handers are more likely to be gifted in certain fields. Within the world of boxing, it appears there is a greater propensity towards left handedness among the sport's elite than in the population generally. Until recently, most of these boxers were 'turned' to become converted southpaws, often because of the difficulties southpaws had in getting fights. Joe Louis, for instance, successfully avoided southpaws throughout his 71-fight career. Those days are largely over (though there are a few converted southpaws among today's world champions, including Oscar de la Hoya and Virgil Hill). Today, in almost every one of the seventeen weight divisions there is a world champion or former champion, along with several contenders, who are southpaws, and these include many of the game's elite. Champions or former champions like Pernell Whitaker, Michael Nunn, Henry Maske, Frank Liles, Michael Moorer, Humberto Gonzalez, Hector Camacho and Mark Johnson, to name a few, may have been helped by the awkwardness of their 'wrong-way-round' style, but one can't help thinking there's more to it than that.

Whatever the truth, Naseem's natural left handedness came in a package that seemed filled with every natural asset a boxer could dream of. What is more, he quickly learnt the Ingle style of switching from southpaw to the orthodox stance and back, and did it with the same effortless grace that Herol Graham had displayed.

By the time Naseem started at middle school in September 1982 he had been boxing intensively for over a year – six or seven days a week, two hours a day – and had reached a point of considerable skill and technical proficiency. He had become an established and accepted presence in the gym, still far too young for formal competition but far too good, and far too cocky, to be ignored.

'I would say we had to work with Naseem, so we got used to him,' Johnny Nelson remembers. 'He progressed and got better and better and better, and after a while, one by one, a lot of people didn't want to spar with him because it was like being hit by a bag of rice and not being able to hit back. He was so fast and skilful. He could talk a good fight, but he could back it up, and if you tried to grab him he was so fast you just couldn't catch him.'

Naz was to spend his next four years as one of 270 pupils at Concord Middle School, and the memories from his teachers' point of view do not appear to be particularly positive. While his sense of humour, vitality and 'untapped potential' are stressed, what seem to be remembered more are Naseem's arrogance, laziness about school work, discipline problems and a predatory tendency. Also mentioned though are the positive roles played by Ingle and Naseem's brother Riath in confronting some of these problems.

Concord's deputy headteacher, Mike Delaney, who was a senior teacher during Naseem's time there, says that throughout these four years staff had problems with the young boxer. 'He was arrogant and . . . well, I'm loath to say he was a bully because he didn't pick on one particular child, but a lot of children were in fear of him and I think he put a lot of pressure on them – emotional pressure if you like – to get his own way, and he always got it because the kids knew that physically they couldn't match him.' He says this with an intensity which indicates Naseem was not one of his favourite pupils, particularly in his first year at the school, when he would get into fights to establish his reputation. 'Initially it was a bit like the old cock of the school thing – the strongest person in the school had to prove himself and the young princes challenge now and then, and this happened with Naseem, and he could handle himself, all right. He was very wiry and was much stronger than he looked.'

Naseem has a different view of his school years at that time. He does not recognize the perception of himself as a potential bully or as a major league troublemaker, and says he seldom had problems with the other children. 'I never really got into many fights at school because I had a a reputation, so there was respect. They gathered that the small one was the effective one who was trained to fight, so I never got into trouble.'

Herol Graham recalls that Naz was not one of those boys who would pick fights, and usually used his gift of the gab to avoid them. 'He used to get into some scuffles,' he recalls, 'but he was intelligent enough to get out of them. He had the speed of his legs and the wit of his mouth, and his sarcasm seemed to get him out of everything, but if he had to defend himself, he could defend himself all right.' John Ingle says that the notion of Naz as a bully is far-fetched. 'It's just not credible,' he says. 'He was weighing four stone when the average weight of guys his age was nearly six stone.'

With Sal spending long hours in the shop and on his community obligations, and Caria raising the younger children, and neither being familiar with the British school system, it was usually Riath, as the oldest son, who was sent to the school to handle things. Riath was barely seventeen when Naseem finished at Concord but the staff were extremely impressed by his maturity and remembered him as being academically inclined and responsible, so they were quite happy to accept his role in this respect.

Brendan Ingle also created a strong, favourable impression, not only through his success in channelling what was regarded as Naseem's aggression, but also because of his occasional visits to the school to find out how his young protégé was doing. 'I remember him coming to us a few times, and asking how Naseem was getting on, and I must say I was quite impressed with the guy,' says Delaney.

At the same time, however, Naseem's teachers felt that his obsession with boxing was detracting from his academic potential. While Brendan Ingle mentions that Naseem's daily Arabic lessons were also partly responsible for this, his son John says that this should not be overstated. 'He would go with his brothers to his Arabic classes after school, but then when he passed the gym he would duck in. Later in the afternoon his brothers would collect him and they'd go home together.'

The school recognized him as a boy with a good deal of unfulfilled academic potential who, overall, produced below average results despite spells of achievement. 'He certainly could have achieved more had he been more focused,' says Delaney. 'There was always this unproved gut reaction on our part that he could do better than he did. But he had to work hard to be average and he was lazy about school work and therefore he struggled.' He also makes the point that, in common with many boys in the school, Naz's intelligence was not reflected in his written work. 'We often find that a particular boy will be brighter than some of the girls, but this doesn't manifest itself in their work. Naseem was like that – he had problems committing things to paper.'

Again, Naseem takes a different perspective on this period, stressing that he already knew he was going to be a professional boxer and therefore did not see much point in putting time and energy into his school work. 'I just couldn't wait for the last bell to ring so I could go down to the gym and train every day, so for me school was just a passing of the time, because from the age of seven I knew what I wanted in life.'

This tunnel vision is certainly not something he has accredited to himself retrospectively. His friends say that right from the start boxing was his only real passion and he would regularly remind them of his glorious destiny. Some say he was so single-minded that he missed a great deal of what is taken for granted in a regular childhood because every day after school and at weekends, without fail, he was in the gym.

Even in class he would find ways of bringing his obsession into the arena. One late Friday afternoon session in 1985, for example, each pupil was required to present a show-and-tell oral on his or her hobby. Naseem, then eleven-years-old, played a hip-hop number on his ghetto blaster and proceeded to fill the time with a non-stop, high speed shadow boxing exhibition which impressed his classmates no end. 'We had never seen anything like it,' one of them, Nick Jones, was quoted as saying. 'We were whispering to each other: "That were great." But we never let on to Naz. He already knew how good he was.'[4]

But if some of his classmates were won over, from the school's perspective 1985 was the year when most of the problems with Naseem came to the fore. It is perhaps no coincidence that this was a year of great frustration for the aspiring young fighter. Amateur regulations only allow boys to begin boxing competitively when they reach eleven, so Naseem presumed that after four years of learning his craft, he would be able to enter his first tournament soon after his eleventh birthday and was devastated to discover he was still 8 pounds too light to be allowed to compete in the lowest weight division. He was quite prepared to fight boys much bigger than himself, but the regulations compelled him to compete within the accepted weight divisions and there were none light enough to accommodate him. So, contrary to accepted folklore, Naseem Hamed did not begin his amateur career as an 11-year-old. He ended up having to wait a full year before he had grown large enough to enter his first competition, and even then, with some intensive eating under his belt, he couldn't quite make the 4½-stone limit. Ingle had a simple, romantic explanation for this: 'It is very difficult to fatten a throughbred and he is a thoroughbred.'[5]

But when Naseem had finally made a enough of a dent in the scales (with a couple of pounds' help from little pieces of lead around his waist), Brendan Ingle was ready with his stories and legends. The local press were tipped off that the next 'Bomber' Graham had arrived, his gym mates were on hand to give him a rousing send-off and the 12-year-old had stars in his eyes and was burning to go.

3

The Professional Amateur

There can be few 12-year-olds in the history of this sport, or any sport, whose debuts have received quite so much publicity and are remembered quite so vividly as Naseem Hamed's. For the stalwarts of the St Thomas's Boys' Club it must have been a bit like waiting for the American boxing authorities to allow Muhammad Ali back into the ring in 1970, or perhaps Mike Tyson to emerge from prison in 1995. Naz had been at it for five years and was already by far the best pre-teen in the gym, and now, finally, on 24 February 1986, at the age of twelve years and twelve days, he was being allowed to prove himself – even though he wasn't guaranteed a place on the bill. The result shows that the 4-stone 2-pound Hamed won a unanimous decision over Grantham's Peter Ironmonger, who outweighed him by 5 pounds, at a dinner show at the Cutler's Hall in Sheffield.

'I remember it very well,' says Naseem. 'I went along as a spare on the night, just to see if there was an opponent for me, because I wasn't really on the programme. Anyway, there was someone to fight, and we boxed and I won in style – stole the show – and ended up being named the Fighter of the Night and winning the cup,' he says his eyes shining from the memory. 'It was my first fight, and it was a good feeling, a good start, a *great* start.'

Brendan watched the fight from the ringside seats, with his son, John, in the corner to keep the amateur officials happy. When he tells the story he gets a similar glow because that first win proved all he had been saying about this young upstart. 'He was tiny, smaller than the other fella, but he boxed absolutely brilliantly. He just dazzled this kid.' Ingle was immediately on to the local *Sheffield Star* reporter at the tournament, singing Naseem's praises, and the paper devoted its entire report to his performance. The first gauche printed words about Naseem Hamed were these: 'Bomber Graham look out – the schoolboy terror is after you!' The story went on to quote Ingle: 'This fella has got it all, just like the Bomber did. He's a natural.'[1]

From then on Naseem was to box as often as Ingle could find opponents of the right size, which wasn't as often as the boy would have liked. They travelled around the pit villages and further afield, matching him against tough youngsters who were usually bigger and stronger than him. By then boxing had become the boy's obsession, something that his parents accepted with some reluctance. Naseem says his father, in particular, did not want him to box, but changed his mind after he started picking up titles.

Three months after his debut, he fought in Hull against against Vince Okenyi who was nearly six months older, several pounds heavier and six inches taller. Naseem and all his team mates thought he had done more than enough to win, but a majority of the judges did not approve of his Herol Graham-like style and gave the other boy a split decision. Okenyi and Hamed never did get to fight again, and his first conquerer (at least on the judges' cards) became the only lad to go and stay one-up on the Prince.

Of that loss Naseem has this to say: 'I beat him, but he got the decision and afterwards he looked at me all funny and I thought, Why's he smiling when he knows he lost? and I said to myself, Is there any way we can get him into the ring again? Then I knew what he was thinking, and I smiled back at him because that was the best thing to do – smile.'

Okenyi's coach, Mick Bromby, has a very different perspective. 'It was a clear, fair, decision – definitely no robbery,' he says. 'Vince won that fight comfortably. He was much taller and had much longer arms and he was able to land straight, hard shots. It was a clean contest, but Vince's longer reach was the telling factor.'

According to Naseem the only reason he never avenged that defeat was because Okenyi retired in order to avoid a return. In fact Okenyi did continue boxing, with some success (winning a senior national schoolboy title in 1989 and only then retiring), but he always fought in higher weight and age divisions than Naseem.

'After that,' says Bromby, 'whenever Naz saw me he'd say, "Where's that tall black boy what I fought?", and the last time, a few years ago, I said, "He still lives around here but he's twice your size now, Naz," and he laughed.'

Naseem continued to fight as often as opponents could be found, and Ingle would inspire him by encouraging him to pretend he was fighting against the big names in the professional game. 'I remember when he was about twelve years old, I says to him before one of his fights: "Naz,think in six years' time, you're making your pro debut. You get a purse of £400 and I take a quarter – £100." He says, "no problem." Then I say, "It's two years on, you're fighting for the British title. You get £4,000 and I get £1,000 of that." He says fine. "Now you're fighting for the world title," I say. "You get £40,000 and I take £10,000 of that." Fine. "Next, you're fighting in Las Vegas for £400,000 – and I'll take a quarter of that – one hundred grand," ' Ingle recalls. 'For once in his life Naz goes all quiet for a few seconds, and then he tells me: "I'm not too sure about that, Brendan. One hundred grand is a lot of money." Then a bit later while we was in the gym together, he comes up to me and says: "I've talked about this with my dad, Brendan, and you can have the one hundred grand." '

By the time he finished at Concord he had been boxing competitively for half a year, had already had several mentions in the local papers and was beginning to make a name for himself within the Yorkshire amateur establishment. Mike Delaney believes this had a positive effect on his behaviour, if not on his schoolwork. 'He was good at boxing and successful, he was getting a lot of praise for it and he was going away to tournaments and winning cups and medals and certificates and getting the odd line in the press – the old "Wincobank 12-year-old wins away" sort of thing – and it became self-perpetuating: the more he was successful, the more energy he put into it. We were pleased because it gave him a controlled outlet. Brendan Ingle had got him into a bit of a lifestyle, with a timetable, and he got a bit more control in his life.'

By the end of 1986 his record stood at 10 wins in 11 bouts, and he still weighed only 4st 7lb, while the minimum weight for competing in a schoolboy championship was 4st 10lb. For the South Yorkshire Schools championship Ingle put him on a strict, four-meals-a-day diet to get him up to weight – a unique situation for a lighter weight boxer. He eventually made the minimum limit and won the title by default, because no opponent his size could be found. The local papers started to adopt him as a kind of mascot, quoting every superlative Ingle threw their way, but still sometimes getting his name wrong. 'Nahim Ahmed is one of boxing's young prodigies,' wrote the *Sheffield Star*, 'a little terror of a scrapper with one problem. He cannot put on weight.'[2] And so it went.

British amateur boxing has three major streams at the junior level, fighting under the same boxing rules, but with each having its own structures and committees. These are the junior ABA tournaments, the Schoolboy Championships and the Boys' Club (NABC) Championships. Soon after Naseem turned thirteen he won his first amateur national title under the banner of his new school, Hinde House Comprehensive, when he narrowly out-pointed the bigger and technically more experienced Kent boxer, Michael Wright in the 32 kg (5st 0.5lb) National Schoolboy Championship junior A finals in Derby.

As had become his custom by this stage Naseem entered the ring by vaulting the ropes, wearing what he called his 'wicked gold gown', complete with shoulder pads and tassels, danced around the ring, did an Ali-shuffle, and put on a bit of a show for the crowd before getting down to business. For David Prior, current chairman of the Boys' Club Boxing Panel and editor of

Amateur Boxing Scene, this was his first encounter with Naseem and one he will never forget. 'I can still see him in that long, shiny, flowing dressing gown, floating around the ring with his hands down. There was always something special about him. He had a slightly different style which was eye-catching, and then he did a somersault after he won.'

The 4 foot 6 Naseem, still only 4st 10 – 4½ pounds lighter and five inches shorter than the favoured Wright – was clipped several times in the opening round by his more aggressive opponent, but his speed and workrate allowed him to dominate the second half to win a split decision. While the *Sheffield Telegraph* naturally felt the decision went the right way, noting that Naz 'recovered from a shaky start to outbox Wright,'[3] Steve Bunce, who was covering the tournament for *Boxing News*, was less convinced, noting that while Naseem 'soon showed he was more than a showboat' and that his 'fast work must have impressed the judges', he felt that 'Wright's pressure had earned him a win.'[4] It was to be the first of four fights with Wright, who is currently an undefeated professional, with Naseem winning all of them.

The unique relation between amateurs and professionals in the St Thomas's gym was shown by the fact that several of the gym's leading boxers, including Herol Graham, travelled to Derby to cheer on their young mascot. By the time Naz's fight was over Graham had lost his voice, and Naseem returned the compliment by telling Sheffield journalists that the 'Bomber' was his model. 'He's got all the style and all the moves and that's how I want to fight. I don't like two people just knocking lumps out of one another,' he said.[5]

Brendan, as always, was ready to capitalize on his charge's success, expounding his virtues to everyone who would listen, and many who wouldn't. These included politicians like local Labour MP, Richard Caborn, reporters with the local newspapers and businessmen like the Harrogate financier Nigel Burrows who was shown a Naseem gym exhibition and then taken to one of his fights. He was bowled over and in September 1987 announced that his company, Analysis Group, was sponsoring Naseem for £300 a year to pay for his training and travel needs until he reached the age of twenty. He was the first of several Yorkshire business sponsors to fall in behind the young boxer over the next five years. Naseem's comment at the time suggested he thought this all as it should be: 'I like people to watch me and sponsor me. It's great.'[6]

This also helped ensure Naseem a spate of fresh publicity. The *Sheffield Star*, for instance, ran a full-page spread on the 13–year-old, complete with a picture of his family, spurious accounts of how he was an A-student at school and a Naz prediction that he would win an Olympic gold medal and then a fortune in the professional game. He made it clear that no other occupation interested him. 'I know I can go on to make it as a professional boxer. These plans won't fall through because I shall just train harder if things get tough,' he is quoted as saying. 'Doing anything else never occurs to me. Boxing is the only thing that matters.'[7]

By this stage Naseem was starting to become a rather gaudy part of the furniture within the professional circuit, touring the country with his trainers to watch Herol Graham, Brian Anderson and Johnny Nelson in action. One of those who got to know him was Des Gargano, the Manchester bantamweight who, seven years later, would become one of Naz's early professional opponents. 'He's one of those guys I feel I've always known because he used to go to all the shows as a little kid, travelling around with Brendan Ingle, and he used to hang around the professional fighters,' Gargano recalls. 'After a while I got to know him quite well and he was always telling us he was going to be a champion. Once he told me that one day he'd fight me, and I said, "You'll have to wait a while", but in the end it happened. I always liked him. He had a lot of spirit and he was really confident, but not cocky. He was great.'

Naseem was spending less and less time at home, though he remained close and extremely loyal to all members of his family. His entire focus, seven days a week, was on boxing, and even within the home he was constantly shadow-boxing. His sister, Noel, then nineteen, would tell of sore arms from his 'friendly' blows. 'He doesn't know his own strength,' she would complain.[8]

During weekends spent in Sheffield, Brendan would have him

over to view videos of Sugar Ray Robinson, Muhammad Ali – particularly during his prime in the sixties – Ray Leonard, Roberto Duran and Marvin Hagler, and Naz would watch spellbound, and the next day would become that 'legend' in the gym. One day Naz would be Robinson, boxing off his toes, firing off pin-point hooks while in retreat. The next he would be Hagler, switching from southpaw to orthodox and back without blinking, or he'd get his squat little pubescent body up close and bang away, slipping the counters, like Duran, or wind up a big right and then sneak in a surprise bolo like Leonard. But most of all he was Ali. Anyone who watched footage of a wide eyed 22-year-old Clay/Ali shouting: 'I must be the greatest!' would recognize immediately the root of Naz's antics, even in the junior amateur ring. Everything about Ali appealed to the youngster: his hands down, taunting and teasing style, his phenomenal speed and accuracy, his arrogance, his shuffle, his clowning, his conversion first to the 'Black Muslim' Nation of Islam sect and later to conventional Islam, and most of all his fame and fortune.

'Sugar Ray Robinson was a great fighter, but at my time he was way back, so for me the main one was Muhammad Ali,' Naseem says today, his eyes sparkling whenever the subject is raised. 'I watched all of the fights of the young Ali, as well as the Robinsons and Leonards, the Haglers and Durans, and Ali was the best – the greatest fighter of all time. He was my idol and I loved everything about him: his style, his charisma, his showboating, the way he succeeded, his class, how he became a world figure, he was a credit to boxing and sport in general. He's made what our sport and all sport is today, especially when it comes to what we get paid. The ball really started rolling with Ali, and I want to be a legend like him – the new Ali – so that when I'm gone they'll say, "There'll never be another Naz." '

Ali's ideas about life and his approach to his profession seem to have rubbed off on the impressionable young Naseem, even though the 'Greatest' was well into his retirement by that stage. When combined with the teaching from family members and Yemeni Community Association activists, and the impact of some of his older stablemates, they contributed to Naseem's conception of himself as a black fighter and his pride in being a member of the broader black community. While he tells you that he personally seldom experienced direct racism, it is something he is certanly not oblivious to. 'I fight like a black man, and at the end of the day, for a lot of white people here, a nigger's a nigger – don't matter if you're black or brown. I identify strongly with the black community here,' he says.'[9]

The combined influence of Herol Graham and Muhammad Ali, as well as Ingle's unorthodox tuition, was also having a decisive effect on Naseem's style. In competition he would dance, hands at his sides, doing the Ali shuffle and moving in and out. He was not planting his feet as he would later in his career and therefore was almost always reliant on the inscrutability of the judges or the patience of the referee. This was not always forthcoming, and between 1987 and early 1989 he dropped another four decisions, all of which he and his people felt should have gone his way, though naturally his opponents and their coaches disagree.

His second loss came against a young star of the Droylsden club, Paul Sweeting, in May 1987 in Derbyshire. Once again, there are two very different versions of what happened that night. According to Sweeting's coach, Charlie Grace, his 13-year-old not only won a unanimous decision, but dropped Hamed for a short count in the first round. 'The scoring was quite close, but I don't think the fight as a whole was close at all. My boy won quite easily,' he says.

John Ingle remembers a very different fight. 'I think Charlie Grace must have very fond memories of his boy, because I was there and it was definitely a majority decision and there was definitely no knockdown. Naz has *never* been knocked down in a fight. I thought Naz beat him easy.'

They fought again in December 1987 and this time a much-improved Hamed won a unanimous decision, which Grace concedes was just and fair. Two years later, when both lads were fifteen, they fought for a third time in the NABC national quarter finals in Newcastle, and this time Naseem won on a third round disqualification. 'Naz was great by that stage – really fast – but he hadn't yet developed his power and strength, so I told Paul the only way he could win was to rough him up,' Grace recalls. 'It was close and I thought Paul was doing quite well, and told him to try and finish Naz off, but instead he butted him and got disqualified.' John Ingle, however, says Sweeting was disqualified for constant holding. 'He was taking a real hiding. He just didn't know what to do.'

Naseem's third loss was even more controversial, this time against Vic Brumehead from Buxton, whom he had already outpointed earlier that year. John Ingle describes this as the worst decision of the lot – one of the most outrageous he has ever seen in the amateur game. 'They absolutely robbed Naz blind,' he says. 'Naz just left the ring laughing afterwards, because there was no other way to react. It was a total robbery. They fought three times and Naz won all three as easy as each other.'

Brumehead's trainer, John Taylor, naturally sees things differently. 'Look, Naz was a better boxer than Vic, no doubt about that,' he concedes, 'but I had watched him carefully in their first fight, and I told Vic, "You must wait for him to get to you and counterpunch," and he did just what I said. Vic fought very well that night. If Naz had attacked more it would have been different but I thought it was a fair decision and I think John Ingle is being biased if he says otherwise.'

Three months later, in March 1988, they fought again and this time Naseem was rampant, picking up an easy win. 'Yes, I've got to admit, Naz was somewhat special that time, and after that Vic didn't have a chance against him,' Taylor concedes.

Naseem's fourth loss came against a tough Darlington lad of travelling stock, Jacob Smith, whom he had already beaten in his first year as an amateur. This decision incensed Naseem's people. 'There is absolutely no way Jacob Smith deserved it,' says John Ingle. 'Naz won by a mile, and in fact with each of those so-called losses we felt that he was a clear winner, but the Smith and the Brumehead losses were the worst.' However Laurie Degnan, Smith's coach, says the verdict was fair. 'I thought it was clear cut,' he says. 'Jacob forced the fight and got on top of him. He chased Naz around the ring and had him on the back foot, and he won clearly.'

Smith, like Naz, went on to win an NABC title, and the pair of them fought twice more, with Naseem winning both fights comfortably, stopping him in 1989 and then breaking Smith's nose and beating him on a unanimous decision in the flyweight final of the North East Counties junior championships in November 1990. 'Hamed had improved tremendously in the eighteen months or so since Jacob beat him,' Degnan recalls. 'By their last fight he was brilliant. The speed of his improvement was unbelievable.'

Naseem won his second National Schoolboy title, with what Steve Bunce of *Boxing News* described as a 'blistering display which rated around a stiff jab thrown as Hamed moved left and right around the centre of the ring,'[10] when he unanimously outpointed Plymouth's much-favoured two-time national champion Scott Dann in the Intermediate National 42 kg (6st 8.7lb) finals in Derby on 25 March 1989.

Two months later, however, on 23 May, he was to suffer his last defeat, to a tough, experienced, come-forward pressure fighter, Dean Pithie. They fought in the 42 kg division of the Class A semi-finals of the junior ABA national tournament in Manchester and Pithie got the nod from the judges.

Naseem had outpointed Pithie earlier that year in the National Schoolboy semi-finals in the Midlands and at the end of three rounds his people felt he had prevailed more decisively in the return, landing the cleaner punches and avoiding most of Pithie's blows. 'He really got robbed against Pithie,' says Brendan Ingle. 'I remember that fight well. Naz was very very flashy and the judges thought he was arrogant, so they just didn't give him credit for how good he was. In fact he never actually lost any fight. He just got robbed because of his flashiness.' To which John Ingle adds: 'It didn't look that close to me. I actually thought Naz beat him easier than the first time they fought.'

But, once again, the opposite corner saw things very differently. 'Both fights were fairly close,' Ron Harkness, Pithie's amateur coach, acknowledges. 'In the first fight I thought Dean's cleaner, harder punching may have clinched it, but I wouldn't argue with the decision because it was very tight. But in the second Dean won every round. He was pressurizing Naz and didn't give him room to move. Naz was trying to wrestle and throw him down because he couldn't do much else. In those days, you see, he was still flicking his punches. The power only came later.'

Pithie himself insists he deserved both decisions. 'I definitely thought I won the first, but I wouldn't complain – it was a majority decision and could've gone either way, but the second fight I beat him easy. It was a very convincing unanimous decision. I knew where he was coming from and I stayed on top of him and stepped on his toes. He was punching quite hard then, but not nearly as hard as he would later.'

These two never fought again, because after this Naseem, who was a month younger than his rival, always competed in a higher weight division. Pithie, like Naseem, went on to box for Young England, won the senior ABA featherweight title in 1994, and is currently unbeaten as a professional. 'I'd love to fight Naz again,' he says, 'but not quite yet – only when I've got a bit more experience.'

Naseem had already developed a healthy degree of cynicism about the inconsistencies in amateur scoring and had become stoical about losing close ones. 'None of those defeats were genuine,' he says. 'I didn't find the fighters who beat me were actually better than me. In my heart I knew I never lost. I never got out of the ring feeling the opponent had been too strong or too good. Never.'

He blames these decisions on the prejudices of the amateur officials. 'The judges in the amateur game didn't like the flash business. They didn't like me because I boxed different from any other boxer in Britain, so when I boxed in championships I either had to stop my opponent or win very easily, because if I won a close one, they'd probably give it the other way, but I never actually lost.'

This perception is certainly not restricted to the St Thomas's Boys Club fraternity. David Prior, who covered the championships for *Boxing News*, agreed there was a bias from amateur referees and judges against Naseem's eccentric style. 'They didn't like the hands-down, floating round the ring type of thing. I queried it and asked, "which rule is it contravening?" and no one could say, but his approach certainly did not find favour,' he said, adding that Ingle's 'anti-establishment' stance may also have come into the equation.

Naseem regularly received warnings from the referees for his tactics and antics, and once, after doing a somersault in the

Yorkshire finals, the referee told him, 'I will sling you out of the ring if you ever do that again.'

Ray Black, a Humberside amateur official who refereed several of Hamed's fights, said he had to warn him continually for 'intimidating' opponents, clowning and not keeping his hands up, but insists there was no bias against him. 'What he was doing was showmanship, not boxing,' he says. 'In the rules it says you have to defend yourself at all times and that meant you couldn't dangle your hands at your side like he did. It was just a case of applying the rules. There was definitely no prejudice against him. In fact I liked him – he was a real character.'

One effect his fifth and last defeat (against Pithie) had on the 15-year-old Naseem was to prompt him to go in search of inside-the-distance wins. From this point on he began to plant his feet more firmly when punching and, having passed through puberty, his strength also began to develop rapidly. The result was that in a matter of about six months he turned from a relatively light-fisted, hit-and-move boxer for whom an inside-the-distance win was a rarity, into a knockout specialist.

The 1995 senior ABA featherweight champion David Burrows, who lost a majority decision to Hamed in 1989, noticed the difference in his power after seeing him in action again the following year, noting that while Naz was always strong and skilful, 'it was only when he was fifteen or sixteen that he started to punch.'[11]

Far larger gym mates, who had previously described him merely as fast and elusive, now became wary of getting into the ring with him because of his newfound power, and everyone at the St Thomas's Boys' Club spoke of his remarkable improvement. He was soon starting to get into serious open sparring sessions with seasoned professionals and was sometimes getting the better of them. His brother Ali, who himself had been drifting in and out of boxing since childhood, remembers returning to the gym in 1990 and being amazed by his brother's improvement when watching him sparring with a far larger professional. 'He absolutely destroyed him, he hammered him and was giving him a lot of abuse, and I thought to myself, How can a 16-year-old do that?, and from then on I realized that Naz was going to be extraordinary because I had never seen anyone like that.'[12]

'Silky' Jones, the former WBO light middleweight champion, and a close friend of Naseem's, has vivid memories of these sessions. They both started boxing at the St Thomas's gym the same day in 1981, when Jones was fourteen and Hamed seven, and continued training together for the next ten years. 'The last time I sparred with him was probably 1991, and he was still a boy then, but obviously a hell of a fighter,' Jones says. 'He used to give me nightmares. There was no one else in the gym I used to dread sparring with, apart from Naz.'[13]

After the Pithie setback there were no more close fights and Naseem dominated every tournament he entered. Twice that year he represented England schools against Wales, winning both his bouts easily, and by the end of the year many were calling him the best junior in Britain.

By this stage in his life boxing had completely taken over Naseem's existence and his family were seeing less and less of him. When he had time he would help out in the shop, but usually he was working out in the gym or touring the country with Brendan Ingle, watching fights or competing in tournaments.

Naseem's single-minded focus had a mixed impact on his secondary school career at Hinde House Comprehensive, where he was one of about 500 boys and 400 girls. On the one hand his relationships with staff and fellow pupils was markedly better than at Concord, but his academic performance suffered. Naseem says he got on well with all his teachers at Hinde House, and that they all made it clear they liked him, and he appears to resent comments from former teachers which stress his arrogance and disciplinary problems, putting this down to 'jealousy'.

Graham Hicking, the current deputy head teacher who taught Naseem during this period, says that while there were never any major disciplinary problems with the young boxer, women teachers found difficulty in getting him to respond. 'If it was me or another male teacher, then he would listen, but he would find it hard to listen if it was a young lady teacher telling him what to do.'

He does not recall Naseem getting into many fights at school, and says that while he was always extremely self-confident and had a quick sense of humour, he usually preferred sticking with one or two close friends, before shooting off to the gym after school.

Most of his teachers stress the role played by Brendan Ingle both as a guiding moral force and as a benign factor in persuading him to toe the line. 'I was warned that he was a bit of a tearaway,' his former head teacher, Graham Elliot, is quoted as saying. 'He got into the occasional scrape, but nothing serious. If I ever had any reason to see him, I always said to him: "I can always ring up Brendan, you know." '[14]

As at Concord this mild admonition seemed to work wonders. Naseem simply had so much love and respect for his trainer, friend and mentor that a gentle word was usually enough for him to modify his behaviour. Graham Hicking believes that if it had not been for Ingle's role, he might not have followed the straight and narrow the way he did. 'He was the sort of boy who could have turned out differently if it hadn't been for the positive influence of people like Brendan Ingle. He had a certain arrogance, an aloofness and a sort of supercilious manner that could get taken the wrong way by teachers and classmates. That arrogance could have turned into aggression if it hadn't been for Brendan.'

Naseem was neither particularly gifted nor very interested academically, though his attendance record and punctuality was good up until his final year (1989/90) when he was frequently away on boxing tournaments.

School records show he began GCSE courses in art (painting and drawing), physical education, home economics, maths, English language, English literature and two science subjects, but only completed the courses in English (grade F) and painting and drawing (grade G). He also completed a non-GCSE (internal) qualification in maths. Today Naseem stresses that his academic aptitude should not be judged by his performance at school, because his entire focus was on boxing. 'I did well at school. I took some qualifications and passed them but the main thing I did was I turned up and never took time off school. I didn't really set my mind on getting qualifications or on being a clever chap, in theory. I just couldn't wait for the last bell to ring so I could go down to the gym and train every day, so for me school was just a passing of time because I knew what I wanted out of life, through and through.'

His school-leaving report describes him as a 'pleasant, well-mannered student . . . extremely confident and outgoing with a good sense of humour,' but adds: 'He has been, on occasions, too confident but recently he has made a more consistent, serious attempt to improve upon his efforts.' It also describes him as 'lively with a friendly personality' and notes that he 'socializes well with peers and enjoys discussions, both giving opinions and listening to others,' and goes on to say that he is 'keen to succeed'.

During his final two years in the amateur game – 1990 and 1991 – Naseem proved himself to be the outstanding flyweight in Britain, even though for most of that time he was not old enough to be allowed to compete against senior boxers. His plan was to remain in the amateur game long enough to get picked for Barcelona, take the flyweight gold medal, and then turn professional.

He started 1990 in fine style by stopping Bedfordshire's Richard Izzard in the second round to win the NABC Class A 48 kg (7st 7.8 lb) finals (his third national title) at the Festival Hall in Basildon on 19 January. Izzard, an experienced fighter with a reputation for heavy hitting, moved straight into attack mode from the opening bell, but Naseem was nowhere to be found. After a minute of moving around the ring, he suddenly shifted stance and connected with a five punch combination, prompting the first of two first-round standing counts. In the second Naseem, his hands carried low, began picking Izzard off with heavy shots, prompting calls of 'stop the fight' from the crowd. A final Hamed right cross persuaded the referee to step in at the 1 minute-10 second-mark.

'Naseem turns on all his power' announced the *Boxing News* headline. 'Hamed now has the power to complement his style and gold-gown image,' wrote Steve Bunce, who added that he 'scored on the move with either hand, from either stance and was powerfully impressive when he set his feet fractionally closer and whipped in three or four shots of hurtful accuracy.'[15] After this performance the paper featured him as the main attraction among the juniors, giving him the epithet 'golden boy'.

On 31 March five weeks after his sixteenth birthday Naseem and his 13-year-old stablemate, Ryan Rhodes, pulled off what the Yorkshire press called 'an historic triumph for Sheffield'[16] by both winning National Schoolboy titles at 48 kg in Derby with inside-the-distance wins. Naseem stopped Darren Williams in 1 minute 50 seconds in his final, for what was his fourth national title. Williams was known as both a banger and a mover and was expected to provide a tough challenge, but it was not to be. He kept on hitting air while Hamed picked him off with jabs and hooks, regularly switching stance to confuse his opponent. He then stepped in with a short lead right hook to drop the Londoner and, after putting him down for the second time with an identical punch, the referee stepped in. The crowd booed as Naseem performed his regular victory somersaults to celebrate his ninth straight win since the Pithie setback and his eighth inside the distance.

Hamed's fifth national final, and his third of 1990, saw him up against his old rival Michael Wright. Naseem had won a disputed verdict in their first meeting in 1987, and a far easier one in their second in 1989. On 26 May 1990 they met in the national junior ABA finals at the York Hall in Bethnal Green, and early in the first round Naseem suffered the first serious injury of his boxing career when he landed a hard right on the top of his opponent's head, and then another on his elbow. For the rest of the fight Hamed was in agony and emerged with his right hand badly swollen (the same hand he would injure in late 1995 when preparing for his first world title defence), though X-rays later showed severe bruising rather than a break.

For the rest of the fight he used his right sparingly, while darting in and out with his left, jumping in to use it as a cracking lead punch and then backing off and using it as a defensive jab, but always moving with both hands below waist level, and mixing up his punches with plenty of clowning. In the third round Wright launched a sustained attack but seldom connected with anything promising.

The East End crowd did not like what they saw and a section screamed abuse at Hamed throughout the fight. 'I was bashing him up,' Naseem recalls, 'and all I could hear from the crowd was: "He's only a dancer, the black bastard! Nigger!" It affected me by making me bash him up harder.'[17] Naseem won a unanimous decision, but afterwards the capacity crowd booed him for several minutes, with the only dissenting voices being his two faithful clubmates, Herol Graham and Johnny Nelson.

Afterwards, several amateur officials attacked referee Billy Phillips for not warning Hamed to box with his hands up and to stop showboating, a complaint which was criticized by Steve Bunce of *Boxing News*. 'That, I believe, is rubbish, because loose moves and low hands are central to Hamed's style,' he wrote. 'If the ABA left the styles of multi-talented, original boxers alone and helped develop their individual talent by not attempting to muffle them and produce a winning formula, then boxers like Hamed . . . might produce at international level.'[18]

Naseem's record now stood at 52 wins in 57 bouts and he was being widely cited as the best 16-year-old of any weight in Britain. 'I have not missed a day in the gym for nine years, I have five national titles and I am on my way up,' he said in an interview at the time. 'I am confident that there is almost no one of my age who can beat me. I want to win the ABA title and the Olympic gold and then I will turn pro. I have no distractions.'[19]

Brendan Ingle, however, could see some of the potential obstacles and said that although Naseem was by far the best flyweight in the land, he did not expect him to get picked for the British Olympic squad because of the 'politics of amateur boxing' – recalling that the same thing had happened to Herol Graham in the 1970s. Instead, he speculated that Naseem would be able to represent Yemen. 'We know he will get picked and we know he will win a gold medal; we know he is the best in the world at his weight. A country just united after twenty years of civil war would suddenly have a sporting hero,' he said.[20]

The influence of 'Old Irish' remained considerable, extending not only to every aspect of his boxing career (which in itself would take up more than twenty hours a week) but to all his life choices. Abdul Shaif of the Yemeni Community Association believes that Ingle's impact on Naseem's life was parental in its scope and implications. 'Brendan is not just his second family, but is as much his first family as his actual family is,' he says. 'He's not only been a carer for Naseem but an inspiration as well. Brendan's trained him, given him everything he has and Naseem needs to relate to him just as much as he needs to relate to his father. It's as simple as that. Brendan has been the dynamic force behind Naseem's success, and Naseem owes a lot to him.'

More than anyone else Ingle could see the potential in the youngster. He had taken Herol Graham and Johnny Nelson to the verge of being world champions, only to see them falter at the summit, and he'd taken numerous other boxers far further than their natural talent would have suggested. He knew that Naseem had far more innate ability than any of them, but he had also seen scores of 16-year-olds rebel or slip through indiscipline. One problem was drink and drugs, which Naseem's Islamic faith had kept him from. Another was 'chasing' girls, something Naseem was already showing an interest in, although he never had a steady girlfriend at this time. Ingle was also wary of his boxers 'hanging out with the wrong crowd' and specifically getting into crime through peer influence. Naseem, however, more than most of Brendan's young fighters, had kept his nose clean, and although he did not like Naseem's sleeping and waking hours or the amount of chocolate and other rich foods he ate, he was delighted with the way things were going.

He predicted at the time that his young charge would one day become world professional featherweight champion, but he also stressed some of the potential obstacles along the way. 'How good is Naseem? If I could get Johnny Nelson winning a Lonsdale Belt and going into the world ring after an amateur career of three wins in thirteen there is no limit to what this boy can do. But one thing we have drummed into him: we have told him if there was anything in drinking, smoking and going around with more than one woman at a time, we would all be doing it to better our lives. Naseem has the greatest talent for his age of anyone I have ever seen, but if he wants to be a champion he must live like a champion. He will win everything provided he can live for boxing in the next nine years the way he has lived for the last nine and I know that will be difficult. From the age of seven he has knocked around with professional fighter. He has seen how champions are made and he has seen the pitfalls. If he is intelligent enough to choose his friends wisely, he has the greatest chance of anyone we have ever had in this gym.'[21]

In his school leaving report Naseem stated he wanted a job in the construction industry 'to learn a trade with my hands', but in the end he opted for the telephone industry after Brendan Ingle persuaded one of his businessman friends, Steve Strafford, a director of Ashford Communications, to sponsor him for a telephone engineer's apprenticeship. The whole idea was that Naseem would be able to take as much time off as he needed to pursue his boxing career and Strafford readily agreed to this. 'This was Brendan's idea,' Strafford acknowledges. 'Naseem had to be committed to the gym and we agreed, even though he missed some excellent tuition in his apprenticeship course because of this commitment.'

He was one of thirty apprentices and according to Strafford mixed easily with his workmates, participated in company activities like fun runs and football games, was keen to learn his trade and showed some dedication. 'He was held back from developing his technical skills by his boxing training, which always came first, but he could certainly have become a telecommunications engineer, given the time, because Naz is someone who will make a success of whatever he does,' said Strafford.

Eventually, the training scheme, which was co-sponsored by the Telecommunications Industry Association, collapsed, but Naseem remained with the company until turning professional in 1992, and learnt enough to install new phones and lines in his parents' house. Strafford, who has known Naseem from the start of his amateur career, says he always had an easy relationship with his young employee. 'You can't not like the lad,' he says. 'It's a shame, all the bravado on TV, because people don't see the other side of him.'

Naseem makes it quite clear that despite working for Ashford Communications for two years, and his high regard for Steve Strafford and fellow director John Ashton, he never had the slightest intention of following a career in this or any other industry. 'The reason I took this job was because he would give me time off whenever I wanted, give me great hours to train and pay me to watch boxing and to box, and though I still served my apprenticeship, and passed my exams and learnt something about the trade, I actually spent far more time in the gym than at work, so I owe Steve Strafford a lot. People would say to me, "If anything goes wrong with your boxing career you can turn around and be a tradesman," and the only thing I'd say to them was, "You must be crazy – the reason I'm doing this for a while is because I know what I'm going to be and do and it won't change in the future, so get that silly statement out of your head because I'll never fall back on any trade." '

The most impressive result of Hamed's amateur career came shortly after he started working, when he completely outclassed the US international, Dan Acevedo, in the 49 kg division, as part of a 12-fight match-up between the American Olympic junior team and the English youth team at Heathrow on 12 July 1990. Naseem, who was ebullient at being chosen as the team captain, landed almost at will with both hands and had the favoured New Yorker bewildered by his constant switches in stance and sudden attacks and he won by margins of 60–55 and 60–56 (twice). After the decision was announced, Naseem did a triple somersault, and this time received a prolonged cheer from the crowd. The only other English boxer to win in what was otherwise a dismal team performance, was his old rival Dean Pithie.

After this, Naseem was chosen by Brendan to be part of Herol Graham's 'camp' in Graham's preparations for his second world middleweight title challenge – this time for the WBC title against Julian Jackson in Spain on 24 November 1990. He spent eight days training with his older chum, specifically to sharpen Graham's timing and improve his mobility, which were seen as the key to beating the slow but thunderous punching Virgin Islander. 'Naseem had the reflexes and speed to help me because I was doing the running and he was doing the attacking,' says Graham, 'so he was making me move my head because I wouldn't hit him back. He really made me work.'

Naseem was convinced his buddy's extremely positive attitude and all-round sharpness would secure him victory this time, after the disappointment of his off colour majority-decision loss to Mike McCallum eighteen months earlier. For three and a half rounds Graham toyed with Jackson, hitting him at will, closing his eye, and taking nothing in return. But just when the referee was about to halt the massacre, Jackson, one of the hardest punchers in the history of the division, connected with a trip-hammer right to end the fight. Graham was to lose two of his next three fights and was never the same again. It's a lesson Naseem remembers well – never to lose concentration, not even for a fraction of a second. This was reinforced in an impromptu sparring session with a 6 foot 4, 16½-stone professional heavy-weight Adam Fogarty not long afterwards, when Naseem was knocked down for what he says was the first and last time in his life – inside and outside the ring. It proved to all his gym mates that the youngster could take a very hard punch and come back for more, but for Naseem it was more a lesson in caution and a source of minor embarrassment. 'That's his claim to fame – that he knocked a 16-year-old kid down when he was around 6 foot 5 and probably eighteen, nineteen stones,' he says with a touch of bitterness. Then he changes tone and tells you what happened next. 'But I got up and if you looked at his face and you looked at mine you would have thought that I had been the winner, which I was. He had a nosebleed and he took some good shots and some *good* punishment on that night.'

Brendan Ingle watched this incident from the far side of the gym with a mixture of horror and amazement, and has since been careful to provide closer supervision for Naseem's sparring sessions. 'I was just coming in the door when Fogarty lifted him off the floor with a punch and put him on his backside, and then Naz backflipped off the floor, hit Adam on the chin and then bust his nose.'

Johnny Nelson, who was acting as timekeeper for that sparring session, confirms this version of what happened, making it clear this is not another Brendan-Naseem talltale special. 'Naz was being his brash, fast self, and he was really taunting and tormenting him, because Adam couldn't hit him. Naz was hitting him, then telling him what punch he was going to land next and each one went off, and Adam got really frustrated, and as Naz went in Adam closed his eyes and hoped for the best and he connected. As Naz went down he did a backwards somersault, springing straight back on to his feet again, jumped back in, hit him with a right cross and just nailed him. He broke Adam's nose and gave him two black eyes. Unless you saw it you would not believe it, but I was there, and it happened.'

Today, Naseem stresses that despite his reputation within the gym for having an iron jaw, he knows the risks of putting himself in a position where it can be tested. 'I think you might as well not get hit, if you can do it. There's no point trying to prove something just to show people you got a great chin. Silly in my eyes.' He touches his chin and continues. 'This is only flesh and bone. Obviously if you get hit you can get it broke. No matter who you are, if you get hit on the chin and get hit properly, you're going to get put down. Look at Mike Tyson. Who would have thought he would get knocked out? So it can happen to anybody and I know it can happen. I know the risks in boxing.'

Hamed ended 1990 by beating Michael Wright for a fourth time, to take his second junior ABA title and his sixth national amateur title, this time in the Class B (16 year old) 51 kgs (8st 0.4lb division). Boxing once again at Bethnal Green's York Hall, he gave a less flashy and more lethargic performance but still won a wide unanimous decision.

On 12 February 1991 he turned seventeen, making him eligible at last to box seniors, though still classed as a junior in the international realm and in some of the national championships. Unfortunately he had been born a month too late to box in the senior ABA championships. The regulations required that boxers turn seventeen before the preliminary regional ABA tournaments, which started in January. As a result Naseem had only a handful of fights in 1991, a factor which helped persuade him to turn professional a year later.

His senior debut took place on 15 April 1991 when he scored a unanimous points win over the Northampton boxer, Chris Robson, at Sheffield's Grosvenor Hotel, after which he concentrated on winning his seventh and final junior title, the NABC Class C (17-year-old) flyweight title.

He reached the finals, held at the Grosvenor Hotel in London, on 13 May 1991 and was up against Colchester's Danny Adams, who, like Naseem, was a former national schoolboy and ABA junior champion and England international. It was a harder fight than most of his others, with Adams landing several solid punches, but Hamed was far too fast for him and had a higher workrate. In the last round Adams was given a public warning for holding as Naseem was rattling home rapid-fire combinations to take a unanimous decision.

The last fight of Naseem's unpaid career came after a relatively long period of inactivity. On 17 October 1991 he accepted a late call to box in Manchester and was given time off from work at short notice make the trip. Together with John Ingle and the 'old man' of the St Thomas's gym, Jimmy Wood, he drove across the Snake Pass in stormy weather to face local favourite and Young England international Michael Brodie, a 17-year-old who, like Naseem, was a national junior ABA and NABC champion, and is currently an unbeaten professional.

The event, hosted by the Ancoats and Miles Platting Lads Boxing Club, where Brodie was the star attraction, and held at the Manchester Club, drew a capacity crowd who booed 'Ahmed', as he was called in the programme, to the rafters. Jimmy Wood, a self-styled 'quarter-millionaire moneylender' who at the age of fifty-six still trains and spars every day and is one of the many eccentric characters of the St Thomas's gym, remembers the occasion vividly. 'Naz came out in his leopardskin shorts and did his vault over the ropes and the crowd went 'Boo, boo' and some of them shouted racist slogans, and then Brodie climbed through the ropes and got a massive cheer. The bell went, Naz circled for a few seconds and then he landed a brilliant combination to the head and Brodie was counted out after 32 seconds, including the count, and there was silence, complete silence.'

At the age of seventeen years and eight months Naseem Hamed's amateur career had effectively come to an end with an official record of 62 wins (18 inside the distance) and five defeats (all on points), and with seven British junior titles to his name. Impressive though it might be, this record is deceptive. First, many of those who followed his career said his real tally should have been closer to 67:0, and it was notable that he went unbeaten for the final two and a half years and 23 fights of his career. Second, while his 27 per cent knockout ratio does not suggest a power puncher, it is worth stressing that almost all of these stoppages occurred in the final, unbeaten stretch, when he established himself as one of the big hitters of the junior divisions. Third, when he entered the professional game he was far more experienced than his fight total would suggest. Although he had only been allowed to compete for the previous five and a half years, he had in fact been active for over ten years, for two or three hours a day, six or seven days a week.

By this stage Naseem and Brendan had already decided he would forgo the Olympics and turn professional as soon as British Boxing Board of Control regulations allowed: on his eighteenth birthday. The decision to give Barcelona a miss was a controversial at the time – with many in the amateur ranks pointing out that for several years Hamed and Ingle had been predicting Olympic gold, only to abandon the unpaid ranks six months before the moment of truth arrived.

Naseem says the decision was motivated partly by his desire to start earning 'real' money as quickly as possible, but also by the suspicion that, despite being the best flyweight in Britain, he would not get picked. It was once even hinted to him by an amateur official that his image might not be right for the British team. 'There was a lot of politics in the amateur game,' he says with a tone still resonating with resentment. 'I would have been the best in the country and I could have made the team easily, but they were always picking those English kids they favoured. It was like they were already picked. In the amateur game, if your face didn't fit, then you wouldn't get in.'

Brendan Ingle reinforces this point, stressing that the amateur establishment's 'hatred' of his club as a result of the feud going back to the seventies, meant that the Olympic selection committee would find a way of bypassing Naseem. Specifically there was a suspicion that whatever happened, Scarborough's Paul Ingle (no relation) would get the Olympic berth, even if Naseem beat him over the next nine months or won an ABA senior title. As John Ingle puts it: 'There was no way he'd get picked. They just saw him as a good junior and they didn't like him because they didn't like us. We got a sense of that a year or so earlier when he was picked for the England squad against Tunisia. They had him sparring with seniors like Paul Ingle and Michael Alldis – one round with one, the next with the other, without a rest – but even then they couldn't get the better of him. Then they made him run with blisters on his feet and they tried to mess with his style: it was clear they had it in for him.'

With the Yemen option having faded, mainly because of the Olympic selection requirements regarding nationality and the weak state of Yemenese amateur boxing, they were reliant on the largesse of the despised British officials whom Ingle regarded as beneath contempt. It is worth pointing out that at the time there was a good deal of infighting in the amateur establishment and widespread allegations of financial mismanagement, malad-ministration as well as favouritism.'[22] 'If you're the national coach,' says Brendan Ingle, 'you're onto a good thing. You've got your system of training and then my kids lick yours, so my system has to be better than yours, but you can't admit that to yourself. They felt humiliated.'

Brendan was also concerned about allowing the British national coaches to tamper with Naseem's winning style, as they certainly would have done if he had been picked; and he was suspicious that attempts might be made to poach Hamed by offering huge financial inducements after Barcelona, as, indeed, started to happen soon after he turned professional. While he was always confident of Naseem's absolute loyalty, the predatory climate made him wary of outsiders with a proprietorial interest in his protégé.

The argument against their decision is that many believe that Naseem might have been selected, at either flyweight or bantamweight, simply because he was by then clearly the best in the country and, given another six months in the senior ranks, would have proved that beyond any doubt, and therefore would have been viewed as an outstanding medal prospect. David Prior, for one, stresses that despite the tensions and history of conflict with Ingle, Naseem was selected to box for Young England, 'so he couldn't have been completely out of favour', though it still appears unlikely that the selectors would have chosen this precocious 17-year-old ahead of more established (and more establishment) seniors. And even if they had picked him, there is no guarantee he would have returned with a medal, given the weird inconsistencies of Olympic electronic scoring.

Today Ingle insists his choice proved to be the right one. 'If he had been picked for Barcelona, sure, he would have gone and won the gold medal, but in the end we proved our point. What is better: to be world champion at the age of twenty-one and a millionaire or to be still fiddling around with the amateurs and have people messing you about?'

4

The Arabian Knight

Naseem had to wait six frustrating months between his last amateur fight and his professional debut. It was not initially intended that the gap would be this wide, but the time was certainly not wasted.

Every day the young boxer would walk the 200 yards from his front door to the St Thomas's Boys' Club gym and work out for three hours or more. Having always trained with professionals, and with his style that was to prove so well-suited to the pro game, it took no great effort to adapt. His training regime therefore remained the same as before – just with more rounds each day, and no one watching could fail to be impressed.

He had one trick he and Brendan liked to show visitors which demonstrated just how fast and agile he was: a combination of 38 punches, with up to eight different foot movements, in eight seconds – nearly five punches a second with a shift in stance or a step backwards or forwards each second. He was once timed throwing 54 punches in 12 seconds and it was not just pit-a-pat stuff either. He had another trick he used to torment his sparring partners: while keeping his eyes firmly fixed on their feet, he would tell them which punch he would hit them with next and despite their best efforts it would land just as he'd promised and without him getting hit in return. Those who worked out with him at the time say his improvement was remarkable. He had by then reached his full height of 5 foot 3 but as his body thickened out, so his strength and power continued to grow.

Johnny Nelson, who sometimes sparred with Naseem himself, said he dented the confidence of several good, large professionals at this stage, including Neville Brown, who went on to win the British middleweight title and challenge for WBO super middleweight crown, and Shaun Cummins, a middleweight contender.

'Naz was sparring with these big men, adults of 12 stone, when he was still a teenager of sixteen, seventeen, eighteen, and he was slaughtering them,' Nelson recalls. 'Neville didn't want to spar with him any more because Naz was hurting him, and Neville couldn't touch him – and he's a decent fighter. Naz just destroyed him, and the same with Shaun. There were a lot of guys who came down here and wanted to join the gym and when they got in with Naz, he ridiculed and destroyed them.'

And like most of Hamed's former sparring partners, Brown himself was happy to sing the praises of the youngster and to confirm his superiority. 'I've sparred with that guy and I cannot believe what he does sometimes in that ring,' he said in interview two years later. 'I have to be on my top form just to survive in there. He's dynamite. I'm pretty fast but he's out of this world. He can bang *and* box, and he's also got the balance to come back with a combination you don't even see.'[1]

For thirty years Brendan Ingle had been developing his unique style of tuition and for the previous decade he had focused on Naseem as his star pupil. Ingle was the basic inspiration for everything Naz did in the ring, but over the years he kept on adding to it and pushing its parameters, with Herol Graham always available for Naz to learn from. The period of intensive tuition between the end of his amateur career and his professional debut, helped to consolidate what had been developed before.

'Brendan told me to be flash, tricky, on my toes,' Naseem

said. 'He told me I was right to think that the point of boxing is
to hit and not be hit. I never want to get hit. Who wants to get
hit? It hurts. I've always wanted to be different. If you are a
normal fighter people can work out how to beat you. I wanted a
style so unpredictable that no one can work out what's going on,
what I'm going to do next. I can switch and lead off with either
hand, from either foot – when you can do that you've got be
special. I wanted to be extraordinary. Extra-ordinary. I've
always wanted to be extra-ordinary, exceptional, supreme.'[2]

Meanwhile Ingle was busy looking for the best promotional
options for his young charge. Naseem already received backing
from several business sponsors, including his employers,
Ashford Communications, his first amateur sponsor Nigel
Burrows and, later, the Yorkshire sports outfitter, Tim Sugg.
For a 17-year-old who had never won a senior national title, nor
any international competition, it was quite a vote of confidence.
Another group which readily came to his aid was the Yemeni
Community Association which, a few days after his last amateur
fight, controversially agreed to loan him £3000 to buy boxing
equipment.

Naseem's parents were not entirely convinced by his choice of
profession, just as they had been uncertain about his decision to
start boxing competitively as an amateur. Three weeks before
the loan was granted, Sal was quoted as saying that he and his
wife had hoped Naseem would retire as an amateur and that they
could not bear to watch him in the ring. 'I wish he would give it
up. I don't like him boxing but what can I do? It's his life and it's
what he wants to do.'[3] It did not take long, however, for Sal to
get with the programme and soon he was a familiar ringside
presence at every Naseem fight, nervously puffing on his
cigarettes and then shouting and gesticulating and grinning
when the job was done, often climbing into the ring afterwards
to give his son a hug.

Naseem's mother, Caria, while still nervous about the risks of
injury, has encouraged him ever since he made his career
decision. 'My mum feels something, just like any other mother
with her son going in to fight and with the dangers in boxing,'
says Naseem, 'but we sit down before a fight and she says, "Which

round do you want to take your opponent out in?" and I say the second or the third round, and she turns to me and says, "It's done – you just keep training, get your mind on the job and you'll do it." '4

But it was not just his family he had to convince. When he started telling people within the fight game of his plan to fight for pay immediately after his eighteenth birthday, the reaction he received was largely negative – the main argument being that he still needed another year or two in the amateur ranks to mature physically. With his old-fashioned, side-parted, short-back-'n'-sides, his childlike face and slight, boyish body, Naseem looked a good two years younger than his age and the idea of him competing in the toughest profession of the lot disturbed some of his followers.

'A lot of people thought I shouldn't have turned pro at eighteen – that I was a bit young,' Naseem recalls. 'They were saying, "You told us you would box in the Olympics and that you were going to do this and that." I was quite young-looking at the time, and they were underestimating me by saying I was too small and too young, so I just couldn't wait to show my ability – that I was strong enough to outbox, outthink, outpunch and outstrength mature men.'

Ingle had worked with several promoters before, but it was decided that the Matchroom boss Barry Hearn had the right style, connections and vision to take Naseem's career forward. The Romford-based Hearn was and is the archetypal Essex Man. Tall and handsome, with his cropped grey hair, easy charm, flashy smile and sometimes flash temper, this chartered accountant was the born salesman, who had made his millions through a business empire that involved revolutionizing world snooker, before he settled on boxing, and then, in 1994, expanding to football.

At the time the deal was negotiated with Ingle and Hamed at the end of 1991, Hearn was the most dynamic promotional force in the fight game. Among the fighters contracted to Matchroom were world champions (or champions-to-be) Chris Eubank, Nigel Benn, Herbie Hide, Steve Collins, Crisanto Espana, Chris Pyatt, Steve Robinson, Eamonn Loughran, Pat Clinton and Paul Weir. But perhaps more important, at that point in Hearn's promotional career Matchroom was putting on more major shows than any other group and his fighters were generally getting a better deal as far as media exposure was concerned.

Naseem's fights would be televised by the satellite channel Screensport, which would give him exposure in Europe, with the prospect of bigger things once he 'took off'. It was agreed that Ingle would not relinquish his rights as Naseem's manager and that Hearn's sole role would be promotional. As with all his professional fighters, Brendan (together with his son, John, the co-trainer) would receive 25 per cent of Naseem's purses for his role as both manager and trainer and $33\frac{1}{3}$ percent when he boxed abroad (though he was, in fact, entitled to take $33\frac{1}{3}$ per cent for all his fights).

Long before Naseem's first fight, Ingle's brain was ticking over with ideas about how he could boost publicity for his young star, and the thought emerged of making a splash out of the mundane business of signing his professional boxing forms. Ingle contacted his friend Richard Caborn, the Labour MP for Sheffield Central, and it was agreed that Naseem would officially launch his career in the House of Commons. A veneer of credibility would be added to the occasion by a meeting between Ingle and Hearn and the all-party parliamentary boxing group of MPs.

Caborn was only too happy to cooperate. For over a decade he had enjoyed a close friendship with Ingle, working with him on a number of projects and providing financial assistance to the gym. He had also built up firm connections with Sheffield's Yemeni community and particularly the Community Association. He first met Naseem when visiting the gym ten years earlier, and was extremely impressed with what he saw. 'I thought there is no doubt this is a very talented lad,' he recalls. 'He was a tough little cookie but he had dedication and his feet on the floor.'

Hearn and the St Thomas's contingent met with the MPs on 4 March 1992 – three weeks after the boxer's eighteenth birthday – following which a prepared laudatory statement was issued, noting that the parliamentary group recognized 'the sterling work which Brendan Ingle, the supertrainer from Sheffield, has achieved for the sport.' After that Naseem signed his forms in the House of Commons in front of the MPs and the press – creating the desired impact, at least in his hometown.

Naseem, Brendan and John Ingle also began to work on creating a more defined image for the young fighter – to add to the rope-vaulting, acrobatics and gold gown of his amateur days. It was only at this stage that the the words Prince and Naseem were inextricably linked – sometimes as 'Prince Naseem – the Arabian Knight', or just plain 'Prince Naseem Hamed' and later simply and majestically as 'The Prince'. The idea was that the name 'Prince' combined images of fistic royalty with those of succession – prince today, king tomorrow. By mixing this image of being heir to the throne with the not entirely consistent picture of the Arabian Knight, an aura of mystique was introduced. This name-association was to become an adman's and headline writer's dream – the kind of instant identity that created a strong, definable image, and was easy to play with – the two favourites, which achieved cliché status, being 'The artist still known as Prince' (a reference to the now-nameless singer) and, of course, 'The Prince born to be king'.

All that was left was to find the right debut opponent and the best bill to feature the fight on. The opening came at the Mansfield Leisure Centre on 14 April, with a bill headed by a fight between Hamed's heavyweight stablemate Paddy Reilly (Clifton Mitchell) and Michael Murray. It was decided to make an instant impression by picking a serious opponent and skipping the usual practice of moving from the three three minute rounds of the unpaid ranks, to four three- (and sometimes two-) minute rounds for novice professionals, and instead to going straight into a fight of six three minute rounds – a move commended by the fight press. After the first six designated opponents found reasons to cry off, the final choice – Dagenham's Ricky Beard – was regarded as a bit risky by some of Naseem's more cautious advisers.

A former North East London senior ABA champion, the tall, tattooed Beard had been a professional for three years and was rated the number six British flyweight, though he did much of his fighting at bantamweight. He was nearly five inches taller than Naseem, altogether bigger, eleven years older, and had a reputation as a bit of a banger. Though his record showed a moderate two wins (both inside the distance), one draw and six losses, most of those defeats had come to top-rated men. He always put up a good fight and had never been counted out, though the then British champion Robbie Regan beat him in a sixth round stoppage in 1990. In his previous outing, six weeks earlier, he had given the former British champion Francis Ampofo a good run in an eight-rounder and despite his age he seemed to be improving with every fight (an impression confirmed by some of his subsequent wins, including an eighth-round stoppage over former Commonwealth champion Darren Fifield three years later).

What is more, unlike most debut opponents for future 'stars', Beard fancied the job. 'I was supposed to be the hardest-hitting flyweight in Britain, I was a lot older than him, I'd been fighting for fifteen years and I was having my tenth professional fight, so I knew I had a big edge in experience,' he said. 'I thought he was just a flashy kid and I could go out, meet him head on and knock him out.'

The day before the fight Brendan did his best to drum up interest in the occasion, making a special pitch to the Sheffield Yemeni community by announcing that Naz would be wearing his ceremonial Arab dagger, shawl and head-dress for the fight (though in the end he came in with only the shawl). 'I wanted to add a bit of colour and flamboyance to his image,' he explained. 'The Yemenis of Sheffield have lost a great deal and he has given them something to be proud of.'[5]

At the weigh-in both men made the contracted weight of 8st 2lb on the button (2 pounds over the flyweight limit). Naseem was in a state of high excitement for the rest of the day, filled with the sense that his destiny was about to begin. 'I had a lot to prove that night,' he says. 'People were saying that I was taking on too much by boxing a grown and mature man who had twice gone the distance with the British champion and that I was getting in the deep end. I'd watched Beard fight against Francis Ampofo, and he gave Ampofo a good fight, so he was a great opponent for me. I had to make people realize I had the skill and the ability to go with my confidence and I just couldn't wait to get into the ring and prove I was going to be a great professional.'

For many fans, and for most of the fight press, his ring entrance provided a first glimpse of Naseem – coming down the aisle with his torso covered by the Arab shawl but still looking tiny and juvenile next to the huge, sullen bodyguards accompanying him, and then vaulting over the ropes and giving the crowd a forward flip. As he stood to face Beard, the instant impression was one of a little boy defiantly facing up to a hard man. They might have weighed the same but, as with most of his opponents, Beard looked so much bigger and stronger than the skinny boy in the fake leopardskin shorts who drew laughter from some in the crowd.

Naseem started out extremely quickly from the southpaw stance, darting in and out, bouncing up and down, twisting and turning to get out of the way of Beard's bombs, leaping forward and landing punches in combinations of five, six and seven. Beard attacked from the start, but only managed to land two punches, both glancing right crosses which connected while Naseem was moving away from him. Halfway through the round he put Beard down for a two-count with a left-right combination to the chin. 'I'd never before been caught in the first,' Beard recalls, 'but his speed and power were unbelievable. I was the number five contender but there was nothing I could do with him and he made me feel like an inexperienced novice.' Hamed's supporters were shouting 'Come on, Nabby,' 'Come on Naz,' but Beard used his experience to survive until the bell.

Between rounds Ingle told Hamed to calm down and set himself more, which Naseem did. Soon after the start of the second Beard's nose began bleeding from a flush Hamed punch. He kept his guard high and smiled, trying to draw Naz into a mistake, but it had no effect and Beard soon took on the demoralized look of a man who knew his own execution could not be stayed much longer. Hamed had the look of a boy eager to pull the trigger as he rained punches from all angles on his unfortunate opponent, every now and then finding time for a little clowning gesture. 'I wanted to put on a show for three or four rounds,' he recalls, 'but I thought, what the hell: he was laughing at me behind his guard, so I let the body shot go and I knew he wouldn't get up.'

The final, almost casual-looking bolo punch did not look particularly devastating from outside the ring, but it was so well-timed, fast and accurately delivered that its effect was catastrophic. Beard still remembers the final moments before Naseem slotted the *coup de grâce* through his forearms. 'He backed me up and I stepped one way and at the same time he stepped the other, and he hit me in the solar plexus with a very good right. It was a perfect punch which could have dropped Frank Bruno, and I doubled up, went down and was counted out for the first time before or since.'

Ricky Beard has always been an extremely brave trooper and despite being dropped heavily and winded, he made a serious attempt to get up, before collapsing forward again. When referee Thomas's count reached 10 at the 2:36 mark, Naseem performed four celebratory somersaults and did a little jig before announcing: 'I am strong enough to be world champion before I'm twenty-one.' Beard had no cause to disagree. 'He was really very, very good,' he said. 'Everything he says he'll do, he'll do.'

Ingle was delighted with Naz's performance, though critical of his over-exuberant first round. 'It was a boy against a man in there, but the boy became a man in the second round.'[6] Later, Naseem was to say that this victory should have revealed his full potential to the boxing world. He had, after all, given a far more convincing performance against Beard than the world rated Regan or the former British champion, Francis Ampofo. 'I carried it off really well, you know. I showed I had it all from day one and people should have realized I weren't a flash in the pan.'

In fact, he had nothing to complain about, getting more press than any debut fighter since Lennox Lewis. The Yorkshire papers were ecstatic and *Boxing News* treated it as the main undercard fight, under the heading, 'Sharp Naz is a class act', while other more established performers like Naseem's sometime stablemate Paul 'Silky' Jones and middleweight contender Martin Smith were given footnote reports. He was now on his way to fulfilling his calling, he had leapfrogged the flyweight rankings and in his first fight had made a name for himself.

All in all it was a pretty good start and a delighted Barry Hearn moved quickly to establish a momentum. Eleven days later he featured Hamed on the undercard of a show in Manchester headed by Chris Eubank's defence of his WBO super middle-weight title against John Jarvis. His opponent was the 22-year-old Leicester boxer Shaun Norman, a former Midlands ABA finalist, who had won one, drawn one and lost three (all on points and all at bantamweight) in his six months as a professional. In his last fight Norman had drawn with former British amateur international Neil Armstrong and in December 1991 had taken the then undefeated Mickey Cantwell (who went on to win the British and WBC international titles) to a close eighth round verdict. He had not been expected to win but was thought to be cagey enough to last a few rounds, and perhaps the distance.

Naseem, weighing in once again at 8st 2lb (half a pound less than Norman), put on a bit of a show at the start and took three right crosses for his trouble, before getting down to work. He dropped Norman with a left cross from the southpaw stance for a count of three. Norman returned to the corner bleeding from a cut under the eye and looking like he'd rather be somewhere else.

In the second Naz continued to play, doing an Ali-shuffle, dancing around with his hands low, making constant shifts in stance and teasing Norman with exaggerated feints. A right hook to the jaw shook the Midlander, after which Naseem pinned him in a neutral corner and pounded him. As Norman tried to escape he took a right which put him down and though he wobbled up at the count of eight, referee Roy Snipe decided he had seen enough 55 seconds into the round. Naseem did three somer-saults across the ring to celebrate.

Once again Naseem had done the job far more impressively and decisively than the top British contenders, and had given the crowd what *Boxing News* described as 'an entertaining and arrogant display of boxing and showmanship which put Chris Eubank to shame'.[7] After this the magazine rated Naseem as its number five flyweight in Britain – placing him within its 'elite' category – and its number eight flyweight in the Commonwealth.

This second victory had another, unintended, but ultimately beneficial spin-off in boosting Naseem's profile. Just as the stuffy amateur establishment had turned their noses up at his style and antics, so the professional establishment began to get shirty. General Secretary of the British Boxing Board of Control, John Morris, gave Naseem a ticking off about his backflips and other acrobatic stunts, warning him to 'cut it out' – just as he would do in rather more deferential terms after the Steve Robinson fight over three years later. Clips from Naseem's fights were being shown on ITV and its main commentator, Reg Gutteridge, used the opportunity to criticize Naseem's behaviour – not for the last time in the young fighter's career. This prompted *Boxing News* editor Harry Mullan to weigh in with an editorial piece entitled 'Carry on Clowning' (complete with a picture of a somersaulting Naz) in which he argued that Hamed was entertaining, the crowds loved him and it made for good TV. 'I see nothing wrong or offensive in what Naz is doing, any more than in Eubank's theatrical posturing and posing,' he wrote.[8]

For a two-fight flyweight to be the subject of such a high profile debate was the kind of bonus that made Hearn and Ingle salivate, and its only effect on Naseem was to prompt him to search for new angles to best display his wares. By nature he had never been someone to shun controversy, but from then on he did his best to court it.

He had his third outing against Andrew Bloomer, a Welsh featherweight of sub-journeyman pedigree, in Birmingham on 23 May 1992. After an amateur career which had once seen him making the Welsh ABA bantamweight finals (only to lose on the scales), the Pontypridd 27-year-old turned professional as a featherweight in May 1991 and had amassed a neat record of 11 fights, 11 losses (all on points). What made him vaguely interesting was his size and his durability. Bloomer stood 5-foot-9 (six inches taller than Naseem) and at 8st 8lbs, had a six-pound weight advantage at the weigh-in.

Fighting against bigger men was something of a hobby for Naseem, and a much-beaten featherweight presented no fears for a fighter accustomed to going head to head with heavy-weights, but Bloomer was a real survivor who had never been stopped and only once dropped, and had lasted the distance against several hard-hitting pros including the ultimately ill-fated Bradley Stone (twice). The test for Naseem was to see if he could go one better than Stone and the unbeaten Alan Ley, and win inside the distance.

This Hamed achieved with ridiculous ease. His first punch was a cracking right hook which connected, followed 10 seconds later by another which missed and sent Naz tumbling in Bloomer's corner. After that minor embarrassment, he toyed with the heavily tattooed Welshman, switching from southpaw to orthodox several times to confuse him, clowning in the centre of the ring and thumping home a lead left uppercut – which after this was to become his favourite knockout blow. It wobbled Bloomer and left him with a nosebleed.

The skinny Welshman threw a few desperate shots at the start of the second, all of which missed, before Hamed stepped in with a right-left combination, followed by another solid left hook. Bloomer took refuge on the ropes but Naseem drummed home a barrage of heavy blows. The final punch, a heavy right hook, caused Bloomer to turn away, his legs slowly folding and referee Jim Pridding jumped in to rescue him at the 46-second mark, giving Hamed his third second round stoppage in a row – a result he celebrated with his obligatory backflips, cartwheels and twirls, before helping the forlorn Bloomer out of the ring.

Naseem's performance completely outshone those of his promotional stablemates Nigel Benn and Chris Pyatt. The main event saw Benn being outboxed by Thulane 'Sugarboy' Malinga, only to be given a gift decision, while Pyatt laboured to a points win over Ian Strudwick. Afterwards Hearn was elated about Hamed's showing while Ingle trumpeted to the press that his charge had 'stolen the show' from the main event.

At this point, Ingle announced that he would be pressing the case for the British Boxing Board to waive its regulation that a boxer must turn twenty-one before being allowed to challenge for a British title and give Hamed special permission to take on Robbie Regan for the national flyweight crown. But though the Board later reduced this ridiculous limit to twenty, it has never shown much inclination for bending its rules, and, needless to say, permission was not forthcoming.

Even before his first fight Naseem expressed disdain for the potential opposition within the flyweight division and he was later to say he regretted he never had the chance to beat up 'those

old-timers', Robbie Regan, Francis Ampofo, Dave McAuley
and Pat Clinton. It was a remark typical of Hamed's mentality –
he found it very difficult to refrain from expressing as
provocatively as possible, his honestly held beliefs, and these
included a conviction that his God-given talents were far
superior to those of anyone else within his range, and even many
of those beyond it. He also had a strong inclination to needle
potential major-league opponents.

At that stage Hamed was a three-fight 18-year-old and the idea
of him even contemplating a fight against the 31-year-old
McAuley (who at that stage had just lost his IBF world flyweight
title), the 28-year-old Clinton (then the WBO's flyweight
champion), the 24-year-old Regan (the British champion with
only one cut-eye loss in twelve fights) or the 25-year-old Ampofo
(the former British champion with eight wins out of ten), seemed
ludicrous to anyone who hadn't seen what he was capable of in
the gym. Certainly the view at the time was that Hamed's claims
were the silly rantings of an overheated teenager, but in
retrospect they look increasingly credible.

The mid-1992 Hamed was far from the finished article – he
still did too much futile jumping around, and had yet to develop
the strength, power and timing he shows today – but he already
had all the basic tools which would make him the finest fighter,
pound for pound, in Britain and Ireland. It was not the results
that counted, but the way he delivered them. Beard, Norman
and Bloomer were hardly world beaters but Hamed was
flattening them in a far more decisive and unequivocal way than
anyone else – including Regan and Ampofo. Even at that early
point in his career Naseem Hamed probably hit harder than any
other flyweight in Britain and was certainly faster and more
difficult to hit, and he was accustomed to boxing up to 20 fast
rounds in the gym without visible signs of fatigue. Also, the way
he handled far bigger men in sparring suggests that his taking
the British title in his fourth or fifth fight would have been
feasible.

But with the Boxing Board's age policy forcing him to abandon
this option, Naseem's natural body growth combined with his
taste for chocolates, junk food and his mother's cooking meant
that over the next seven weeks he filled out by over 5 pounds to a

little over the bantamweight limit. With the realization that the flyweight title option was a no-go, Ingle and Hamed decided there was no point keeping his maturing body within range of the 8-stone limit, and he stepped up to bantamweight.

His fourth opponent, exactly three months after his debut, was another B-list Welsh featherweight – Nicholas 'Miguel' Matthews of Ystalyfera. He was, and is, one of those British boxers who get plenty of work from promoters because they're always available at short notice, they know how to survive in the ring (and usually last the distance) and there's little danger of them pulling off an upset, though they're honest triers who provide a good show.

Matthews, then twenty-six, had amassed 51 fights in less than four years by the time he fought Hamed, with his record showing a paltry six wins (two inside the distance), eight draws and 37 losses (four inside the distance). It was a deceptive record, however, and he was far better than his official tally suggested, as is indicated by a recent late-career winning streak. A good number of the draws and the decisions against him were out-and-out robberies, with around half of them being by half point or one point margins, and his conquerers included some of the best in the business, among them WBO world champions Colin McMillan and Johnny Bredahl and others like Richie Wenton and Johnny Armour who made their mark on the British, European and Commonwealth scene. He was four inches taller than Hamed and, at 8 stone 10lb, had a 2½-pound weight advantage.

Making his London debut in a benefit show for Michael Watson (crippled after his return fight with Chris Eubank ten months earlier) at Mayfair's Grosvenor House on 14 July, Naseem had yet another effortless ride, though this time he let things last one round longer, explaining later that he liked to give the crowd a bit of a show.

After a playful feel-out first round he got down to business late in the second, dropping Matthews with a heavy right to the side of the head for a five count just before the bell. In the third he poured on the punishment, with referee Roy Francis stepping in after 65 seconds. Afterwards Naseem was presented a trophy for the 'Outstanding Prospect of the Year' in the annual ProBox

awards for Screensport fighters – the last time Naseem would
box for them.

To the astonishment of many in the boxing fraternity, this fight
was Naseem's final effort under the Matchroom umbrella. Six
months after their high profile House of Commons signing, Ingle
and Naseem (along with others in the gym) decided to sever all
ties with Barry Hearn and instead to accept an offer from rival
promoter Mickey Duff to fight under his National Promotions
banner.

To say that Hearn was incensed by this defection would be to
put things mildly. Interviewed for *Boxing Monthly* over a year
later he was still expressing his dismay at Ingle's decision, calling
it 'a mistake of colossal proportions', and complaining that he,
Hearn, had built Hamed to the point where he was known all
over Europe and was about to become a household name in
Britain. 'I'm possibly the worst trainer in the world so I don't
train fighters. Brendan should take the same approach to his
managership,' he was quoted as saying.[9]

Even today this defection rankles with Hearn, who was clearly
deeply offended by Ingle's apparent preference for Duff,
arguing that Ingle's motive was entirely pecuniary. 'We were
doing a lot of work together in co-promoting shows, but then he
sold his promotional rights in his stable to Mickey Duff without
even discussing it with me . . . I wasn't disappointed for Naseem
because obviously he's always been a quality fighter and he was
always going to get there. I was disappointed that at any time in
your life you have to do business with people like Brendan
Ingle.'

Hearn is not even prepared to acknowledge Ingle's prowess as
a trainer. 'I prefer to acknowledge the old adage that great
fighters make trainers great,' he says with a half smile – and then
adds, with the self-deprecating humour that is part of his
undoubted charm, 'It's also true that great fighters make
promoters great.'

He claims he had a 'fine relationship' with Naseem and insists
he knew better than anyone else how to channel his skills and
personality to the best promotional effect. 'I had no problems
with Naz at all. He's an outgoing young man and he's extremely

talented and has the potential to be a phenomenon, and I would obviously have done a fantastic job on him,' he says before catching himself again. 'But then what would you expect me to say? He was going to get there anyway and I think, to be honest with you, he's made it in about the right time.'

Ingle sees things rather differently, arguing that Hearn's desire for greater control was the cause of the breakdown in relations, and that the Essex man's sales pitch exceeded his service. Furthermore, Ingle was extremely wary about other managers and promoters 'poaching' his fighters and had faced several defections. He was particularly resentful about the departure of the promising, though erratic, Paul 'Silky' Jones to the Hearn stable and saw this as a precurser to what might be attempted with Naseem – and it's worth bearing in mind that he'd already had to contend with several managerial offers for Naseem, including one from Chris Eubank. 'I'd had Silky Jones since he was a kid of 14, and I'd taught him everything he knew, and then I sent him down to work with one of Hearn's fighters, and all of a sudden Silky leaves me and goes to Barry Hearn,' Ingle says in a tone which matches Hearn's on the bile scale. 'And then with the contract that Hearn wanted me and Naz to sign, he would have had control of him, lock, stock and barrel, and there was far too much work gone into him for that, so we went to Mickey Duff.'

In his first three months as an active professional Naseem had four fights, which had lasted a total of less than nine rounds. But the changeover in promotional control meant that while contracts were being signed and options considered, the eager young fighter was not fighting, and it was to be almost three months before he was in the business again – a big gap by Naseem's standards at the time.

He remained in serious training throughout this period, but the long break – and this was the first of several over the next eighteen months – also provided the chance to extend the range of his appeal in his hometown and to give more time to his family, his community 'obligations', his own social life and his religion.

Naseem acknowledges his regular fight schedule during his

first three months in the professional game – and again since
1994 – had some effect on the time and focus he could devote to
his Islamic faith, particularly when it came to two of the 'pillars'
of the religion which every Muslim is expected to practise:
praying five times a day facing Mecca and fasting during the
month of Ramadan (which involves abstaining from all eating,
drinking and sex from sunrise to sunset). 'There are allowances,
where you don't have to pray at the exact time, as long as you
follow up and do a prayer at a different time,' he explains, 'but
you can't really fast if you're boxing. Obviously if you're fighting
it's going to interrupt the schedule of your eating, so, yes, that is
one clash with my religion, but it's the only one.'

He still carries a copy of the Koran in his kitbag to fights, and
says he reads it occasionally, and he sometimes attends his local
mosque in Rothay Road, half a mile from his parents' home,
when in town. He has never had even a sip of alcohol, a puff of
a cigarette or taken any recreational drug, he refuses to eat pork,
ham and bacon, and he makes it clear that one of his post-boxing
options is some kind of full-time Islamic commitment (though
he also talks about a future career in 'show business').

It would, however, be incorrect to overstate the rigidity of
Naseem's current religious views and practice. What is clear is
that he seldom lets it go as far as curtailing his pursuit of and by
women, or restricting his personal style and musical taste, and in
common with most Yemenis the few views he has expressed on
social issues are relatively liberal.

Dr Abdul Shaif says that Naseem tends to 'take the best out of
religion' – particularly the discipline, the work culture and the
respect for elders – and sift out a good deal of the rest. 'Naseem
spends a great deal of time in the gym,' he says, 'and I know he
has his own private life as well, which may contradict what is
happening in Islam. But he has certainly absorbed many things
from Islam, and his identity stems from this. Being Yemeni
means being Muslim, and I think he has picked the best bits
out.'

Early in his amateur days Naseem developed a reputation as
something of a night owl. As a teenager he liked to go to an out
of town snooker hall, often until the early morning, and would
spend many hours playing and invariably winning. His best

break is between 30 and 40 and, as with boxing, he hates to lose and loves to demolish the opposition. As Ingle puts it: 'If he plays you in snooker, you'll play ten games and he'll beat you nine in a row, and you'll tell him you've had enough. But you can't do that with him. He'll say, "You're still playing," and you'll have to wait for ten, and then, when he's beaten you for the tenth time, he'll commiserate with you. That's how he is.' Naseem would regularly watch major snooker tournaments and later struck up a friendship with snooker world champion Stephen Hendry, who gave him tips on his game and remains one of the few sportsmen Naz comes close to hero-worshipping.

It was during this period that Naseem started to become more vocal about another passion – his fascination with fashion. This first received publicity when the women's editor of a local paper used him as an extremely willing clothes horse for a Sheffield boutique – the first of numerous fashion shoots.'[10] It did not take long before Naseem's views on menswear became a staple of just about every interview he granted. He would tell you his hobbies were 'shopping, shopping, looking good and shopping', and later he began designing his own line of clothes.

After completing his schooling, and particularly since turning professional, he also established a reputation as a regular at 'Josephine's' and other Sheffield nightclubs, and a bit later started making frequent trips to London's West End clubland as well – attracted by the music, the women, the prestige and the late night excitement. Inevitably, given these environments, his size, his reputation as a cocksure professional fighter, as well as his sometimes vainglorious attitude to his growing fame, there were young men tempted to have a go at him, though it's an aspect of his past he prefers to underplay. 'I get a lot of respect out there,' he says. 'People realize I'm a boxer, that I can fight, and they leave me alone – even earlier in my career. I don't have no problems whatsoever, and anyway I got friends around me all the time, but I've never had bodyguards except when I was in the Yemen. I think, who's going to bodyguard the bodyguard?' He points to himself with a knowing smile, prompting the response of, 'You!'. 'Exactly, exactly', he says with a nod.

Some of those around him are rather more equivocal on the subject, claiming that people leave him alone because in the past he's been forced to prove what he's capable of. Brendan Ingle makes the point that Naseem has generally managed to avoid trouble because he hangs out with good people and because from the start his boxers are taught to walk away from insults and to avoid proving themselves in the street. 'But, you know, it's very difficult because people see him on television, and the only crime you can't be punished for is envy and jealousy. You get a small element who get jealous, but he handles it well.'

There are several legends in Sheffield about what handling things well can mean – about large men, sometimes more than one at a time, swinging at fresh air before getting their decisive come-uppance and others about Naseem being flattened. One oft-repeated tale has him beating up an aggresive drunk twice his size at a local disco. There is even a much quoted urban myth, which seems to grow with each telling, of Naseem teasing two women (in the more vivid versions, 'a pair of lesbians') having a scrap outside a Sheffield club, and getting pushed/punched/decked/knocked cold for his troubles, though Naseem is quite clear that except for the incident with the heavyweight Adam Fogarty when he was sixteen, he has never been dropped in the ring, the street or the playground by any man, woman or child. John Ingle insists that Naz has never been in a street fight and has several stories of how he avoided fights. 'Once we were playing five-a-side football and this guy from the other team went for him. Naz could have knocked him cold, but he just danced away and laughed. Another time this kid went for me and Naz could have taken him out with one punch, but instead he just calmed the kid down.'

Despite his occasional displays of petulance, Naseem has long been a popular figure in his hometown. One reason for this is that early in his professional career he established a reputation for 'doing his bit' for Sheffield. He received his first favourable public notices in this regard in late 1992, and since then has regularly appeared for or given public backing to a wide range of civic and community projects including charity fun runs, anti-crime and anti-graffiti campaigns, children's hospital fund drives, community gym openings, Christmas lights switch-ons and others.

Much of his sense of place and community and his willingness to get involved has been a result of Ingle's connections and his many years of activism on behalf of Sheffield's poor. It was standard practice for Ingle to involve as many of his boxers – amateur and professional – as possible in these projects. Perhaps the most popular have been the inmate versus teammate sparring sessions at the sports centre in the nearby Doncaster Lindholme Prison which he organizes once or twice a year to raise money – around £1000 a time – for various charities. He started this programme in 1991 after several years of doing a similar exercise with Herol Graham and other boxers in local pubs and schools. Each time he picks ten or twelve of his boxers, who are put in with a team of prison boxing hopefuls for a round apiece, with the rest of the inmates (sometimes up to 600) paying £1 (and since last year £2) for the privilege of watching their hardman heroes try to land a glove on Brendan's lads (who wear headguards, just in case). The rules, as Ingle explains it, are simple: 'My lads can't hit the prisoners, but if the prisoners hit them the Governor is supposed to give them £50 and if they knock any of my lads out, he gives them £100. There's great excitement and the prison fellas go mad, but after two minutes they're completely knackered.'

Ingle's boxers spend hours in the gym learning to avoid being hit by each other and seldom suffer the indignity of taking a solid punch from an inmate during the two-minute sessions. As Ryan Rhodes, a regular at these sessions, puts it: 'With our training, if you get caught, then it's your own fault. It does happen occasionally, but really, it's a good laugh. They go wild and the other prisoners cheer for them, but they cheer for us as well.' Naseem has done his prison duty six times and has never been hit, and his presence has made him a huge favourite with the inmates and screws, some of whom are ex-boxers themselves.

Naseem has always held a great deal of genuine affection for his hometown, and can also be extremely defensive about it and, as he showed a little later in his career when being criticized for a supposed slight on Sheffield fight fans, exceedingly sensitive about any contrary impressions. While he tolerates the tired phrase 'the Yemeni Yorkshireman', like most South Yorkshire citizens, he stresses that his identity is city-bound rather than regional and will tell you he does not know what it feels like to be a Yorkshireman but that he's truly proud to be a son of Sheffield.

Even from his early professional days he has been careful never to antognize any section of the local population, right down to refusing to state publicly his football team preference, despite fairly regularly attending Sheffield Wednesday's games. When pushed on this issue all he offers is a wry smile and a vacuous answer: 'I support Sheffield Wednesday *and* Sheffield United, and the Sharks in basketball, the Stealers in ice hockey and the Eagles in rugby because at the end of the day I support the whole of Sheffield and anything to do with Sheffield because I'm born and bred in Sheffield.' And when this raises an eyebrow he'll point a finger and insist: 'You should definitely mention that.'

In 1992 he also began making intermittent appearances at various Yemeni community projects – opening an exhibition on Yemen at an inner city school, giving his name to an organizational fund-raising drive and later allowing his merchandise to be sold for community fund-raising purposes. The publicity given to him in Sheffield, first as an amateur and more particularly since turning professional, established him as a heroic and inspirational figure for the Yemeni youth at a time when rising unemployment as a result of the closure of the steel mills was exacerbating the social problems in the community.

'Our young people see him as their king, as doing something they would once have only dreamt of doing,' says Abdul Shaif. 'Now they don't have to dream; it can become reality because Naseem has done it. So when Naseem started making a name for himself a lot of young people began channelling their energies into sport – energies which could otherwise be aggressive, or which would have been wasted playing cards in a café. He has given them an element of hope.'

5

Waiting for Mickey

Naseem began his fifteen-month relationship with Mickey Duff and National Promotions soon after the Miguel Matthews fight. It started out with great promise but turned out to be the least productive and most frustrating spell of his professional career.

Duff was very much a known quantity for Brendan Ingle – a streetwise wheeler-dealer who had fought his way up from the bottom, had done the business in every department and seldom missed a trick. They had worked together for many years, particularly with Herol Graham, and though there had been several disputes, there always seemed to be a basic respect between the the philosophically inclined, yin and yang grey haired Irish ex-pug and the wily, witty red-haired Londoner.

Duff is an institution in British boxing – a man who seems to have been around for ever – as a fighter, trainer, cornerman and manager, and over several decades as Britain's pre-eminent promoter and matchmaker (while retaining his managerial and cornerman roles). For many years he and his partners enjoyed hegemony in the promotional field, and although their organization, National Promotions, had conceded some ground to their rivals, they were in August 1992, nevertheless a significant force to be reckoned with, and, indeed, remain so. Among those fighting under their promotional and managerial control were several British, European and Commonwealth champions and world-rated boxers, including Frank Bruno, Henry Akinwande, Billy Schwer, Johnny Armour, Gary Jacobs, Henry Wharton, Andy Holligan, Duke McKenzie, Lloyd Honeyghan, Herol Graham, James Cook and Richie Woodhall.

The deal with Duff provided for Naseem's fights to be screened on the satellite channel Eurosport, and offered him the promise of regular work on National Promotions undercards. That, at least, was intended to be the start, with the hope of bigger things in the future. Once the contacts were signed, Duff and Ingle moved quickly to ensure the momentum was maintained and decided to put Naseem on the undercard of a bill featuring Billy Hardy and Andy Holligan in Sunderland on 7 October 1992. Naseem's opponent was the Manchester bantamweight Des Gargano, an old friend of his who came in as a late substitute at less than twenty-four hours' notice.

Nice guy Gargano, then thirty-one, is known in the game as a 'runner' – a ducking and diving southpaw whose general *modus operandi* is to circle the perimeter of the ring and stay out of trouble. The Des Garganos of this world exist in every sport and profession – good, honest buck survivors, who can be relied upon to make up the numbers and to be available whenever they're called up.

When Gargano fought Hamed his record stood at 26 wins (two inside the distance), 58 losses (three on cut-eye stoppages) and two draws. He had been the distance with some of the best little men in Britain and Europe – Pat Clinton, Jimmy Bredahl, Bradley Stone and Joe Kelly. Every so often he managed a three- or four-fight winning streak (and won nine out of 14 in a 1990–91 run), and once he fought an eliminator for the Central bantamweight title, but mainly he was a tough, elusive loser. The challenge for Naseem was to catch him and put him away. It has to be said that the 5-foot-5 Gargano, who weighed in at 8st 8lb, one pound less than Naseem, was already a bit weak in the legs when he entered the ring, having trained the previous night, before being given his call-up at 10.20 p.m.

Hamed, fighting in a pair of bright green and black satin trunks as a temporary change from the leopard spots, went straight into attack mode and soon had his man down for a six count, and though the Mancunian soon got on his bicycle, he went down again from a push-punch combination shortly before the bell. 'He gave me a terrible first round,' Gargano recalls. 'He would stand in front of me with his head a few inches from mine, and I just couldn't find a way to catch him. He would fake and feint a lot and look at the canvas or at his corner and then catch me with a punch at the very same time, and he was hurting me with some really big body blows, and winded me a few times. I managed to cover up when he wound up for most of his big punches, but he would catch me with the little ones.'

For the rest of the fight Gargano fled and Hamed pursued. In the second round Naseem leapt into the air to drop Gargano with a surprise punch, but he was up immediately. He was dropped again in the third and finally Naseem caught up with him for long enough to finish things in the fourth, pinning him in a corner and ending it with thumping left to the solar plexus which felled the veteran and prompted referee Gerry Watson to call a halt at the 2 minute 6-second mark. 'I just doubled up and went down,' says Gargano, 'and when I struggled up the referee could see from my face that I couldn't breathe – I just couldn't suck it in – and he stopped it.'

Having told Gargano seven years earlier that he would one day fight and beat him, Naseem had delivered just as he promised. Gargano, still boxing at the age of thirty-five, and now with 115 fights to his name, is not a man to take a beating personally and was happy to acknowledge he was enormously impressed. 'I've boxed with a lot of champions and I thought I was indestructible,' he says. 'I take a lot of pride in going the distance and I'd never been knocked out, but Naseem was really classy. He was extremely difficult to hit, he had very quick reflexes, moved a lot and he hit really hard. And I've always liked him too. He has a lot of spirit and I think what he's doing for boxing is just great.'

Hamed's sixth and last fight of 1992 featured him as the main undercard attraction on a poorly attended Andy Holligan bill at the Everton Sports Centre in Liverpool on 12 November. Naseem was given another awkward customer, Peter Buckley – perhaps his most difficult opponent yet.

The 23-year-old Birmingham spoiler was the Midlands super featherweight champion, though he did most of his boxing at featherweight and occasionally at super bantam. He had a so-so record of 18 wins (three inside the distance), 18 losses (two inside the distance – both to Duke McKenzie) and five draws, though he was considered unlucky not to get the nod on several occasions. After making a fairly promising start to his professional career, losing only two of his first eleven fights, he soon settled into the 'opponent' grade. He was good enough to beat the lesser hopefuls and to give a frustrating night to the likes of Johnny Armour, Drew Docherty and Johnny Bredahl – slippery, hard to hit and extremely adept at grabbing, holding and wriggling out of trouble – but lacking the power or ambition to do much more.

The 5-foot-8 Buckley weighed in at half a pound over the super bantam limit – three more than Hamed, but looked several weights heavier when they stepped into the ring. Naseem made his usual flashy entrance but gave what was certainly his worst performance to date, being unable to break Buckley's negative rhythm for long enough to put him away.

After taking a couple of stiff punches, the Birmingham boxer decided the only sane course was self-preservation. He tucked his chin behind his forearms, grabbed, held, ducked and dived, but threw very little in return. Naseem tried everything – shifting from southpaw to orthodox and back, throwing surprise punches from unusual angles, the Naz-shuffle, dropping his hands and inviting his man in, and talking to Buckley and even to the ringside press, but nothing seemed to work. He became frustrated, lost his gumshield in the second and third rounds, was warned for holding and hitting and finally descended into what was, by his standards, a sloppy performance.

His only real moments of success came late in the third when he dropped Buckley for a two-count, and followed up with a combination of three right jabs and a left cross. He also managed to wobble him with a solid left shortly before the final bell. Referee Phil Cowswill scored the fight 59½ to 58, indicating that

Naseem won four rounds to Buckley's one, with one even – a clear win and a fair score, but by no means a flattering performance.

For the first time in his short professional career, Naseem received bad press for his boxing. *Boxing News* headed its report 'Not so princely this time, Hamed', noting that it was 'a contest that fell sadly short on entertainment value'.[1] Hamed's own view is that Buckley was entirely to blame. 'Sure, he took me the distance, but I wouldn't say he was my toughest opponent,' he says. 'It's just that when you get in with a fighter who's not going to commit hisself to fight, whose goal is to lose and to go the distance by holding, covering up, doing things he wouldn't use to win with, then obviously you going to have a bit of a problem. If he wanted to win he would have to throw punches back but he was just trying to make a name for hisself by going the distance with me, even though he was taking a beating in every round. Now to me, that's silly.'

Buckley, however, does not share this rather egocentric view of 'making a name' for himself by surviving with a novice, and believes he boxed an extremely sensible fight. 'I wasn't intimidated by him and I think that's why it went the distance,' he says. 'He'd had only five fights and I'd had over forty, so he didn't really give me no problems. He wanted to dictate the pace but I was just messing him about. He was more of a showboater in those days – he's settled down now – but I just tried to keep my chin down and to keep close to him. I've got a good defence and when he came close I just tied him up. He won the fight all right, yeah, – no complaints about the decision at all, but he didn't hurt me.'

Despite this, however, he came away with the impression that Naseem was a boxer of enormous potential. 'I'd been in with former world champions, but even then he was something special, and I could see he was going to go all the way. He might have been lacking in experience, but he had all the natural ability and I knew he would be a world champion.'

If the Buckley fight was a bad end to an otherwise excellent year, 1993 started on an even more dismal note – though this time outside the ring and not of Naseem's own making. For the first seven years of Hamed's boxing career he was the darling of the

Sheffield business and political establishment and, more particularly, the Yorkshire Press, which was only too happy to fill its pages with gushing reports of the young boxer's exploits inside and outside the ring. Naseem is not an avid reader, though he very occasionally makes his way through a boxing biography or a pacy novel (*Papillon* is still his all-time favourite), devours the fight magazines, skims the tabloids to see what they're saying about him and gets the *Guardian* or *The Times* at home. But of all the papers it is the *Sheffield Star* which he reads most regularly, and which has been most attentive to him, so it came as a bit of a shock when he woke late in the morning on 4 January 1993 to find a triple page investigative spread of a decidedly different tone.

The headlines were just the sort the aspiring professional did not need: 'Boxing star caught in row over £3000 loan', 'Yemeni cash row' and, to balance things a bit, 'The meteoric rise of the Arabian Knight'.[2] The nub of the controversy concerned the £3000 loan from the Yemeni Community Association to Naseem, to help him train and buy boxing equipment, at a time when his father, Sal, was a prominent office holder within the organization. £1000 was presented to him shortly before he completed his amateur career in October 1991 (when Sal was sitting on the association's nine person management committee) and the remaining £2000 in May 1992, shortly after his professional career started (when Sal was its chairman).

One of the complaints from three prominent members of the association was that the group's auditor was not told that Naseem was Sal's son – a fact dismissed as irrelevant by its spokesman Dr Abdul Shaif, who stressed that Sal had played no part in discussing or voting on the loan, and that the loan was made because it was felt that Naseem was an important symbol of the community and that it would identify him with the association.

The suggestion from the complainants – who were subsequently expelled for making 'baseless allegations' and being 'disruptive' during a 'power struggle', – was that there was favouritism at work and that the association's 'haphazard' financial procedures allowed the loan to pass through unnoticed. Following their expulsion, the three made a vociferous public call for Sheffield City Council – which had made substantial annual grants to the association – to re-open a 1989 council investigation into the group's finances, in which it was cleared of any wrong-doing, but warned to improve its accounting procedures. A December 1992 council report said that while there might be legitimate concerns about the group's accountability, there had been improvements and that there was no evidence of mismanagement or that cash advances had been given to family members.

According to the association the money for the Hamed loan came from its own funds, and not from the council grant and it was stressed that in return for the loans, Naseem had agreed to pay back the £3000 at 15 per cent interest by the end of March 1993 and to allow the association to sell fund-raising T-shirts bearing his name and picture, which by the end of 1992 had raised £900 – prompting Sal Hamed to comment that the purpose of the arrangement was, in fact, to make profit for the community,[3] a position that was subsequently affirmed at the association's Annual General Meeting.

Viewed from outside the incessant internal political rumblings of the association, the whole controversy seems extraordinarily overblown. Today Dr Shaif insists the complainants had 'their own axe to grind' – not because of any opposition to Naseem, but because of his father's position in the association and its internal conflicts. He argues, however, that despite the brouhaha, the whole issue helped to cement relations between Naseem and the organization. 'For us this was a very good investment – not necessarily in business terms – but as an investment in confidence for the community, and I think we've got more than that back because Naseem has not only been an inspiration to the Yemeni community here, but to Yemenis wherever they are in the world. Naseem will always remember the community supported him at a fundamental turning point in his life, when he was just an amateur turning professional. He'll never forget that.'

Nevertheless, the accusations continued to simmer for some time in the local press, and were, inevitably, picked up elsewhere. As late as May 1995 an editorial in the South Africa-based *Boxing World* magazine by the British boxing

writer Peter McInnes made substantial reference to the
controversy. Naseem has avoided commenting on it, but it
seemed to have the effect of making him more cautious with the
press, and more wary of their motives. From then on, those
surrounding Naseem, and the boxer himself, became more
protective of his reputation – often politely requesting lists of
questions from would-be interviewers, as well as copies of draft
feature stories, and insisting that questions of a personal nature
not be asked. While Naz often likens his public style to that of
his hero, Muhammad Ali, this is one of many areas where the
two men simply cannot be compared. Despite his love of public
acclaim and attention, by early 1993 he had already become
diffident and suspicious with the public and the press. Ali, in
contrast, seldom refused an interview, a signature, a hug or a
kiss.

What was needed after the Liverpool letdown, and more so after
the funding controversy, was a quick return to action in order to
re-establish his earlier breakneck momentum. Instead, it was
three and a half months after the Buckley fight before he was to
step through the ropes again – a delay that would become part of
a pattern over the next year. The consolation was that he was to
appear at the Wembley Arena against an unbeaten opponent,
and on a more substantial bill than the previous two under
Mickey Duff. This time he was up against the 24-year-old
Newport bantamweight, Alan Ley, on the undercard of a 24
February 1993 bill headed by the British lightweight title fight
between Billy Schwer and Paul Burke.

Ley, a former Welsh ABA flyweight champion, had turned
professional in September 1991 and had a record of four fights,
four wins and no knockouts. He shared two opponents with
Naseem – Andy Bloomer and Shaun Norman – and had outpointed both of them (while Naseem had knocked them out). He
was known as a skilled southpaw, who was a bit lacking in the
power department.

The fight was made at the 8st 6lb bantamweight limit, and
with Naseem's inactivity and his habit of eating as he pleased, he
had a struggle to make it. Two days before the fight he was
surprised to find himself three pounds over the limit, prompting

Brendan Ingle to give him a ticking off about his undisciplined diet. To help him shed the excess weight Ingle offered to join him for 36 hours of complete abstinence from food and water.

When they arrived in London the night before the fight, Naseem was still two pounds over, and neither of them allowed each other to sneak even a sip of water, and just to make sure of not failing, they went for a brisk walk before the weigh-in. Naseem weighed in at 8st 5½ lb, half a pound within the limit (which Ley made on the button), while Ingle was down to 11st 9lb – 5 pounds less than when the deal was done.

'The trouble with Naz,' Brendan recalls, 'was that he was still growing but he was continuing to eat as he pleased, and the wrong foods too, and let me tell you, this is a fella who could eat for England.' Though the lesson was never entirely absorbed, Naseem was never to leave his weight-making duties this late again.

The fight itself proved much easier than many expected, and once again showed off the Sheffield teenager in the best possible light. From the opening bell he had his fellow southpaw in trouble, pumping out his right jab and firing home left leads and right hooks from unexpected angles without taking anything in return.

Halfway through round one, after several changes in stance, he banged the Welshman over with a left-right combination. Ley was up at eight but soon after was dropped again, this time with a bone-jarring right. The Welshman decided the best strategy was to grab and not let go, a move which kept him buoyant until the bell. In the second round Ley continued to hit and hold, but it was clear his legs had gone and Naseem dropped him twice more. After the fourth knockdown Ley chose to remain on his knees for the full count, still conscious but too shaken and demoralized to rise.

Twelve days after his nineteenth birthday Naseem had given his most impressive and polished performance since turning professional and did not waste the opportunity to let the London press know what he had in mind. 'I'm good enough to win the British bantamweight title right now,' he said, in what was the first of several public salvoes directed at national champion Drew Docherty. And with Schwer having lost his title on cuts to

Burke, Ingle did not lose the chance to press home to Duff his claim for a better billing for Hamed, announcing that his charge was the 'new star' and best bantamweight since the heyday of Alan Rudkin – a rare understatement by the Irishman's standards.

Hamed, who had been leaping the ropes ever since his junior amateur days, soon added another element to his expanding acrobatic repertoire – his trademark forward somersault over the ropes ring entrance. In fact, though he is now the primary exponent of this method of arrival, he did not invent it himself. That singular honour belongs to his close chum and sparmate, Ryan Rhodes, then still an amateur. 'I first tried the frontflip over the ropes in the gym ring in about 1993,' Rhodes recalls. 'A few people seen it, and then a couple of guys tried it, and then Naz started doing it, and he got really good at it and then a little while later he started doing the flip in his fights, but I was the one who invented it.'

Naseem, who scornfully claims that Chris Eubank borrowed his rope vault after visiting the St Thomas's gym in 1991, acknowledges his debt to his buddy for the somersault variation. 'I'll tell you the truth about that: the first time I saw that frontflip, it was Ryan who did it. I'll never tell a lie where I got something from. End of the day, when I get something from him, he should get the credit. I seen him doing it and I thought that was a wicked way to get into the ring.'[4]

But 1993 was not be the year Naseem's acrobatic skills and pugilistic talents were shown off in the way they deserved. Mickey Duff's vast promotional experience and network of contacts were proving to be less valuable than Ingle had hoped, and his relations with Ingle, while never plummeting to the Hearn depths, were not quite as warm as a few months earlier. By this stage they were starting to argue incessantly, with Ingle wanting more action and profile for Naseem, and Duff saying this depended on National Promotions getting more security for their investment.

It took over three months before Naseem's next fight – against yet another Welsh loser, Kevin Jenkins, on another Andy Holligan undercard at the Mansfield Leisure Centre on 26 May 1993. Jenkins, twenty-two, had started his professional career with some promise in December 1989, picking up two wins and a draw in his first three outings, but after that he quickly settled into the tomato role, losing, usually on points, to bigger name prospects. The high point of his record of 3 wins, 12 losses and three draws was a draw with future Commonwealth flyweight champion Darren Fifield three months earlier, and he had been the distance with some live ones like Robbie Regan, Paul Weir and Joe Kelly. He possessed a firm chin, with only Danny Porter having knocked him cold, but hardly qualified as a stern test by this stage in Hamed's career.

Eager to put on a show after so long out of the ring, Hamed made the most of his boogy down the aisle, his rope flip plus forward roll ring entrance and his eyeball stare-out of the Ammanford week-end warrior. Jenkins responded with a phlegmatic grin and later explained he had never heard of Naseem before the fight and knew nothing of his reputation. In the opening round Hamed (8st 7½ lb) put on an exhibition, dancing around, shooting from surprise angles, getting warned for slapping and then going into an exaggerated breakdance routine which Jenkins imitated. In the second the fun was over and he fired hard punches through the gaps in his opponent's tight guard, hurting him on several occasions. Jenkins (8st 6½ lb) gallantly tried to fire back but towards the end of the round was trapped in a corner and hammered with a volley of very fast punches.

As the bell rang for the third, Ingle told Hamed, 'This is the round'. A vicious left hook to the body felled Jenkins for a nine-count. Seconds later Naseem was warned for a low blow, but the next punch, this time a sickening right to the solar plexus, knocked all the wind out of the Welshman and he collapse in obvious agony, prompting his corner to throw in the towel. For reasons known only to himself, referee Pridding kicked the towel out of the ring and ordered the boxers to fight on, but after one final punch, he came to his senses and called it off at 1 minute 58 seconds. When he had recovered, a sulky Jenkins said he was unimpressed with the beating he took, claiming that Danny Porter hit harder.

Today, however, he remembers things differently, and acknowledges Hamed's brilliance. 'He was way too good for me and more or less beat me up, didn't he? He's a totally different kind of fighter – much better than any of the other top-rated men I'd fought. I tried my hardest to hit him but I didn't connect once in four rounds,' he says, stubbornly insisting that he lasted until the fourth, rather than the third, when the fight actually did end. Today he tacitly acknowledges that his sour-grapes post-fight remarks were not entirely accurate. 'He's got immense power, more than anyone else I'd fought, and I'd been in with some strong featherweights before, so I didn't want to stay in there too long because I knew the score – that there was no point staying in there and getting hurt when there was no way I could win. I really thought he was something else.'

While Naseem received good trade and hometown press for this victory, and was promoted to number five in the British rankings by *Boxing News*, he was once again forced to twiddle his thumbs, train and wait for Duff to come up with another morsel to chew on. It took another four months and this time he was 'lent' to the new Irish promoter, Brian Peters (who had a business relationship with Duff) for his first-ever show at Dublin's National Basketball Arena on 24 September.

Ingle was delighted to show off his protégé in his old stomping ground, even though Naseem had to face the mild indignity of appearing on the undercard of a bill headed by a fighter he was convinced he could beat, and who had turned professional exactly a year after he had. Wayne 'The Pocket Rocket' McCullough, the Shankill Road bantamweight, had won the silver medal at the Barcelona Olympics, and after only seven months in the ring he was already having his eighth fight, and drawing an over-capacity crowd for his Irish debut. Naseem, by contrast, was having his third, and last, fight of 1993. It was a comparison that was hard to avoid, and Ingle and Naz certainly took note.

Naseem's opponent was the 26-year-old Central featherweight champion, Chris Clarkson from Hull. He had been a fine amateur – twice winning National Schoolboy titles – but had not quite cracked it in the professional ranks. By the time he fought Hamed, his record showed 18 wins (2 on stoppages), 21 losses (4 on stoppages) and 2 draws. Over the previous three years he had beaten several middle-ranking fighters, including former Hamed opponents Gargano and Buckley. He once fought for the IBF

Intercontinental bantamweight belt and his conquerers included several of the best men his size in Britain, Europe and the world – and with most of them he had taken the pain and gone the distance – but he was hardly the man to test Naseem at this stage of his career. All that Naz could do was to put up an absolutely scintillating performance in the hope of outshining McCullough, and this is precisely what he did.

Weighing in at the super bantamweight limit of 8st 10lb, his heaviest yet, Naseem was still 2 pounds lighter (and an inch shorter) than Clarkson, but from the first minute it was clear that this was of no consequence. Hamed demonstrated a few of his old tricks and some new ones – like looking at his opponent's feet while hitting him on the chin – but for the most part his opening round was far more businesslike than usual.

Clarkson remembers it well. 'From what I'd seen of him before, he was flashy and I thought I'd go out and give him one straight away, but he did none of that dancing around with me. He came out to do the job with a crouched-down style, face lowered, and he did the job. He slipped everything I threw with his head movement and then countered with a right jab through my guard which hurt and straight away I thought, What have we got here?' Things rapidly deteriorated for the Hull fighter and with just over a minute to go he was dropped with a left cross, over the top. 'I was badly dazed,' Clarkson remembers, 'but I somehow survived till the bell, and when I sat down in my corner I said, "Every time I move he hits me," which was true because he can land from any angle.'

Early in the second Hamed was on to him again, putting Clarkson down with a perfectly timed right cross. He was back on his feet when referee Barney Wilson reached the count of eight, and he knew the end was near. From the safety of a few years' distance, he remembers his own demise as a thing of beauty. 'Naseem got straight on top of me, worked me round to the corner without throwing a punch, and just as I heard my corner screaming, "Out of the way!", he whacked a left hook right underneath my heart which was so hard that I don't remember the next few seconds, but as I started getting up I heard the referee counting ten. The man's a devastating puncher.' At 1 minute and 50 seconds, Naseem had scored his eighth stoppage in nine fights, and his fifth in the second round, and the Irish crowd roared their approval.

Soon afterwards, McCullough put up an impressive, but less spectacular 'homecoming' performance in beating Algeria's Boulem Belkif on a fifth round technical knockout and inevitably the comparisons were made – which, in fact, was the whole idea of putting them on the same bill. Clarkson, who had recovered sufficiently to watch 'The Pocket Rocket' in action, left in no doubt as to who would prevail. 'I watched Wayne very carefully and afterwards I thought that Naz would tear him apart, and I still think that. McCullough's workrate is exceptional but the problem would be Naseem's power. He will punch right through McCullough.'

Immediately after the two fights were over Naseem made his opening salvo against his Belfast rival, announcing to the Irish public that he would win a world bantamweight title in 1994 and then successfully defend it against McCullough, to which the Irish star responded that he would be a double world champion by the time Hamed challenged him. Hamed and Ingle stayed for another couple of days in Dublin and found that their efforts had been worthwhile, with Naseem frequently being congratulated by well-wishers when walking in the city centre. 'When we arrived no one had heard of him, but he stole the show, and I tell ya, they really loved him in Dublin,' Ingle says.

One of the upshots of this extended stay was that Naseem and Clarkson became firm friends after the fight, as so often happens in boxing. They were staying in the same hotel and for a couple of days had a fine time hanging out together, an experience which suggested to the Hull boxer that Hamed was not quite as egocentrical as so many assume. 'We really got to talking and when I got to know him, he wasn't like I expected at all,' he says. 'I've got two sons and he was talking about them all the time and was very interested to know more about them. He's not the big, upfront person everyone thinks he is. He's got a heart, and he's a funny guy as well. Basically he's a real nice kid.'

After this impressive outing Naseem's career went from slow to halt, and when 1994 arrived he had been out of action for four months. By this stage McCullough had seen off 11 opponents in eleven months, while Naseem's record showed only 9 victories in twenty-one months, and a paltry three outings in 1993, and his opponents were strictly of the B- and C-list variety.

It is not the way that careers of all-time great professionals are meant to proceed. Joe Louis won 27 times and was the number one contender by the end of his first year and a half. Sugar Ray Robinson won 31 fights in his first eighteen months, beating four world champions in the process, while Willie Pep won 33 fights in the same time – all well before his twentieth birthday. Henry Armstong had 27 wins, 26 on knockouts, in the year he won the world featherweight title. Harry Greb managed 43 fights without defeat during one eleven-month spell. And among the recent 'greats', Tommy Hearns knocked out 17 men in his first fifteen months while Mike Tyson packed in 28 fights and had won his first world title after twenty months as a professional.

There were many excuses for the lulls in Naseem's first two years, but one reason was the ongoing dispute between Duff and Ingle over the nature of their deal. Duff was holding out for a joint involvement in Hamed's management, with National Promotions arguing that their existing agreement provided insufficient protection in the promotional contract, because, as Duff put it, 'otherwise the boxers can just tell you to fuck off after a while'. In effect, the group was not prepared to make a major league investment in Naseem unless a more advantageous contract could be secured, and Ingle was not prepared to budge.

Today both men are magnanimous about the dispute and there is little of the hard feeling there was with the Hearn bust-up. 'I wouldn't say they left me; I think parted is the better word,' Duff insists. 'We parted ways because Naseem had to go into another league and at that particular time there were people who I was involved with – not me, but others – who weren't prepared to put up the funds necessary, and Frank Warren was in a position to sign a long-term contract and to guarantee larger amounts of money than I was.'

Duff says that while their contract lasted he had a good business relationship with Ingle and a healthy, though not particularly close relationship with Naseem. 'Listen, let me put it to you this way,' he says. 'Nobody around at the time or now has or had a bigger opinion of Naseem than I. I always thought he was an exceptional fighter and nothing has changed my mind. I didn't get to know him that well at the time, and you don't need the fingers on two hands to count how many times we've met to date. In fact since we parted I've probably met him more often than when we were together, and what I'd say is that I found him eccentric and quite jovial. There's nothing wrong with him, and we still get on reasonably well.'

At the time Ingle said the main reason for the move to Frank Warren was the promise of live coverage through ITV. 'Mickey Duff was paying well but Naz wasn't getting the exposure he needs,' he said at the time.[5] Today he still stresses that despite their disagreements, he respects Duff for being open with them, and for having no hidden agenda, and points out that the signing of the contract with Warren did not mean a complete end to his relationship with Duff.[6] 'To be honest with you, Mickey was very fair with us, and that's important. But the agreement ran out and he wanted to do another agreement, and Frank Warren offered us a better deal, so we went there.'

The year of 1993 was, however, not entirely wasted. Naseem's progress in Britain may have been far too slow, but he was making big waves in the Middle East and particularly in the Yemen. For several years Brendan Ingle had been talking about promoting his young fighter in his parents' homeland, and had used the family connections to ensure that the groundwork was well laid. In 1990 – the year after the Republic of Yemen was established as a single unified state, Ingle started sending videos of Naseem's amateur fights, along with all his results and stories about his prowess, to the Yemen.

By the time Naseem turned professional he was already a figure of national repute, despite the fact that boxing had been virtually an unknown quantity there. His fight films (including some from his amateur days) were shown on national television, a video of his life and career was produced, and the president, Ali Abdullah Salah, became a personal fan. Ingle had boned up at the local library on the country's geography and history, and reckoned that the time was right for a high profile tour of the Five Cities, complete with several exhibition fights, all of them televised throughout the Gulf region.

The Yemeni government was delighted to have acquired its own sporting hero and bent over backwards to facilitate and fund the trip, not only for Naseem, Brendan and Alma Ingle, but for a delegation which included Sal, Riath, Nabeel and two sparring partners.

This was officially announced in a rather odd full-page advertisment in *Boxing News*, publicly sponsored by the government of the Yemen, which provided details of the tour and issued a public challenge to British bantamweight champion Drew Docherty in the following terms: 'THE ARABIAN KNIGHT PRINCE NASEEM HAMED – Nine fights, Nine wins, Eight KOs – will be 20 in February. He sends out a challenge to: DREW DOCHERTY For a £5,000 sidestake to defend his British bantamweight title in Sheffield. Hamed's manager/trainer Brendan Ingle has backed the Prince to win FOUR LONSDALE BELTS OUTRIGHT within the next five years at weights from bantamweight to lightweight.'[7] A week later Ingle himself made a public offer to bet £500 that Naseem would win four British titles, from bantam to super feather. Needless to say Docherty did not respond, no one took up the wager, the fight never took place and Naseem never got his shot at any British title, let alone a clutch of Lonsdale belts.

For Naseem, the Yemen had previously been a place where the vaguest of childhood memories had intermeshed with his parents' stories, and had taken on a distant and romantic hue. The two-week visit, starting on 26 November 1993, was the first since his return at the age of four from an extended stay, and he had little idea of what to expect. What he got was a reception which astounded him and the entire delegation.

When he arrived he found himself mobbed by thousands of admirers who wanted to touch him and hug him, before being whisked off by heavily armed bodyguards for VIP treatment at the presidential palace, where, among other gifts, he was presented with a gold Rolex watch (subsequently valued at over £10,000), and a jewel-encrusted ceremonial dagger by the President.

Brendan Ingle thoroughly enjoyed himself, delighted in the knowledge that everything he had been saying about Naseem's support there had been proved, and more. 'Naz came there and it just absolutely took off,' he recalls. 'It was marvellous watching it. You get thousands of people out there to meet him, and all over the country we were mobbed by people and very well received. It was unbelievable.'

He and Alma were happy to take a back seat and view the experience with a distance that was not available to Naseem, who had to make do in his halting Arabic, and constantly meet up to the colossal expectations he was confronted with. Brendan, however, has never been over-impressed with pomp and ceremony, and finds it hard to ignore disparities in wealth and privilege, and it was the connection with the ordinary Yemeni which he relished more than any other aspect of the trip. 'It gives you such a lift. It's a beautiful country and the people are lovely, but like everywhere else you got your problems,' he says with unaccustomed diplomatic understatement. 'It's a Third World country. Very, very poor and very, very rich.'

During this visit, crowds estimated at almost 10,000 turned up to watch Naseem's six exhibitions with his sparring partners and Yemeni amateurs and, perhaps for the first time in his life, the young fighter felt a little overwhelmed. 'I was a bit surprised at first, but I had to get used to being mobbed by these massive crowds, and protected by these bodyguards,' he recalls. 'It was great in that you get the people out there basically admiring your skills and talent, and they think I have brought great things to their country and basically that I've put it on the map, but it was very hectic out there.'

The Yemeni government was delighted by the success of the venture, and eager to extend the contact with the young fighter to a permanent basis, building Naseem a house and setting up a training camp, with the idea of having him back to fight there – a plan that has yet to materialize. The Yemeni government's view was that Naseem was an example to the youth of the country and a unifying figure in a nation with a history of political conflict and division. 'Boxing is not much practised in Yemen but we are talking about an achievement by a young man who was reaching the top of his profession through hard work, strength of character and perseverance,' says the country's London embassy spokesman Mohamed Beshr. 'He's a good example to follow – not necessarily to become a boxer but as an example of what can be achieved through dedication. He became a role model to the people because of this, and there is universal admiration for him in Yemen. We regard him with pride and admiration and it is like he is a national hero.'

Ever since returning from that visit, Naseem has stressed the Yemeni connection more forcefully, fighting under both the British and the Yemeni flags, and always making a point of mentioning his Arab heritage and of being 'part of the Arab world' – an oft-used phrase which endears him to the other Arab countries where his fights are screened (though to date the only other country in this region that he has visited has been Quatar, in late 1995).

Some of those in Sheffield's Yemeni Community Association would like him to take a slightly more distanced and critical perspective on the region, though given his continued excitement about his VIP treatment there and the flow of official gifts that have been coming his way, this is not likely to happen soon.

Despite his generally dismal year in terms of progress with his career, Naseem returned home elated, and a fortnight later was to get a further boost when the London-based international magazine, *Boxing Monthly*, ran a brave and perceptive four-page cover story hailing Naseem as the sport's finest prospect – better than Oscar de la Hoya and Roy Jones – while expressing the view that he had been regrettably under-exposed. Among the claims about Naseem's prowess carried in the story was one by British middleweight champion Neville Brown who said Hamed was 'the best thing to come out of this country, by far'[8] – a bold assertion for a 9-fight 19-year-old in a country which can boast of the likes of Jimmy Wilde, Jim Driscoll, Ted Kid Lewis, Benny Lynch, Randolph Turpin, Ken Buchanan, John Conteh and Lennox Lewis, among others. For the previous seven years he had been receiving enthusiastic coverage from *Boxing News*, but had barely been mentioned by any of the other major fight magazines. The *Boxing Monthly* story served notice that he was a major force to be taken into account and it certainly contributed to the explosion of interest from the national broadsheets and tabloids which followed in 1994, frequently being quoted or referred to.

Brendan Ingle also received his own coming home present, when at the end of 1993 it was announced that this former professional boxer, once condemned by his Catholic high school as a 'slow learner', was to be awarded an honorary Master of Arts degree by Sheffield University for his three decades of community work in Wincobank. 'The [St Thomas' Boys'] club has become a beacon of hope for many young people and a passport to fame for a few,' the university's citation stated. 'It is a meeting point for all colours and creeds, the unemployed, the hooligan, the hopeless and often the helpless case . . . Mr Ingle believes that if these youngsters can be motivated to look after their bodies, he can train them to look after their minds and become responsible citizens.' It went on to mention some of the details of Ingle's work outside the gym. 'Not content with his role in the club, he also goes to court with young offenders who, in the majority of cases, have no one else to turn to. Magistrates respect him to such an extent that in the past they have placed young offenders in his care,' the statement read.

6

Frank Warren
and the Big Breakthrough

As boxing promoters go, and it's a major qualification, Frank Warren is surprisingly forthright in appreciating the difference between self–interest and reality. He has his convenient blind spots – Don King certainly being one of them, the current WBO hierarchy another – but for the most part he communicates a disarming candidness about the world, his profession and himself.

When you first see him in public, the instant impression is not entirely sympathetic. There's a softness in his 43-year-old face, but those almond-shaped eyes seem, at first, to communicate a suspicious wariness about the world and a hard inner core. On the one hand it's no more than you'd expect from a man who survived a volley of assassin's bullet through the lung, a 'smear' campaign from the *Sun* and a financial wipe-out that almost left him bankrupt, and who stoically re-emerged, more powerful

133

than ever before. On the other hand, it's also no more than you'd
expect from a partner of Mister King.

The major reason for his dominant position in British boxing
today has much to do with his connections with King, and the
fact that he succeeded where others failed – in sewing up Sky
Sport as an outlet for his fighters. But business success also has a
great deal to do with trust, and whatever disquiet there might
still be about aspects of Warren's past, the word from most
boxers, managers, sponsors and fellow promoters is that he's a
man you can cut a fair deal with: a hard-driving wheeler dealer
certainly, but also a straight talker in an often bent business. In
addition he has a well-proven flair for spotting talent and
exploiting it, and an inclination for taking chances and putting
his money on risky wagers.

It is this predilection for a flutter which brought Warren into
boxing in the first place. The product of a large, tightly knit
working-class Islington family, he left school at fifteen and in his
first job worked as a Smithfield meat market porter, before
setting up his own business renting vending machines to pubs.
But he has always been a prodigious gambler, and came into the
game after winning a £25,000 even-money bet on an unlicensed
fight. 'It was all a bit of an accident really,' he says. 'A friend of
mine was involved and he couldn't come up with the money, and
I stepped in and got bitten by the bug.'

He began promoting unlicensed shows – not the bare-knuckle
variant but gloved fights with rather laxer rules than their
licensed counterparts – and he did this with considerable
panache, putting him on a war footing with the Boxing Board of
Control and the rest of the sport's establishment. Soon, however, he ensured that the medical dimensions were tightened up,
and in the late 1970s his organization narrowly missed being
elected as the WBA's British representatives at its Florida
convention – a move which prompted the Boxing Board to make
its bed with the association. At this point he realized that the
unlicensed universe was about to implode and decided to 'go
legit' by taking out a promoter's licence with the Board. Over
the next nine years he established himself as one of the country's
busiest and most successful promoters, breaking Mickey Duff's
promotional headlock, signing up many of Britain's most

successful fighters and staging ten world title bills between 1985 and 1989 – a record no other promoter at the time could compare with. He also set up several companies, became a major investor in the London Docklands Arena development and became the first promoter to acquire a stock exchange listing. With his mansion on several acres of choice Hertfordshire real estate, the Rolls-Royce and the fur coats, he had the aura of the ultimate eighties high-flying entrepreneur.

But if he had not known it already, on the last day of November 1989, he discovered that his wheeling and dealing had won him at least one potentially mortal enemy. Arriving at Barking's Broadway Theatre in London's East End to attend one of his boxing shows, a man with his face covered by a woollen hat stepped out of the shadows, pumped four bullets through his chest and left him for dead. Somehow he hung on and remained conscious, knowing that if he didn't he would never wake up. He underwent emergency surgery, keeping his life but losing half a lung. And that was just the start of his troubles.

His attempted murder was a catalyst for a collapse of his already extremely shaky business interests, with investors and clients running scared after hearing the news that there was a price on the main man's head. The man charged with Warren's attempted murder, his first 'world' champion, Terry 'The Fighting Fireman' Marsh (the Basildon light welterweight who retired, undefeated, after one defence of his IBF 'world' title), was acquitted in the Old Bailey. With his broken ribs still aching, Warren discharged himself from hospital after ten days to try and salvage the situation, but this time he failed. By early 1991 the entire Warren empire had collapsed, and he was in debt to the tune of £30 million – much of it from the collapse of the London Arena scheme.

Then in April 1993, when Warren was already down and struggling, Kelvin MacKenzie, then editor of the *Sun*, decided he was ripe for a kicking, and ran a story over nine days focusing on an extra–marital affair Warren had. They broke the tale by driving his former mistress to his home for a doorstep set-to with Warren's wife, providing a blow by blow photo-story of the event.

Today he is still seething about the intrusion. His hatred of

MacKenzie is unabated and he feels a good deal of vicarious satisfaction in the fact that after MacKenzie was relieved of the editorship of the *Sun* (which, through its connection to Sky, now sponsors his tournaments), it was the 'fantastic deal' (Warren spits out those words with a tone of deep sarcasm) that MacKenzie made on behalf of the satellite network with Chris Eubank and Barry Hearn which contributed to his departure from Sky.

With his marriage in tatters, and with the threat of bankruptcy proceedings and of eviction from the Hertfordshire mansion looming, things could hardly have been worse at that stage, but, somehow Warren held on and survived. 'I'd lost a helluva lot of money, my businesses, my health, my personal life, but I worked hard trying to get myself back in the game, and I've worked hard at keeping the family together, which I've managed to do.' He co-promoted a couple of world title bouts with Barney Eastwood, used the profits to begin satisfying his creditors, and by the end of 1995 had paid out over £10 million in settlements. Nevertheless, as a result of his dealings at the start of the decade, in February 1996 the High Court banned Warren from taking up a position as a company director for seven years, following a four-year Department of Trade and Industry investigation into the financial collapse of the London Arena.

What pulled him back from the brink, was the spin-off from his relationship with Don King, who arrived in his life just at the right time, and Warren remains grateful for this fortuitous intervention. King was one of the first to wish him well after he was shot, and over the past three years Warren has made an enormous amount of money from their partnership (and the Don has made a good deal more in return), so it is not hard to see why he treads lightly in this area. His view is that, sure, King went to prison, but he served his time and has never been back and he suggests that the antagonism to him from the 'white' press amounts to racism. He'll point out that the reason boxers flood to King is that he offers them the best deal, and he delivers on it.

This, however, is only a small part of the truth about the enigmatic American. Don King may be the greatest promoter in the history of the sport, but there is another side to the story.

Other promoters have done their fair share of ignominious deeds, but none on the scale and with the audacity and consistency of the Don. It's easy enough to dismiss his links with organized crime as a thing of the past, or his criminal record as old hat, and to be bamboozled by his grandiose gestures, comical verbosity and sense of fun, but behind the malapropisms there has also been a pattern of violence and corruption which takes some hard swallowing, even for those who admire his intelligence, chutzpa and flair.

Yet for all this, the title of 'Promoter of the Century' – given to him by the WBA in 1994 – has a ring of truth to it, and at no time was this more apparent than in his four 'wilderness' years, after he lost control of the heavyweight title after Buster Douglas knocked out Mike Tyson. He promoted like crazy – bigger, better–attended, more exciting bills than any of his rivals, breaking just about every promotional record in the sport's history. He promoted 47 world title fights in 1994 (twice putting six title fights on one show) and by 1995 King (together with the Showtime cable network) had regained control of the heavyweight division.

Despite his bad name and his legal troubles, the dominance of the shock-haired Svengali seems secure – and this is exceedingly good news for Frank Warren, and by proxy, Naseem Hamed – as long as he doesn't fall too far under King's spell.

For Warren this partnership happened partly by design, and partly by being at the right place at the right time. Early in 1993 King, still in the cold as far as the heavyweight titles were concerned, and having been temporarily removed from his throne as the world's number one promoter by Dan Duva's Main Events organization,[1] was taking a long-term view by trying to sew up as many of the sport's other major fighters and divisions as possible. At the time Warren was just beginning to claw his way back by promoting Colin McMillan and Paul Hodkinson and had connections with Barry Hearn through his involvement with ITV as well as with Barney Eastwood.

King wanted to extend his empire to Britain and Ireland, and had established a periodic working relationship with Warren after they co-promoted the Azumah Nelson–Pat Cowdwell fight in October 1985. He saw in Warren a man he could work with –

well connected, dependable and, at the time, not sufficiently established in his own right to offer much competition. Specifically he asked Warren to negotiate a British terrestrial television deal through ITV.

The British promoter jumped at the chance, secured a favourable deal, and became King's partner, though they continued to retain their own organizations. Warren moved quickly on signing up the best and brightest in British boxing, taking over Andy Holligan and Duke McKenzie from Mickey Duff (and through the King connection taking Holligan straight to a WBC title shot with Julio Cesar Chavez), then Nigel Benn, Robbie Regan and Steve Robinson from Barry Hearn. What he offered at that time was considerable: higher purses, the ITV connection and all the largesse that came from the King connection. At the end of 1993, when Warren made his offer to Brendan Ingle, his comeback had succeeded, and he was once again one of the most effective forces in British boxing.

At this stage the options for Ingle and Hamed were limited: either sign with one of the remaining major promoters or follow the dead end route of trying to go it alone. Having been through Hearn and Duff, the only big time promoters left were Frank Maloney (Lennox Lewis' manager and the promoter of several British and American hopefuls) and Frank Warren. Some of Ingle's boxers had previously fought on Warren bills and it was Warren who made the first move and struck the right note. It was a splendid coup for the Hertfordshire promoter and one he'd had his eye on for several months. He first watched Naseem on television and was enormously impressed. 'I just couldn't believe it. He came across with so much confidence that I thought, This kid's going to be a star. He was with Mickey Duff at the time and I was a little disappointed because I thought to myself, Well, I missed one here, but as things turned out he saw the light and came over.'[2]

In fact what happened was that as soon as Warren heard the Duff contract had expired he invited Ingle and Hamed to his home for a long chat about Naseem's future. The Sheffield pair did not need persuading that things were not moving according to plan under Duff, and the offer put forward by Warren and his Sports Network company was enticing: a one year or 10 fight contract (with the option of a second year) and with the promise of live ITV exposure, purses of an order neither Hearn nor Duff could contemplate, and the sweetener of a new car for Naseem. The subtext was also reassuring to the suspicious Ingle. 'The agreement was we'd work as a team – he is the promoter, I'm the manager and trainer, and my son John the co-trainer, and he said to us: "I won't steal him off you",' Brendan says.

Warren, in fact, stressed that he was not interested in Hamed's day to day business management – his contracts with sponsors, advertisers and his press relations – and has been delighted with the role played by Riath Hamed in this respect. 'I made it clear I didn't want to get involved with the commercial side of fighters,' he says. 'I just haven't got the time. If I can help them I help them, but Riath and Naz have done some cracking deals that I'd be proud of doing, so good luck to them. It's nice to see that and it's good for boxing.'

With the relationship now well into its third year, all the parties have been delighted with the way things have evolved. 'Frank Warren has been as good as gold,' says Ingle, a manager who is not averse to criticizing his promoters even while his fighers are still under contract to them. 'This is important, and I emphasize it: after we first sat down together, everything he promised, he's done, so we've had a good relationship.'

Naseem, with his love of money, title belts and sparkling displays of wealth (like the jeep he received after winning the European title and the solid gold Cartier watch Warren gave him after the Robinson fight), also seems satisfied with the service he's received. Interviewed last year on Channel 4's *Big Breakfast* by Frank Bruno, he made it clear in his idiosyncratic style that as long as the shiny things were rolling in he would remain an extremely happy camper: 'Yeah, he's the main man. He's doing the business . . . He's the best promoter in the world, I reckon. Respect to Frank Warren! Respect, Frank – you're a badarse! Love it, Frank! Two time Frank! Just get me another belt!'[3]

Naseem's first fight under Warren was against Peter Buckley, the only man to have taken him the distance, in Cardiff on 2 January 1994 – four months and five days since his previous outing. Fighting on the undercard of the Nicky Piper–Leonzer

Barber WBO light heavyweight title bill, Naseem's task was to make a good impression on television and to do significantly better than first time around.

In the fourteen months since their previous encounter, Buckley had fallen more squarely into the 'opponent' role. In his first outing after losing to Hamed, he challenged Harald Geier for the WBO's vacant Pentacontinental super bantamweight title, and though he lost on points he did surprisingly well, even dropping Geier in the ninth round. After that, however, he lost nine in a row, though he went the distance each time and a couple of those defeats were disputed. This brought his tally to 29 losses in 52 fights. Both boxers weighed in at the super bantamweight limit of 8st 10lb (despite press reports that Buckley had a weight advantage of anything between nine and 14 pounds).

This time Naseem approached his task with more resolve, dispensing with some of the clowning and showing far more patience in his bid to take the Birmingham man out as soon as possible. He frequently changed stance and used every punch in his arsenal, including numerous thumping body blows, but Buckley was unmoved and remained in his shell, his head well covered. He seldom attempted anything meaningful in return despite Naseem's willingness to tempt him by hanging his chin well within Buckley's range, and most of what the Midlander did throw missed (though Hamed's right eye was slightly grazed).

Having won the first three rounds easily Hamed piled on the punishment, and at the end of the third referee Mike Heatherwick asked Buckley if he was all right. 'I'm fine, but thanks for asking,' he replied. But at 1 minute 48 seconds of the fourth, after Buckley took seven unanswered blows, ending with a right to the head which twisted his neck around, the referee decided he'd seen enough, bringing the fight to what the crowd and much of the press felt was a premature end.

Nobby Nobbs, Buckley's manager-trainer, was incensed. 'There's not a mark on him. God help you if you'd had to referee Galento–Louis,' he shouted. While Hamed was winning pretty much as he pleased, Buckley did not seem to be stunned or in serious trouble, and may even have had an outside chance of surviving the distance for a second time.

Today Buckley is quick to acknowledge that he was outclassed and that Hamed had improved considerably in the interim. 'He tried to stop me from the first bell and really tried to take my head off,' he recalls. 'He's very fast so you don't see the punches and he throws them from really awkward angles, so you can't tell where they're coming from, and he uses plenty of tricks, like staring at your feet and then throwing a punch, but I wasn't really fooled. I even tried my own trick – treading on his toes – but he said to me, "I know that one," and he trod on my toes.'

It was only the second time Buckley had been stopped in his long career (the first was against Duke McKenzie in five rounds, over three years earlier) and he remains irritated about it, arguing that he was starting to get into his rhythm in the fourth. 'He's very hard to fight because no one else fights like him, so you can't find anyone to spar with who'll really help you, but the longer the fight went the easier I thought it was getting to avoid his punches and work out his style. I don't argue with the referee, but I was all right, I wasn't really hurt, and I think he stepped in too soon, with no good reason.'

Hamed and Ingle were both well satisfied with his effort. While it was not a spectacular display, he had shown marked improvement since their first encounter – more patience, less unnecessary movement and more effective punching, particularly to the body. Frank Warren claimed that he would have Naseem fighting for a world title before the end of the year and shortly afterwards announced that his next encounter would be at Earls Court in London four weeks later.

This was a major opportunity for Naseem. His opponent was to be the former British featherweight champion Peter Harris, but more important, this bout would give Naseem the kind of British and international exposure he needed at that stage. The 26 February Don King–Frank Warren co-promotion featured Nigel Benn's WBC super middleweight title defence against Commonwealth champion Henry Wharton and Michael Nunn's WBA super middleweight title defence against Steve Little, and also featured Oliver McCall, Lloyd Honeyghan, and Dennis Andries – a combination which would mean that Naseem would be displayed before a full contingent of the capital's press as well as several of the major American boxing writers and commentators. But, for the first time in his professional career, he sustained a training injury, spraining an ankle on the eve of the fight, forcing Ingle to pull him out at the last moment, leaving Naz extremely frustrated at the way his destiny kept on being interrupted.

Warren was determined to establish a momentum for his young protégé and initially put him up against the unbeaten Dominican, Laureano Ramirez, for the IBF Intercontinental bantamweight title at Mansfield on 9 April, which ITV agreed to screen live. Ramirez dropped out two weeks before fight time but Warren succeeded in persuading the ITV sports bosses that Hamed was still worth featuring at the top of the bill (co-promoted by Alma Ingle), which included some of the brightest prospects in Britain.

Hamed's new opponent was a 26-year-old Belgian of Sicilian extraction, John Miceli, who had a record of 10 wins (four inside the distance) two losses and a draw. Miceli was known as a capable and aggressive fighter with a good chin (he'd never been stopped) but a bit lacking in the power department and fairly easy to hit. He had lifted the Belgian featherweight title in June 1992 but after one defence had dropped down to bantamweight to challenge the world rated Vincenzo Belcastro for the European bantamweight title and, though he lost a clearcut decision and was dropped in the sixth round, he put up a sound display and succeeded in cutting Belcastro. He had been 10 or 12 rounds four times, while Hamed had never been beyond the sixth. Naseem made an unusually cautious prediction: 'He'll fall in six,' later changing that to eight on Alma Ingle's advice.

Once again wearing his leopardskin trunks (having decided these were a more distinctive trademark than the green and black pair he had worn for his previous few fights), Naseem made a dramatic impression from start to finish, treating the capacity crowd to a short and explosive rendition of his repertoire.

Coming in again for the third time in a row at the super bantamweight limit (1½ pounds more than his opponent), Hamed nailed the Belgian with a short right-hand counter soon after the bell. Miceli was up immediately and went into attack mode, but failed to land a single punch on the phantom in front of him. Twice Hamed stared at Miceli's feet and then fired a crisp combination into his face, and it was clear the visitor had little clue how to deal with his tormentor.

Halfway through the round a right hook to the top of the head put Miceli down for the second time. He was up at eight, still wobbly, but launched another futile tilt at the windmill, before it began punching back with a vengeance, landing from astonishing angles and with remarkable timing and precision. With 20 seconds to go Naseem ended his night's work with a right hook to the body, right hook to the head and finally a devastating southpaw left which somehow found its way through Miceli's high guard and deposited him face-first on the canvas where referee John Coyle counted him out.

After performing his somersaults, Naseem wasn't going to let the moment slip. 'I'm going to be a legend, a legend,' he announced to his national ITV audience. 'Let's forget the world title – three world titles, that'll do me, but I'm aiming to be a legend and I will be!' Frank Warren backed this up by saying Naseem would become 'the best fighter from this country' and comparing him favourably to the past decade's stars of his promotional stable – Barry McGuigan, Colin Jones, Tony Sibson, Nigel Benn and Colin McMillan. The performance won prominent accolades in the Yorkshire press and boxing magazines, but far more important it introduced him to millions of ITV viewers. With this victory he had established himself as an instant star.

Ever since moving up from flyweight two years earlier, Naseem had set his heart on winning the British bantamweight title, and particularly on taking out the then-unbeaten champion, Drew Docherty. But on 2 February 1994, ten days before Naseem's twentieth birthday, Docherty was soundly outpointed by the extremely tough European champion Vincenzo Belcastro. Warren and Ingle gambled on their view that Naz was ready for Docherty's conquerer, and announced that he would challenge Belcastro at the Ponds Forge International Arena in Sheffield on 11 May, in a fight to share ITV live national viewing with Chris Pyatt's WBO middleweight title defence against Steve Collins.

This decision caused consternation among some of Naseem's well-wishers who argued that the Italian would be too experienced, too strong and too cagey for a 20-year-old novice, just as he had been for the well-regarded Docherty. As Ingle remembers it: 'We had an element in Sheffield particularly, saying to me, "What are you doing putting him in with Belcastro? He's had fourteen world-title and European-title fights," so I was a bit on edge and discussed it with Frank Warren, but then Naz says, "What are you worrying about? I'm going to bash him up." '

Belcastro, at thirty-three, was at the peak of his boxing career (as well as being at the start of an alternative career as a qualified chartered accountant). His record showed 28 wins (four on stoppages), six losses and three draws, but several of the losses and draws were disputed and, more important, the quality of his opposition, including those he had beaten, had been of a quality Naseem had yet to encounter. In addition to Docherty he had outpointed and then drawn with Billy Hardy (Britain's former world-title contender and current European and Commonwealth featherweight champion) and knocked out Fabrice Benichou (who went on to lift the IBF world super bantamweight title) and had twice fought for IBF world titles himself, being outpointed by José Sanabria for the bantamweight crown in 1988 and, more controversially, by Robert Quiroga for the super flyweight title in 1991.

Moreover he was enjoying a three-year winning streak which suggested that despite his age he had improved rather than slipped – a view reinforced by his subsequent achievements. After the Hamed fight he lost a split decision to Harold Grey in a bid for the IBF super flyweight title and then lifted the European super bantamweight crown and defended it against British champion Richie Wenton among others to earn a top-ten super bantamweight world ranking with both the WBC and WBA. At the time he fought Hamed, he was rated sixth in the world at bantamweight by the WBC and the July 1994 edition of *Ring* magazine rated him as one of the ten fighters in all weight divisions 'most likely to surprise the champs'. He was extremely wily and hard to tag, had an impressively high workrate, an excellent chin (having never been stopped or even dropped) and was one of the strongest and dirtiest bantams in the world.

He was, indeed, a big risk for an 11-fight 20-year-old and

Ingle was taking no chances. Naseem had not fought within the bantamweight limit since facing Alan Ley fifteen months earlier, and Ingle remembered well the final two days of thirst and starvation to make the weight for that one. With Naseem's love of chocolates and his mum's Arab cooking, he feared they would have the same problem again unless he watched his charge, day and night. They set up camp at the Rotherham United Hoosten Roberts training ground, which Ingle said was ideal for their requirements, and got down to work three days after the Miceli blowout. Today Ingle says Naseem has never again trained quite as hard or as consistently as he did for the Belcastro fight. He made the weight on the 8st 6lbs limit without much trouble while Belcastro was 1¼ pounds lighter.

For Hamed it was a huge occasion: his first professional fight in his hometown, his first title fight and his first outing against a world-rated opponent, and he was to be paid the biggest purse of his career to date – £12,500, excluding perks and expenses – and he had been promised £40,000 for a first defence plus a place on the second Frankie Randall–Julio Cesar Chavez bill in Las Vegas if he won.

Arriving in his gold gown and a new pair of leopard-spotted trunks, he delivered a performance which, for all the controversy it generated, was one of dazzling brilliance which completely eclipsed Collins's impressive fifth round stoppage over Pyatt. There was barely a second in the fight where Naseem was not in absolute control, though he chose to squander some of this by clowning his way through several rounds, and doing everything in his power to belittle and humiliate the Italian.

Right from the start of the first round – when, at the 25 second mark, he dropped Belcastro with a right jab-left cross combination, it looked as if he could end the contest any time he pleased, but that he had set his heart on proving his ability to box twelve fast rounds at a trot. Though it was obviously not quite as simple as this, it was certainly clear by the end of the opening stanza that Belcastro was devoid of ideas on how to do anything other than, at best, survive, against the man-child in front of him. Towards the end of the round the Italian fired a purposeful jab which missed, and suddenly from what seemed like way out of range, Hamed was upon him with a heavy,

looping southpaw left which hit the mark. The European
champion looked utterly perplexed as to where this came from,
and how a boxer with a 63-inch reach could find his face at such a
distance.

From then on the Italian's strategy was to make himself as
tight a target as possible and fire his right cross at Hamed's
inviting but seldom to be found head. When that failed,
Belcastro would use his own head at close quarters, sneak short
punches at Naseem's crotch when the Belgian referee Bob Logist
was unsighted, and grab Hamed around the shoulders whenever
he came close (though Naz himself occasionally replied in kind –
throwing the Italian down a couple of times, landing an elbow to
the throat at one point, a backhander at another, pulling
Belcastro's head down and dropping his own occasionally).
Naseem emerged with a graze under the right eye (courtesy of a
headbutt in the second), and a small cut on the side of the left
eye (another butt in the seventh) and a slightly bruised groin
from at least four dangerously low blows, as well as sore hands
and an aching stomach. Other than these little triumphs, and a
pair of right crosses to the chin in the ninth and tenth, the
European champion had no success and a thoroughly miserable
evening.

Naseem just did exactly as he pleased – pouring it on, then
easing off, here some pain, there a taunt, now fast, then slow.
Every time he chose to open up Belcastro was hurt. In the
second he was wobbled by a left hook. In the fifth, another left
hook caused him to lose his balance and go down, though it was
ruled a slip. A round later Naseem concentrated on his body
attack, firing off damaging hooks and bolo punches which
thudded heavily home, after which Ingle told him to pace
himself. 'Relax it, you're trying too hard. Come off the jab,' he
said.

In the ninth, after taking a right, Naz cracked home yet
another left hook which left the Italian's legs in pasta mode. He
wobbled him again with a right uppercut in the tenth and
dropped him with a lead right cross-left hook combination from
the orthodox stance in the eleventh. Belcastro rose wearily at the
count of seven, nodding to acknowledge the legitimacy of
Hamed's effort, and Naz probably could have finished it had he

chosen to do so. Instead he opted to dance and display his amazing reflexes and uncanny ability to read an opponent's thoughts, anticipate his moves, and evaporate in the face of his attack.

In his corner at the end of the eleventh round, after a performance that was extraordinary though by no means flawless, Brendan told Naseem: 'Naz, you've done it. Go out and enjoy yerself,' and Naseem pranced out, his hand in the air, then on his hips, then waving Belcastro in like a matador trying to coax a well-lanced bull into a final charge, and all the while pulling faces at the ITV cameraman and chatting away to Brendan. Basically, he had a good deal of fun at the other fellow's expense. In the final fantastic and most controversial minute of the fight – neither boxer landed a punch; Belcastro because he couldn't, Hamed because he wouldn't. As the new champion put it, echoing his mentor: 'I had done all the work and I wanted to enjoy myself.'

The unanimous decision was surprisingly generous to Belcastro. Bob Logist made it 120–109 (scoring two rounds even), Pentti Rautatnen of Finland scored it 120–107 (making just the last round even) and Walter Schall of Austria somehow found it within his heart to give the Italian the last round, scoring the fight 119–110.

Afterwards Hamed gave cursory praise to his victim, and a great deal of praise to himself. As he was quick to point out: 'Belcastro never caught me with a flush punch all night. I could have stopped him, but now I know I can do twelve rounds in my sleep.'

Throughout the fight sections of the crowd including some in the press benches shouted abuse at Hamed for his tactics. 'Fucking wanker' was a frequent catcall, and the man from the *Irish Times* mumbled: 'It's fucking disgusting, I'd have him out of the ring.' In addition, ITV commentators Reg Gutteridge and Jim Watt as well as many of the leading boxing writers made it clear they felt rather ambiguous about the morality and taste of this display.

The effect of this controversy was that Naseem gained unprecedented exposure for a 12-fight bantamweight. The national broadsheets, not usually accustomed to giving European title fights, particularly in the lighter weights, much more than a results footnote, devoted page leads to pontificating about Hamed's tactics and talent. They castigated Naseem for what was viewed as a vulgar and sadistic humiliation of a worthy champion, while at the same time acknowledging and praising the young man's brilliance. In a long feature on Naseem in the *Sunday Times*, Hugh McIlvanney described Hamed as 'a spectacular talent' and noted that 'his effortless mastery of Belcastro . . . was an astonishing feat', but at the same time he bemoaned Naseem's 'eagerness to treat his demoralized victim as if he were no better than something you wipe off your shoe.'[4] Other papers ran similar critiques, and for the next couple of weeks *Boxing Monthly*'s mail was packed with anti-Naz hate letters.

Ingle, who seemed genuinely perplexed that anyone should want to criticize Naseem's showing, mounted several disparate defences. He said variously that Naseem's tactics were his answer to those who said Belcastro was too experienced; that it was Naz's response to the many fouls committed by the Italian; that Naz wasn't really Naz in that last round – he had put himself in the shoes of the greats, and for this one he was Sugar Ray Leonard outhustling Marvin Hagler, or Muhammad Ali making a fool out of George Foreman, and that he was 'still a baby of twenty years old', and therefore should not be blamed for putting on a show; and finally that Belcastro took it all in his stride (and in fact the pair of them went out for a meal together afterwards).

Naseem himself offered no immediate excuses or apologies, but insisted he did not intend to humiliate Belcastro and that the Italian's camp did not take offence. And when that was ignored he announced: 'I will not change my style for anybody,' and suggested that the Sheffield and British publics should be proud of him. 'I showed him respect by letting him get in the ring with me,' he asserted, with yet another extraordinary display of arrogance. 'I'm Mr Nice-Guy outside the ropes. Inside the ring I've learnt an art and mastered it. Either people want to see me win or lose. Either way I don't mind as long as people are buying tickets for my fights. It was show time and at the end of the day there are things I have to do to put bums on seats.'[5]

A few months later, however, in a rare display of contrition, he reluctantly acknowledged he had pushed things a bit. 'I'm sorry when people think badly about me,' he was quoted as saying. 'I'm not a bad person. I made a mistake against Belcastro. I know I went a little too far. If I could have that last round back I'd do things a bit differently. I would do a lot of the same stuff again but I wouldn't push it as much as I did.'[6]

With this fight Naseem Hamed had arrived as ITV's new young 'superstar' – a boxer capable of attracting viewership figures of between five and ten million people, with his status as the channel's prime attraction established after Chris Eubank defected to Sky.

He had suddenly become a point of discussion way beyond the sport's traditional confines. In Sheffield itself, where he was given a full civic reception by the City Council after his victory, he was now the most recognizable citizen, his fame having surpassed even that of the major Sheffield Wednesday football stars.

Nationally he had established a significant youth and women's support base, attracted as much by his boyishly appealing looks (the alternately flaring or doleful dark eyes, cruel and sensuous mouth, prominent nose and cheek bones, even the jug ears), as by his limbo dancer's grace and acrobatic dexterity, his taste in music and clothes and his sheer exuberance and obvious love of life and self. It was noticeable that the average age of those attending Hamed's fights was considerably younger than those of most other bill-headers, making him an attractive commodity to advertisers, sponsors and magazine editors. Soon the major national papers and radio stations, men's and trends magazines like *GQ* and *Esquire*, teen fanzines, all the general sports magazines, and the international fight press were paying attention. And Naseem was loving it.

Growing up in the small, crowded, storeside house in Newman Road, Wincobank, and watching the likes of Herol Graham acquire and then lose riches way beyond his reach, made Naseem intensely aware of the connection between his two fists and the world of his dreams. 'Money equals freedom, and I want to be free,' he would say. For a long time before turning professional, Naseem had talked about becoming a millionaire, but now the figures needed revising, and his love of money and the goodies it can buy, became an overt and frequently cited motivational mantra.

'I'm very ambitious, so there's no knowing what I might do,' he said. 'I can't predict just how much money I'm going to make from this business, but I want to be financially secure and have a great standard of living for the rest of my life. I will make so much money my family will live like royalty.' When pushed on a figure he said £40 million would just about do it, though some time later he revised that to £400 million.

Asked what he wanted to do with all this lolly, he stressed he was a good saver and a careful custodian of money – frequently making mention of how he nurtured his bank balance far better than the spendthrift Chris Eubank – before telling you of dreams and habits that would put him close to the Eubank level of extravagance. 'I'm interested in doing a lot of shopping, spending plenty of money on the right clothes, the right houses, the right alliances in life, and nice cars – ' the first of several, the jeep arrived shortly after the Belcastro fight – he said. 'And one day I want to have my own island in the sun, in the Middle East or the Caribbean, with a huge mansion, and a new house for my parents and a mansion of my own here in Sheffield, and a house to hire out to students. It's one of my main ambitions to be the richest sports person ever from Sheffield.'

And just in case this wish list left you with any doubt on the matter, this shop owner's son from a socialist background pressed home the general point: 'I've always been completely confident I would be very rich. Wealth is part of success, and I love wealth.'

After the Belcastro fight Naseem broke into the world rankings for the first time, making it to a rather disappointing number ten on the WBC's list (despite having whipped their number six contender) and number nine in the WBA's. Naseem, Ingle and Warren were confident he could fight for a world title before the end of the year, and felt at that stage he could already beat any of the three world champions – the formidable Texan Orlando

Canizales (IBF), Thailand's Daorung Chuwatana (WBA) and Japan's Yasuei Yakushiji (WBC) without any problem. Meanwhile Warren had started speaking to Mickey Duff about a European and Commonwealth 'showdown' with Johnny Armour, but, knowing just how good Hamed was, Duff wasn't biting.

At the same time, Naseem kept on raising Drew Docherty's name, mainly because of his determination to win the British title and then go on to win 'one of those beautiful Lonsdale belts' outright. Hardly surprisingly, Docherty and his management showed no inclination to allow Naseem on their turf, particularly after the way he lifted the European crown.

It took until July 1994 before the Boxing Board got it together to accept Hamed as official challenger for the British title, and at this point Docherty's management insisted on a 60:40 purse split in the British champion's favour, despite the fact that Hamed held the European crown. Warren lost interest for a while but eventually, at Naseem's strong prompting, he and co-promoter Katherine Morrison offered the British champion by far the highest purse of his career (£30,000) to face Naseem in Scotland on 21 January 1995 with both titles on the line. Docherty's promoter, Tommy Gilmour, turned them down flat, preferring the safer but far less lucrative option of WBO bantamweight champion Alfred Kotey, who nevertheless easily stopped the feather-fisted Glaswegian in four rounds. As a result of all this the Docherty fight never happened and Naseem never got his chance to fight for a British title.

For Naseem, the big one – the opponent who really riled him – was Wayne McCullough, who had just outpointed Victor Rabanales in a final eliminator for the WBC title (making him the mandatory challenger), after stopping Javier Medina for the NABF title. He was also rated number four by the IBF. For Naseem, McCullough's higher ranking, the fact that he was based in Las Vegas under the man rated as the world's best trainer, Eddie Futch, and his mere existence as a marketable fighter in the same division, made him a constant source of irritation and inspiration.

'Wayne McCullough is a good fighter,' he reluctantly conceded, 'but there's no doubt in my mind he would get beat,

just like the rest.' Warming to his subject he could not resist the
impulse to insult the Ulsterman. 'He's not in my class at all. He's
hiding in Las Vegas, knowing that if he fights domestically he's
going to come up against me and will get stopped. I missed
boxing him as an amateur, but I would have knocked him spark
out even then,' he added – an astonishing assertion considering
that McCullough was a senior bantamweight who won an
Olympic silver medal and Hamed was a flyweight in the junior
ranks. Dropping his earlier pretence at respect, Naz made the
first of many predictions of the 'The Pocket Rocket's' demise.
'He's nothing, and all I can say is that it's going to make him a
very rich man if he fights me, but he'll get beat convincingly. He
won't be able to lay a glove on me and I'll carve him up, and I'll
do it in his backyard in Belfast if he wants. He'll get stopped
inside four rounds.'

But, as Naseem was quickly to discover, the gap between
wishes and wish fulfilment can be very wide, even for the best
connected boxers. For one thing there was the question of
tiptoeing through the minefield of the international control
bodies, each with its own particular interests and agenda. Then
there were also promotional alliances, control by rival television
networks and regional and national fiefdoms to negotiate.
Warren had, by then, become the most powerful promoter in
Britain, but this did not change the fact that Johnny Armour,
Drew Docherty, Wayne McCullough, Orlando Canizales and
the rest were tied to rival promoters who knew only too well that
Naseem Hamed was an opponent to be avoided at all costs.

While Warren and Ingle were searching for appropriate
morsels for their young fighting cock to devour, it was decided to
allow him to rest for a couple of months, which gave him a
chance to slot in scores of interviews and make several public
appearances in Sheffield.[7] He also travelled to London on several
occasions – once to appear at the Professional Boxers'
Association dinner, where he won the Prospect of the Year
award.

Warren and Ingle finally settled on the idea of getting the
official European title defence out of the way by defending
against the mandatory contender, another Italian, Antonio
Picardi, on 30 July, before making a bid for bigger things. With

Early days: Naseem Hamed and Brendan Ingle first met in 1981 and hit it off immediately. *(John Marshall)*

ɔsing at the St Thomas's Boys' Club gym. *(John Marshall)*

From his early amateur days Naseem sparred with far bigger boys and men. *(David Muscroft)*

Herol 'Bomber' Graham *(left)* was Naseem's first hero at the St Thomas's Boys' Club gym. Here he is seen with his daughter, Natasha, Naseem and Brendan. *(David Muscroft)*

The 18-year-old Hamed soon after his professional début. *(David Muscroft)*

Naseem's old friend Des Gargano gets the treatment in October 1992.
(Nick Potts/Action Images)

A victorious Naz. Behind him are *(left to right)* the BBBC's John Morris,
promoter Frank Warren, Brendan Ingle (in the 'Flintstones' shirt) and,
far right, Sal Hamed. *(David Muscroft)*

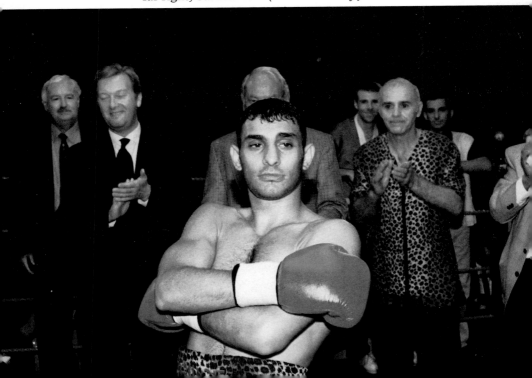

Naseem taunts and teases his way to a shutout against Vincenzo Belcastro to lift the European bantamweight title in May 1994. *(Action Images)*

Hamed pumps a lead right into the face of Freddy Cruz, shortly before stopping him in the sixth round to lift the WBC International super bantamweight title in October 1994. *(Action Images)*

Naseem bangs home a right to the chin of former British and European cruiserweight champion Johnny Nelson in a 'full contact' sparring contest.
(Nick Potts/Action Images)

Naseem walks away from the prone Sergio Liendo after their March 1995 fight was allowed to continue several potentially damaging punches too long. *(Action Images)*

Taking it on the chin: Naz training with young hopefuls at Brendan's gym. *(Ian Bradshaw/Colorific)*

A snarling, sneering Hamed pours it on to the wounded Steve Robinson in the final round of their September 1995 WBO featherweight title bout. *(Action Images)*

The new WBO Featherweight Champion. *(Action Images)*

The prince who would be king is crowned by Frank Bruno.
(Action Images)

the full-house success of the Belcastro fight, they decided to use his hometown of Sheffield as a base for his next couple of fights, this time picking the Hillsborough Leisure Centre, 200 yards from the Sheffield Wednesday ground. Although it had only 1200 seats, co-promoter Alma Ingle pointed out that it was holiday season and many of the usual punters were away, while Brendan said they wanted to reward the support shown for him from the west of the city, and to use the occasion to project Sheffield as the 'sporting capital of the country'. It was the kind of stuff to win them further brownie points at home, not that they needed them. Once again the fight was to be screened live by ITV, with Hamed to head the bill.

Picardi, a 31-year-old Neapolitan veteran, was a credible though unthreatening opponent, with a record of 24 wins (five inside the distance) and 10 losses in an eleven year career which had taken him no further than the Italian title. He managed to outpoint Belcastro in June 1987, but was outscored by his fellow Italian in 1988 and twice in 1993. Four of his losses had come inside the distance, but three of those were on cuts (the fourth, in 1991, came through a one-sided, five-round beating by France's former WBC world super bantamweight champion Thierry Jacob). He was rated number 25 in the world by the WBC and number one by the European Boxing Union, and over the previous five years and 17 fights, only three boxers had succeeded in bettering him – Belcastro, Jacob and WBO junior bantam champion Johnny Bredahl. He was a strong, durable fighter, with an upright style and a fair array of skills, but not much power and a tendency to cut.

Three weeks before the fight Picardi suffered the same injury Naseem had had in his preparations for the aborted Peter Harris fight – a twisted ankle – and the promoters had no option but to postpone the fight for eighteen days, until 17 August, a decision which adversely affected the live gate and meant that for his second hometown fight Naseem had a less than capacity hall which irritated him no end. He could take some consolation, however, in the fact that he had attracted an ITV audience of over seven million – his biggest yet and a remarkable figure for a Wednesday night fight. Despite the delay, which upset Naseem's training routine, he made the weight with relative ease, coming in at 8st 5¾ lb, three quarters of a pound more than Picardi and his lightest in eighteen months.

Before the fight Picardi said he had trained harder than usual and had come to Britain to win, which is about as modest as pugilistic predictions come. Naseem said he did not feel like going the full twelve rounds again, and announced: 'I would like it to be three – yes, three rounds, that's my prediction. I have respect for my opponent but I'll knock him out.' And he tacitly acknowledged that all the criticism of his antics in the Belcastro fight had affected him, by reassuring everyone he would tone it down. 'I will have to ease off,' he said. 'At the moment the public are thinking, "Are we going to love him or hate him?" I want people to like me.'[8]

True to his word, this time Naseem downplayed his vaudeville antics, though he found it impossible to dispense with them altogether. He mothballed his gold, tasselled-gown and his frontflip entrance, but this time arrived clad in nothing but his leopard-spotted trunks and an orange turban around his head.

When the bell rang Naseem moved out quickly, his thick legs, as always, wide apart, and suddenly lunged in with one of his speciality punches, the twisting lead uppercut, this time thrown with the right. It missed and Picardi, fighting from behind a peek-a-boo guard, tried to counter, but despite the fact that Naseem was completely open and exposed, his magnificent reflexes ensured that the punch sailed harmlessly past. It did not take the young champion long to find his range and he began whipping in his surprise punches, shifting now and then to the orthodox position, and back again without missing a beat, and soon the Italian was on the canvas from a snappy right hook-left behind-the-head combination. He was up immediately without a count but was hurt again with a left, seconds before the bell.

In the second Naz stepped up the punishment regime, using his right jab and hook effectively, and then banging home with big southpaw lefts. One of these sent Picardi back and Hamed tripped him up as he looked like going down, causing referee Knud Jensen to rule it a slip. When Picardi rose, the young man in his face had changed his stance and was firing off fast left hooks – two to the body and one to the head landing in quick succession. He followed with another left to the body and a right hook which just seemed to nick the back of his head, and Picardi dropped to his knee and took a count, despite protesting that he was pulled down. After taking another left uppercut, the Italian champion had his sole moment of success, landing a left hook, which prompted Naz to give a little bum-wiggle in mock appreciation.

In the third there seemed to be absolutely nothing Picardi could do to get out of his predicament. Hamed swayed, twisted and gyrated away from his punches in a display of amazing elasticity, shifting stance time and again. The visitor went down from Hamed's momentum after avoiding a punch, which was followed by a legitimate knockdown from a short, fast, southpaw left. Using the ropes, Picardi picked himself up at the count of four and Naseem pounced on him with an eight-punch combination, six of which landed, including a cracking right and three thudding left hooks. Picardi sunk to the canvas, and though he bravely dragged himself up again, Jensen waved it off at the 1 minute-26 second mark, while Naz did his somersault.

'Didn't I predict the round would be the third?' he asked his millions of newfound television followers, before taking them through the final moments. 'Boom. See that? Oh Yeah! Baby, good shot . . . He didn't want to know after that. Oh baby, you looked *so* good,' he said directly to the camera, and from there to seven million living rooms. Frank Warren looked on with an expression of total wonderment on his face. 'I genuinely believe he is the best fighter I have ever been involved with,' he enthused.

Even Mickey Duff was willing to share in this enthusiasm, noting that 'nobody could have done a better job on Picardi'. And to highlight this point, eight months later Duff's unbeaten Commonwealth bantamweight champion Johnny Armour took eight rather more competitive rounds to subdue the still vertical Picardi in a fight for Hamed's former European crown.

Naseem was convinced he was already by far the best bantamweight in the world and after this victory his management shared his confidence. He'd previously told everyone how easily he would be able to handle local rivals like Docherty, Armour and McCullough, but he was also absolutely adamant he could whip any of the four 'world' champions, including the IBF and generally recognized world champion, and one of the greats of the division, Orlando Canizales, who was about to make his sixteenth defence of his title. Hamed's view was that the 28-year-old Canizales would provide him with some competition but, in the end, would be too old and slow for him. Today he still regrets never having been given that opportunity and says he is certain he would have soundly beaten the Texan. In retrospect, it looks like a realistic view. Canizales was by then past his peak and in January 1995 lost a disputed decision to Wilfredo Vazquez, in a bid for the super bantamweight. Vazquez in turn was soundly whipped by Juan Polo Perez (only to be granted the decision by the WBA), while Hamed later destroyed Polo Perez in two rounds.

Perhaps it is pushing things to make too much of such a convoluted form guide in a sport that has so much to do with competing styles, but in Hamed's case this argument is reinforced by a pile of corroborating evidence, including the way he was able to handle far bigger and more experienced fighters from the British champions and contenders – Johnny Nelson, Neville Brown, Chris Saunders, Kevin Adamson – in sparring sessions. Even at that stage of his career, after only thirteen fights, the combination of Naseem's balance, his fighting rhythm, his extraordinary time–distance and hand–eye coordination, the speed of his reflexes, his feet and his hands, his natural power and strength, his solid chin and his unique but highly adaptable fighting style, seemed to make him unbeatable at the weight, and it is not hard to imagine that he would have done a real job on Canizales or any of the other bantamweight champions.

Unfortunately, he was never to get the chance. Like Sugar Ray Robinson, who in the first year of his career beat all the top lightweights in the world but never got a shot at that title, Hamed eventually had to leave a division where he was the best in the world, without getting a chance to prove it. With his ambition of winning up to five world titles (and several more if Ingle has his way), this was a significant setback.

It might be argued that Frank Warren did not try hard enough to secure a bantamweight title shot. At the same time, it must be recognized that it would have been extremely difficult for him to secure a shot for Naseem. It is true that Don King seems to have the ability to get exactly what he wants for his fighters, but Hamed was a Warren rather than a King fighter and the influence of the Don on the control body bosses did not seem to spread by osmosis through his English partner. Also, each of the champions was handled by promoters outside of the King–Warren ambit. Canizales was promoted by Cedric Kushner, who at that stage was one of King's principal rivals, and King was not at that time able to influence the IBF (which was the only organization at that stage to leave Naseem out of its rankings).

Without King's muscle, the only way to be sure of securing a title shot was to follow the McCullough route of working his way to the number one contender position and then waiting up to nine months for a mandatory challenge, and Naseem's management knew they would struggle to keep his weight within the bantam range that long.

Shortly after the Picardi fight, it was announced that Naseem would next defend his European title against Johnny Bredahl, Denmark's unbeaten former WBO super flyweight champion and European bantamweight champion, who, a year later, would give Wayne McCullough more of a headache than he was expected to before being controversially stopped in the eighth round. It was a fight that kept on being postponed, the first time when the more attractive option of fighting for the vacant WBC International super bantamweight title against Freddy Cruz emerged.

In December 1994 it was again announced that the Bredahl fight would take place at The Point, Dublin on 4 March, after Frank Warren won the purse bid by putting up £285,000 (including £175,000 for Naseem), but when it was found to clash with the Ireland–France rugby game the venue of the fight was switched to Glasgow. By this stage Bredahl was the mandatory contender, and the European Boxing Union, through its affiliate the British Boxing Board, was insisting that the fight go ahead. Finally, however, Warren, Ingle and Naseem decided to drop the plan, partly because of Naz's weight troubles (although it was felt he could continue to make the bantamweight limit, albeit with some strain, for a few more months), but more importantly because they felt a victory over Bredahl would bring them no closer to a world title challenge, and that the more profitable option would be to take on a series of super bantamweight contenders. As a result, the Bredahl fight never happened and at the end of February 1995 Hamed officially relinquished his European bantamweight title. The Picardi victory was therefore his last at the 8st 6lb limit and for the next year he would do all his fighting at super bantamweight.

It is worth noting that at that point that Hamed's walk around weight when out of training was around 8 st 12 lb. This is a stone less than both the current IBF bantamweight champion Mbulelo Botile and the WBC champion Wayne McCullough. With the right combination of diet and dedication he could certainly have continued fighting at bantamweight for at least another year (particularly with weigh-ins being held twenty-eight hours before fight time).

A week after beating Picardi, Naseem made one of his regular trips to London, which he began describing as his 'second home'. This time, however, the main purpose was for him to 'network' with Don King and the American fight crowd who were in town to see the Oliver McCall–Lennox Lewis fight. According to Ingle, the McCall camp were so impressed with the stories they heard of Naseem's prowess that one night they woke up the future WBC heavyweight champion to show him what this cocky little buzzfly could do in the ring, and McCall came away enthralled.

Warren felt that Naseem's ability to impress and bedazzle, even when outside the ring, and his complete absence of youthful bashfulness, would serve him well on the American fight circuit, and the talk in his camp began to turn towards getting him major league exposure on the King-connected cable network, Showtime. Before he jubilantly returned home, King gave Hamed his seal of approval, and in so doing indicated a hint of future proprietorial interest. 'This kid's so great he's gonna go all the way. We're taking him to America! Yessirree! The Prince is Vegas-bound!' to which Naseem responded: 'I'm the best bantamweight in the world. No one can touch me. I wanna get to America and show them Yanks how to kick ass.'[9]

With this in mind Naseem made his first-ever trip to the

United States for a ringside seat at Don King's six world title bill at the MGM Grand in Las Vegas on 17 September, headed by the Julio Cesar Chavez–Meldrick Taylor return. He was also able to put in an appearance at the Wayne McCullough–Andres Cazares fight two days earlier at the Silver Nugget hotel, which the Ulsterman won impressively at the end of the third round – a performance which nevertheless reinforced Hamed's view that he could cut down 'The Pocket Rocket' with the greatest of ease.

The idea behind the brief visit was to show Naseem off to the American boxing writers and fight personalities, get him acquainted with the US fight scene generally, and for him to watch some of the best boxers in the world in action in what was probably the finest boxing bill in the history of the sport. Finding himself short of kudos or even recognition from the American fight fraternity, Naseem became increasingly eager to display his wares in the United States, believing he could be an even bigger hit there than in Britain.

Two months later it was announced that Naseem would definitely be fighting in the United States early in 1995, and would have a place on Mike Tyson's first comeback bill in Las Vegas in mid–1995. This prompted a rare display of modesty from Naseem, who acknowledged, 'It will be pretty hard to steal the show from Tyson.' But like so many firm plans, this one too went awry, and the closest Hamed came to the Tyson comeback ring was another ringside seat, as part of another PR and networking visit.

Hardly surprisingly, given the kinds of things that impress him, Naz came away enamoured with King, and, more particularly, King's achievements, and saw these as something to live up to. 'I like to be different, I like to be unique. I like to be number one, the original article, a Don,' he would later say.[10]

Right from the time he beat Belcastro, Naseem had his eye on Steve Robinson. Though he had ambitions to win world titles at bantamweight and super bantamweight, he felt that WBO featherweight champion Robinson had a style made for him, and that even at that early stage of his career he could take the Welshman out. In June 1994 Robinson made his fourth defence of his title against Freddy Cruz, and though he won a unanimous decision, he was taken the distance by the Dominican, who was really a natural super bantamweight and who had only ten days to prepare for that challenge. Hamed naturally felt he could do considerably better and saw the Cruz fight as a way of needling Robinson, as well as the quickest route to a title belt.

The day after Naseem returned from Las Vegas, it was announced he would be fighting Cruz. The bill was initially scheduled for Stevenage, but at the end of September it was moved to Sheffield's Ponds Forge Arena. The choice of Cruz as an opponent caused mild surprise in boxing circles because of the size and experience differences between the two men. At stake was the WBC's vacant International super bantamweight title, a belt and honour of extremely dubious significance.

International, Pentacontinental and Intercontinental titles were ostensibly invented by the various control bodies to give fighters outside the top ten contenders a chance to fight for a title as a preliminary step towards a world ranking. This made little sense, because invariably the new 'international' champion would make the organization's contenders list, and if he was any good would defend against other contenders. The real purpose, of course, was to spread the gravy train, and to find a way of pulling in more revenue from sanctioning fees. With promoters, and more particularly television executives, being unduly obsessed about the need for their fights to have some or other 'title' status, and boxers like Naseem always eager to add another belt to their collection, this made everyone happy – everyone except the ordinary punters who have every reason to be more and more confused and despondent about which title is which and what it all means.

Cruz came into the Hamed fight with an understated record of 44 wins (fifteen inside the distance), six losses and six draws, but these stark figures told very little of the full story of his considerable ability. This Italian-based boxer from Santo Domingo in the Dominican Republic turned professional in 1986 without knowing a great deal about the game, and only managed to win three of his first ten fights. After that, however, he got down to the business of winning in a big way, going thirty-nine fights without defeat before losing a disputed majority decision to the little Puerto Rican darling of the WBA, Wilfredo

Vazquez, in his bid for that organization's junior featherweight (super bantam) title. After that he won nine in a row before being outpointed by Robinson at a higher weight.

Although he was thirty-two years old when he fought Naseem, and had been a professional for over eight years, he had shown no sign of slowing down – a view confirmed by his post-Hamed showings, where he went undefeated for his next five fights before losing yet another eyebrow-raising decision, this time in Britain in December 1995, against Alfred Kotey, once again for the WBC International super bantamweight title. Cruz was an extremely cagey customer – hard to hit, awkward, with a tight defence, a very firm chin (he had never been stopped) and a good workrate, especially when he was well-prepared, as he was for this one. He was not a huge puncher, but had stopped six of his last fourteen opponents.

Though he put in only three and half weeks of unbroken training for Cruz, Naseem was, as usual, in superb condition. His work regime was inconsistent, often relying on a late night whim to get back to the gym, but on most days he would get up around 10 a.m., and spend an hour in the gym after a light breakfast. His next session would usually start at around 4.30 or 5 p.m. and last up to two hours. For supper he would eat whatever his mother cooked, and follow this with a sauna and a swim. At around 10 p.m., he would train again, sometimes running (though seldom long distance jogging), but more often having a general workout. He would go to bed whenever it suited him, often well after midnight.

After six months of trying to keep Naseem's weight down, Ingle was happy to let him eat virtually as he pleased, including traditional no-nos like chip butties, but he made the weight without any problem coming in at half a pound under the 8st 10lb limit (half a pound more than Cruz, although, as usual, he looked far smaller).

For anyone outside the bizarre world of professional boxing, and for everyone with a sense of the absurd, the shenanigans of 'head-to-head' press conferences and weigh-ins for major fights, tend to come across as little more than comical farces, invariably full of melodramatic sound and fury, and signifying absolutely nothing. Ever since Muhammad Ali turned his pre-fight weigh-in for his first Sonny Liston fight into a madhouse, major promoters have cottoned onto the idea that getting the fighters to have a go is bound to impress the punters. The boxers themselves, however, do not always see it this way. Joe Frazier, for example, could never quite laugh off the jokes at his expense that Muhammad Ali sent his way.

For prize fighters, their choice of profession is seldom solely about money. Each fight is a test, not against some objective gauge like a tape measure or clock, but against another man. Partly, it is a test of their skills and preparations. By weigh-in time, if they have done their job properly, they would have put in weeks of intense training and abstained from many of the pleasures and temptations of life. If they fight in the lighter divisions, they may be hungry and thirsty when they step on the scales. It is also a test of a very traditional notion of virility, or at least that's the way it is often viewed by its participants.

The final press conference and weigh-in is the last occasion the two men will get to see each other before attempting to beat each other up. If you are a bill-heading boxer, even one with a well-developed sense of irony, which is rare in this sport, it is hard not to take these theatrical occasions just a little bit too seriously – to see the man next to you at the front table or at the scale as not just another opponent, but as an enemy who will be trying to take away your earning power, your sense of self-worth and your manliness, which is why so many fighters say they hate their opponents before a fight, even though they may embrace and console them afterwards.

To an observer outside the loop, the final pre-fight set-to between Hamed and Cruz was just one of those occasions where the promoters got their money's worth through a few neat soundbites, fit for television packaging and pre-fight reports. For Naseem, a boxer with a more inflated ego and a more defined sense of purpose than most, it represented something else: a slight to be avenged. For the first time in his career he was just a little bit upstaged, and he was insulted. He began by predicting he would win in style, and take Cruz out in four or five rounds. The Dominican smiled, patted him on the cheek and, with his manager, Rafael Guerrero, as interpreter, responded: 'I thought I was coming to fight a man. I am not sure

I can fight with a child. I don't want to end up in jail.' Naz seethed. When you're a 5-foot-3, 'boyish' (albeit increasingly hirsute) 20-year-old, and you believe you're the best fighter in the world, you do not take kindly to being demoted to childhood. Naseem spoke to his audience, not to the out-of-line foreigner across the row: 'When he gets in the ring, he's going to realize that it's a man punching him; a very strong man.'

Naseem headed the bill once again, and drew a better Sheffield crowd than last time though still not at capacity levels. This was partly because of the late rescheduling and partly because the seats were too expensive, but was no reflection on Hamed's general drawing power. ITV revelled in a viewership of nearly five million – not far behind that of the BBC, whose coverage of the England–Rumania football match started fifteen minutes before the fight.

Naseem, with 'Prince' on the front of his trunks and 'To be King' on the back, made his usual pantomime entrance, with his cornermen adding some colour by arriving in their own top-to-toe leopardskin outfits, which Ingle dubbed their 'Fred Flintstone suits'. Ingle also made a point of handing out a few Flintstone ties before the fight.

From the first bell Hamed moved straight in with a long southpaw right jab, which missed, but he soon started connecting. He changed his stance several times and the confusion in Cruz's reddening face was soon evident. He managed to avoid several of the punches but was still getting hit hard and often. At the halfway mark in the opening round, Hamed landed three thumping left hooks in a row, and then a right, and Cruz seemed hurt. The 5-foot-8 Dominican did succeed in connecting with one solid left hook to the head, but Naseem was completely unperturbed. Later in the round the homeboy landed a left lead, followed by a five punch combination which left Cruz looking wobbly. At the bell he graciously held out his gloves in a gesture to acknowledge his opponent's superiority, as if to say, 'So I accept, you are a man after all.'

Guerrero later said he asked his charge during the inter-round break: 'Why aren't you throwing any punches?' To which Cruz replied: 'I don't know where he is. First I see him on the right. Then he's behind me on the left. What happened?' Implored by his mentor to attack, Cruz came out purposefully in the second, throwing a barrage of punches, but Naseem, crouching low, effortlessly swayed from side to side, and every one of Cruz's blows missed the mark. And then it was Naz on the attack again and Cruz running for his life, trying to counter but always missing. After pulling back from three consecutive jabs, Hamed dug in a pair of left hooks and a right hook to the body before the bell.

The third was a less tidy affair. At one point Naseem threw a low blow and Cruz complained, at another he landed a big left and then effortlessly threw Cruz to the floor, as if to say, 'Look how strong I am, boy.' The veteran did have some success, particularly with one right cross which landed flush, but by the end of the round Hamed was putting on a master class, displaying his full repertoire of punches and there was nothing in the visitor's long experience that had taught him how to cope with this lot.

In the fourth Naseem did some clowning then cracked home a big right uppercut which caused Cruz to clutch for safety, though he managed to come back with snappy left hook to the head and several body blows which the Englishman appeared not to notice. In one wonderful moment near the end of the fourth, Hamed's momentum carried him forward and both men tumbled to the canvas in an undignified heap. For any other boxer, this might have caused embarrassment, but not Naz. He rose with a spectacular backwards somersault, landed on his feet, and his home crowd roared their approval.

The fifth was a slower, more methodical round, with Hamed concentrating on his strength-sapping body attack. He seemed to be taking a breather for a minute but Freddy looked beyond the point of substantial resistance – his hands were dropping, he was gulping air in through his mouth – the effect mainly of all those hefty hooks to the short ribs, liver, kidneys and stomach. He tried holding and hitting and was warned by referee Larry O'Connell. Other than this misdemeanour he had no success.

At the start of the sixth Naseem picked his final weapon of destruction: the lead right uppercut. This time it just grazed past, but soon after he threw it again, feinting with a left while dropping his right shoulder and starting from low as if about to fire a jab to the body, and then bringing it up with a twisting motion, impeccably timed and with all his weight behind it, to connect perfectly just under Cruz's unguarded left cheek. It was perhaps the best single punch Naseem had thrown during his entire career – he later called it a 'pearl' – and it prompted former WBC world lightweight champion Jim Watt, who was sharing the commentary for ITV, to enthuse: 'Hamed seems to have the ability to change the direction of a punch after he starts to throw it. That looked as though it came out as a jab and he just switched it into an uppercut bang on the chin. I've never seen that done before.'

Cruz was out on his feet and Hamed launched a relentless attack to the head and body – a bit wild, with several of his punches missing, but still compounding the earlier damage. All the Dominican could do was grab but Naseem pushed him hard in the face with both gloves and wobbled him with a right and left hook. After a final right uppercut thudded home at the 2 minute-03 mark, referee O'Connell called it off. Brave to the last, Cruz protested, but it was clear he was in no condition to continue. It was the first time he had been beaten inside the distance in 57 fights.

Naseem, remembering the earlier slight to his maturity, was quick to gloat. 'He called me a child. I showed him I'm a man tonight. He's going home knowing that I'm going to become a king. I'm the best featherweight, super bantamweight and bantamweight. I'm the best in the world.' And with Steve Robinson at ringside, he was quick to let the WBO featherweight champion know that soon he would be getting the treatment.

Once again the victory helped to raise Naseem's public profile, not only through its success on ITV but also in the way the press dealt with it. This time it was the punches rather than the antics which were the subject of focus. The *Observer*, for instance, provided its readers with two diagrams of that decisive uppercut, along with a story focusing on that single blow. The difference between Naseem's reception, and that of Chris Eubank – who most thought had been clearly beaten by a low-rent American, Dan Schommer, in Sun City, South Africa, three days later, only to be gifted the decision by the WBO judges – could not have been lost on Sky Sports. *Boxing News* provided an apt comparison: 'Stunner and the Stinker' their front page read, together with pictures of a triumphant Hamed and a struggling Eubank.

Frank Warren is a promoter who believes that in boxing, big is best – that the days of the small hall show are over, and that what works today is quality large-scale events. He showed his confidence in Hamed's drawing power by placing him at the head of his biggest bill of the year at the Cardiff Ice Rink on 19 November. Relegated to supporting status was a showdown for the vacant British heavyweight title and the WBC International title between Clifton Mitchell and James Oyebola, along with a fight between the popular Welshman Nicky Piper and Crawford Ashley for the vacant British light heavyweight title and the challenge by Cardiff's Robbie Regan for the European flyweight title.

The early options for Naseem's opponent included the Russian Alexander Yagupov and the former WBC bantamweight champion Victor Rabinales, who earlier in the year had been narrowly outpointed by Wayne McCullough. Eventually, however, they settled on the unbeaten Laureano Ramirez, who had been seen as a possible option for some time and had been in constant training for the previous seven weeks.

Ramirez, at twenty-eight, had, like Hamed, just moved up from the bantamweight division, where he was listed as the number three contender in the IBF world ratings. Raised in the Dominican Republic and based in Spain, he came in with fine amateur and professional credentials. At the age of eighteen he had reached the flyweight quarter finals of the 1984 Olympics in Los Angeles, but he waited until 1990 to turn professional. His record showed 17 wins and a draw (in his fourth fight in 1991). After seven wins in 1992 he went on to outpoint Indonesia's Junai Ramayana for the IBF intercontinental bantamweight belt early in 1993. Hamed was his third opponent of 1994, having knocked out his other two. Known, uncharacteristically, as 'Padilla' (after the mercurial Californian WBO junior welter-weight champion), he was an elusive southpaw with quick hands and a tight defence.

Naseem's preparations were adversely affected when he went down with a severe bout of flu a week before the fight. Ingle considered withdrawing him, but this would have meant yet another setback to his progress. By the end of the week his temperature was back to normal but he was still feeling a little weak from the effects of the virus. You would not have known this, however, before the fight. He made the weight bang on the super bantam limit (while Ramirez was 2¼ pounds under) and was his usual confident, strutting self.

To the boos of a significant section of the 4,000 strong capacity Welsh crowd, he came in once again with orange turban, and this time flashing a red, white and blue gum shield, and made his usual frontflip entrance, followed by his dancing and strutting routine. The torrent of boos and obscenities continued during the fight's three rounds, which were Naseem's least impressive since the first fight with Peter Buckley two years earlier. Perhaps because of the effects of the flu, he struggled to find his range and rhythm and his timing seemed off.

Starting from the southpaw stance, Hamed barely landed a solid punch in the opening round, though he did not take one in return either. He pushed out his jab now and then, but Ramirez was fast and slippery. Whenever the visitor tried something in return Naz would bend back, Ali-style, and sway out of range. This unsatisfactory pattern continued in the second, with Ramirez attacking from behind his quick southpaw right jab, but still not getting home. Naseem would just stand in front of him, swaying rhythmically in slow motion, occasionally attempting something himself, but missing most of his punches.

Finally, in the third, he got down to business, landing a solid left hook early in the round and then another 10 seconds later, both of them catching Ramirez coming in, though Naz himself was clipped by a quick left. He became frustrated when Ramirez held, pushing him back with his forearm and then petulantly throwing him hard to the floor. Referee Mickey Vann gave Naseem a stern, finger-wagging rebuke. Soon afterwards, Hamed connected with a thumping lead right hook to the mouth, followed by a fast three-punch combination, and Ramirez turned away and walked to his corner in a '*No Mas*' gesture.

After a few seconds' delay, Vann waved him to fight on, and Ramirez ran for his life. By this time Naseem had found his

range and as his challenger was back-peddalling, he connected
with a short, devastating right hook high on the jaw and Ramirez
fell as if he'd taken a slug from an AK47. Somehow finding the
courage that had been lacking 15 seconds earlier, he dragged
himself up at the count of eight, but Vann waved it off at 2
minutes 45 seconds.

'Oh baby, it hurts to be this good,' Naz bubbled. 'I have the
skills to be the greatest boxer this country has produced. I am
another legend coming through.' It had been a brilliantly
decisive end to an otherwise off-colour performance, though the
Hamed camp saw it a little differently – as a brilliant end to a
brilliant performance. Perhaps the point to make about it is that
even at his worst, Naseem was in a different stratosphere from a
man who in 1995 would go on to outclass top British prospect
Michael Alldis for the WBO Intercontinental super bantam title
before losing on points against the highly regarded IBF world
super bantamweight champion Vuyani Bungu, after being given
only a week's notice.

When it emerged the press were not entirely satisfied with
Naseem's showing, the fighter and his people displayed their
irritation. 'How can you win in this game?' Naz asked in the tone
of a boxer who had, say, been robbed by the judges once too
often. 'Everything went to plan, it was all correct. I made my
prediction to win in three rounds and it happened. This man has
never been stopped or beaten. He's number four [sic] in the
ratings. I change my tactics for different fighters. If you don't,
they soon realize what you are doing and you end up getting
beat. From the first round onwards I went out and snapped my
jab out coolly and calmly and round three came and I did the
business.'

Ingle's conspiracy antenna was also up, and he castigated the
press for missing the point. 'I'm supposed to be the Paddy, but
you guys are making me look intelligent,' he said. 'He's in front
of them, he makes them make mistakes and then he punishes
them. You won't ever see anyone like him again for a long time,
so you may as well enjoy him while you've got him.'

The Hamed–Ramirez fight drew a viewership of over five
million for ITV, which delighted them considering that it came
at the same time as the BBC's inaugural coverage of the National

Lottery. It received better ratings than BBC1's *Match of the Day*, which focused on Bruce Grobbelaar's first British game since the allegations of match-throwing surfaced.

After this victory Naseem's standing continued to grow, both in terms of establishing himself as a top-drawer British sporting 'personality' and in starting to establish a name for himself in US boxing circles.

He made his first of numerous television appearances on shows within the popular entertainment, rather than the sporting, realm. Being interviewed by Terry Christian on Channel 4's *The Word*, he suffered a rare moment of obvious embarrassment when a set-up in the audience tossed her knickers at him. After this he became a regular 'celebrity' television and radio guest. His attempts at humour or at retaining his 'cool' persona were sometimes less successful than others, but he could always be relied on to provide a lively and spirited presence.

By the end of 1994 he was rated in the bantamweight or super bantamweight divisions by all three major international control bodies as well as all the independent publications. In December 1994 one of the major American magazines, *Boxing Update*, included Naseem in fifteenth place in their 'best pound-for-pound' in the world list. For Naseem such a low ranking might have been regarded as an insult, but what it suggested was the beginning of an American recognition that this 20-year-old was a British fighter cut from a different cloth from the upright, jab-and-move bleeders of past reality and present prejudice.

Hamed's rise to 'legendary' status did not happen as hoped in 1994, and the year had its share of setbacks and disappointments, but in many respects it had been a spectacular success. Under Frank Warren's promotional umbrella, Naseem had risen from a six-round preliminary fighter to a bill header capable of filling a hall and drawing several million television viewers. His six victories were all impressive and he was now ready to capitalize financially on his talent and fame. Even without that longed-for world title belt, The Prince had arrived.

7

From Glasgow to Sana'a

Frank Warren had two parallel strategies to get Naseem Hamed a world title shot in 1995: first, do everything possible to entice one of the champions into the ring; second, put Naz in with a regular diet of rated opponents to try and force his way into the mandatory contender's position with one of the control organizations. The idea was to find opposition which would be taken seriously or at least would provide a yardstick to Hamed's progress.

By the beginning of 1995 they were close to abandoning the plan to get him a shot at a bantamweight title, though there was one option they had yet to try. Alfred Kotey held the low-rent WBO bantamweight title, but was widely regarded as the best of the pack – a real class act. This British-based Ghanaian had received plenty of kudos with his title win over Puerto Rico's Rafael del Valle and his defences against Mexican contender Armando Castro and later British champion Drew Docherty. Kotey did everything he could to tempt Naseem into the ring with him. 'If he wants to prove himself, let him fight me,' he pleaded after outclassing Docherty in four one-sided rounds. 'I'll take on Hamed, anywhere, any place. He won't have to come looking for me. I'll even fight him in his hometown of Sheffield. He's very good at dancing but there's more to boxing than a circus act.'

After arriving in Britain in 1993 Kotey had been managed and promoted by Mike Jacobs who worked for Roger Levitt, who was convicted of fraud and made insolvent. When, in 1995, their KOPRO enterprise collapsed, Jacobs' promoter's licence was taken away by the Boxing Board, and it emerged that Kotey had received a total of less the £20,000 for his four fights in Britain, including three WBO title fights (and, in fact, ended up paying £259 for the privilege of defending his title against Docherty, after taxes and training expenses were deducted). Eventually Kotey severed his connections with the set-up and joined Warren's rapidly expanding stable. He was finally set to fight Naseem after one more title defence against Daniel Jimenez, which he surprisingly lost on a close points decision.

However, in early 1995 Kotey's name was still in the hat, at least as far as the press was concerned. *Boxing Monthly*, for instance, ran a story 'How about Kotey?' in their December 1994 edition, after Kotey outclassed Armando Castro, winning every round on two of the judges' cards, and Naseem was regularly regaled with questions about how he felt he would fare against the man from Accra, to which he would respond with his usual dismissive sneer and the reply, 'Four rounds, that's as far as he'll go.'

But if, at that stage, Kotey's promotional connections made that fight an unlikely prospect, the next best thing was to do a job on one of his recent opponents, just as they had done by picking Freddy Cruz after his points defeat against Steve Robinson. They settled on the seasoned old veteran, Castro, for a 21 January date at Glasgow's Scottish Exhibition and Conference Centre and once again Naseem was to head the bill.

Castro, then aged thirty-one, was one of those fighters who had been around forever, giving good service but never quite cracking it at the top. In thirteen years as a professional, most of it spent in the super flyweight division, he had compiled a record of 42 wins (36 inside the distance), 17 losses and three draws.

After several years as a Mexican champion, he had on three occasions fought for world titles. In December 1991 he challenged the formidable Thai Khaosai Galaxy for the WBA super flyweight title, knocking him down before losing a close decision, then in December 1992 he travelled to Japan for a second shot at the WBA crown, this time being outpointed Katsuya Onizuka and ten months later he was outpointed by Kotey. Though past his best, he was extremely tough (having never been stopped in 62 fights) and hit hard.

No one other than his manager and, perhaps, the fighter himself expected Castro to win but he was given a good shot at repeating Belcastro's success by going the distance. The challenge for Naseem was to become the first man to knock him out, which he confidently predicted he would do. 'He will not go beyond round five,' he announced before the bout.

Naseem trained for almost six weeks, sparring over 200 rounds and even breaking a habit of abstinence by doing some running while on holiday in Tenerife. He was under the weight limit over a week before the fight (later coming in at 8st 9¾ lb – a quarter of a pound less than the Mexican). When Naseem arrived in Glasgow he was concerned he would get the kind of reception he had received in Cardiff two months earlier, but instead found himself being hailed on the streets and treated with respect by the Scottish press. Having just been told he was to be presented with a new Mercedes sports convertible, courtesy of the president of Yemen, he was in a buoyant mood when fight-time arrived.

Staying in the £175-a-night honeymoon suite of Glasgow's Marriott Hotel, he woke up at just after midday, showered, washed his hair and his new goatee beard and moustache, and took his tea and toast in the bedroom. The afternoon, spent with Chris Saunders and John Ingle listening and dancing to music, went slowly, as it always does. Finally, at 5.30 he took a taxi to meet Frank Warren at another hotel and from there to the arena.

A couple of hours before the fight he borrowed a new theme song, 'Here Comes the Hot Stepper' from Ryan Rhodes, who was originally due to make his debut on the bill, but was scratched at the last moment. 'I'd brought the "Hot Stepper" tape and was going to come out to it,' Rhodes ruefully recalls, 'but my opponent pulled out, so I gave it to Naz and he really loved it, and ever since then he's been using it for himself.'

In his tiny dressing room at 10 p.m. Naseem was, as always, dancing to his music with the ghetto blaster at somewhere near full volume, waiting – with his shades on and his greenish tartan kilt well fastened, his multi-coloured gumguard in place – for the call. Entering the ring he looked like he was having a great deal of fun and instantly endeared himself to the 3000-strong capacity crowd who roared their approval and clapped to the beat of 'Hot Stepper'. Brendan Ingle once again came out in his 'Fred Flintsone' outfit, after being advised by a ring steward not to wear the Irish green and white he favoured, as these were the Celtic colours, and this would upset the Rangers fans present. Castro, oblivious to such symbolism, knelt in his corner to pray and glowered at referee Mickey Vann when he patted him on the shoulder, indicating it was time to take his knocks.

Coming out from the southpaw stance Naseem immediately got down to serious work banging in two long left hooks and then scoring at will with both hands, deliberately telegraphing some of his punches and somehow still landing them. Castro managed to connect with a solitary left hook in return but, soon after, a short right hook wobbled him and he wandered around with wooden legs, dazed for the next minute.

From that moment Naseem looked like he could take his man out at any moment he chose, but instead opted to prolong the affair, put on a show and fulfil his prediction. A left hook sent the Mexican into the ropes. He beckoned Naz in and another big Hamed right landed flush. Castro looked finished, but at that moment Mickey Vann decided it was time to remonstrate with the Mexican about why he shouldn't be beckoning Naseem. Vann's little chat lasted 17 seconds. Naseem lunged in wildly, missing two hooks but banging home several more and Castro was saved by the bell.

In the second Naseem started southpaw, switched to orthodox and smashed in an uppercut followed by a left hook and Castro went down. Referee Vann ruled this clear knockdown a slip. Fifteen seconds later a cracking southpaw left hook-right uppercut-push combination put the Mexican down again. Castro complained and Vann warned him about this. Naseem then slotted in a right uppercut and poured on the punishment, landing eleven unanswered punches, but the visitor, his face already marked up, bravely motioned Naseem in, jeering at him.

Castro came out defiantly for the third and made a courageous attempt at an all-out attack, which Hamed treated with utter contempt, slip-sliding out of the way and banging in long, surprise punches in return, prompting the Mexican to beckon the Englishman in for a rumble. It was apparent Naseem was carrying his man, but he was doing it with such panache that no one minded, and the packed arena responded warmly both to Hamed's brilliance and to Castro's bottle.

In the fourth Naseem moved out from the orthodox position with the obvious intention of ending the mismatch. He soon landed a stunning lead right cross which dumped Castro on the canvas for a count of four, and then performed a little jig, strutted about like a peacock and moved in with a jab. Moments later he began letting go with both hands, at one point twirling his right, Sugar Ray Leonard style, and still landing it on Castro's head. Switching to southpaw he smashed home a half-hook, half uppercut which deposited the challenger on the second strand of the ropes, allowing Naseem time to land two more huge hooks to Castro's jaw and face. Mickey Vann stepped in and it looked as though it was all over, so much so that Naseem did a backwards somersault to celebrate. However Vann, obviously determined to make an evening of it, gave the Mexican a count. With a dazed and confused look in his eyes and his mouthguard half out, Castro made one final attempt at glory but Naseem was all over him, missing more than he was landing, but connecting with enough to put Castro in danger of being seriously hurt. Finally after a right cross-left hook combination thudded home, Vann decided he had seen enough, and at 1 minute and 52 seconds, called it off and Naseem gave the crowd another backflip.

With his wonderful instinct for television, Naseem took his 5.8-million-strong ITV audience through the final moments before telling them in a Yorkshire-Yankee hybrid especially cultivated for such occasions: 'He's gone. Goodnight viewers, because you know I'm champ.'

The comparisons with the WBO bantamweight champion

could not be avoided, and Naseem did his best to bring them home. 'This was the man Alfred Kotey could do nothing with – he went twelve rounds,' he said. 'They said before I'd be doing well if I could match his performance, but I beat him inside four. I was going to do it in five, but he was getting a bit too cheeky so I did it in four. He had no right to showboat like that if he couldn't back it up.'

Like so many top boxers Naseem has an impulsive generosity which was displayed again after the Castro fight. While still in Glasgow he was told of an 82-year-old blind pensioner who had been robbed of £1000 – her entire life's savings. His response on hearing this story was immediately to write out a cheque for the full amount and hand it over on the spot.

He was so delighted by his reception in Scotland that, for once, he let his normally impenetrable hometown guard slip a fortnight after the fight, when, on 2 April, it was announced that his next fight would also be north of the border. 'I can't wait to get back to Scotland because the Scottish people like their boxing,' he said. He should have left it there but he could not resist adding: 'The Sheffield public is not a real fight crowd. I think only now the Sheffield people have realized what a fighter they have.'

Naseem was met by a barrage of criticism at home. The editors of the *Sheffield Star*, his longest-standing and most faithful media backer, felt this insult deserved a backpage editorial along with a 'What do you think?' invitation to readers. After praising his talents they got down to business: 'What you may not expect to hear is Naz having a go at the Sheffield public. Perhaps you may think it's a blow below the belt,' it suggested, before going on to argue that despite its lack of a pugilistic tradition, Sheffield had been fulsome in its support for the Prince, just as it had been for Bomber Graham. 'The city wants Naz to succeed and when he fights here again, the Sheffield public would no doubt be happy to prove him wrong.'[1]

Clearly stung by the response Naseem was quick to explain away his remark, claiming it referred to the fact that the arrival in Sheffield of the Eagles, the Sharks and the Steelers, along with Sheffield Wednesday, Sheffield United, the Owls and the Blades, had divided the attention of sports followers. 'I am

definitely committed to Sheffield,' he pleaded. 'It is my home.
I'm based here and I always will be. Those comments were taken
out of context.'[2] Later, after returning from Cardiff where he
watched Ryan Rhodes's professional debut and an off-form
Steve Robinson outpointing Domingo Damigella, he explained
further: 'Far from knocking the Sheffield people, I have one
dream – to take Steve Robinson's world title from him here in
my own city,' he said.[3]

One of the first major advertising contracts Naseem signed was
with the German motor manufacturers, Audi, for an initial fee of
£10,000. They had approached him at the end of 1994 after
Lennox Lewis, their first choice, was knocked out by Oliver
McCall. Two weeks after the Castro fight, however, there were
fears that the deal would be scotched when Naseem was
convicted in the Sheffield Magistrate's Court of driving at 70
mph in a 50 mph zone on Sheffield Parkway – his third
conviction for speeding in the past year. His solicitor, Chris
Cooke, pleaded that a driving ban would 'give him extreme
hardship', by seriously jeopardizing the Audi sponsorship deal.
He argued it would also adversely affect his extensive charity
commitments for the Sheffield Children's Hospital. The court,
however, was unimpressed, banning him from driving for three
months and fining him £150 with £20 costs. 'It was what I
expected,' Naseem conceded afterwards. 'It will probably make
things difficult while I'm banned but at least I did not get six
months.'[4]

The jeopardy level, however, had been overstated. A week
later Naseem was back on his charity circuit – providing backing
for an anti-crime drive in a local estate and further support for
the Children's Hospital. And far from dropping Naseem, Audi
opted to use him more extensively, placing an advertisement in
all the national newspapers and magazines with Naseem in his
leopardskin trunks alongside their A4 model car, above the
slogan: 'They're both the most powerful in their class.'

Audi retained the rights to use the picture until the end of
1995, and after Naseem drew nearly ten million viewers for his
next fight, Audi offered him one of the £21,000 cars he had
become associated with, but he turned them down, opting

instead for full payment in cash. In the tradition of an Audi television advertisement of the time, featuring a crass, yuppie whizzkid, who says of the car: 'It's not my style', Naseem publicly snubbed his advertisers. 'I could have had an Audi but I didn't want it. But I would have taken a Mercedes sports car,' – which, in fact, he was in the process of receiving from the Yemeni government. However, Hamed did not seem to learn his lesson from the driving ban. In May 1996 he was again banned from driving, this time for 12 months, after being caught speeding at 110 miles per hour on the M1 in his Porsche. He was fined £160 with £30 costs.

After the Cruz fight, the sponsorship and advertising offers poured in. He signed a long-term contract with Joe Bloggs clothing, which later included provision for Naseem's designer talents under the label 'The Nas Collection' (to be marketed in Britain and the Middle East and involving a royalty for Naseem for every item sold). There was also a £100,000 contract with Sony Playstation and further offers – some accepted – from car and chocolate manufacturers, fast-food chains, sports equipment companies and sunglass designers, with the figures they were offering coming close to the £1 million range. For a while he had a ghosted column in the *News of the World* and later signed a major contract with Adidas sportswear.

Naseem was also doing regular fashion shoots for a range of magazines, advertisements for Sky and a spate of one-off commercials for the highest bidder. In June 1995, for instance, he completed a 16 hour filming session to make a Jetstar Records commercial for the VH1 cable television channel, advertising a jungle music compilation album, after which he announced he was reconsidering his plans to become an actor after retiring. Among the other offers he received was one to cut a rap CD for Polygram Records, the first of five labels to pursue his signature after hearing his rap promotion record.

He was also being besieged by radio stations, British and Asian television companies, newspapers, and sports, teen, style and men's magazines for interviews. In August 1995 Sports Network and Polygram Videos released Naseem's *Natural Born Thriller* video which went straight to number one on the sports list, later winning the Gold Disc as the top-selling sports video of 1995.

This was followed at the end of the year with a second video, *Prince Naseem: The Making of a Legend*. At the same time The Naseem Hamed Fan Club (managed by his brother Nabeel and offering T-shirts, caps, autographs and a newsletter) was launched, and soon after he consolidated his commercial empire within the company, Naseem Hamed Enterprises.

Naseem was advised to allow a London agency to handle his growing account, but he turned this down, resisting the idea of a pack of boxing-ignorant southerners telling him what they had booked him for. Instead, in 1995, he handed over this side of his affairs to his brother, Riath, who, in addition to being a Yemeni community activist, had a business degree and the commercial acumen needed for the job. He was sometimes assisted by John Ingle and had a team of six solicitors and tax advisers.

What was remarkable about all this was that it was all put in place before Naseem won his first world title. At the time boxing in Britain was supposed to be on the decline (though this claim was regularly contradicted by television viewership figures) and even some of the elite in the sport, like Chris Eubank, had struggled to find sponsors and advertisers to endorse them throughout their careers. Featherweights traditionally don't draw flies, especially when they're still in the early stages of their careers, but in every way Naseem was an exception.

With all this money coming in, Naseem's lifestyle and spending habits changed considerably. He started his fleet of cars with his £15,000 Wrangler Jeep (a gift from Frank Warren) in 1994. In 1995 he added the Yemeni Mercedes and an Alfa Romeo Spyder (also from Warren) and, soon after winning the WBO title, he traded in the Alfa towards a Porsche 211 Carrera 4. He also built his parents a mansion in the Yemen, and, at the end of the year, bought his own mansion in Sheffield. He would only wear designer clothes (Armani, Moschino, Nicole Farhi, Versace and Dolce E Gabanna among his favourites), and would dispose of £100 designer jeans after wearing them once – throwing them in the family wash basket for his younger brothers to rescue and wear.

On his regular visits to London he stayed in a luxury flat in a Mayfair apartment block, but by the end of the year was looking to buy a flat of his own. He liked to be seen in London clubs like

Scalini, Emporium, Malibu Stacey, Hanover Grand and others, and regularly travelled overseas, making several fully sponsored trips to Europe, the United States and the Middle East during the year.

Even before that otherwise obnoxious aristocrat the Marquess of Queensberry had the good sense to put his name to a set of rules to 'civilize' prize fighting, authors and sports writers of varying calibres had been straining to have a go at the best and brightest the pugilistic profession could produce. Byron went as far as taking lessons from the old bare-knuckle champion 'Gentleman' John Jackson. Paul Gallico tried his luck against Jack Dempsey and survived to tell what it felt like to be knocked unconscious, and George Plimpton did it with Archie Moore. And once, Ernest Hemingway, an insecure fellow who fancied himself as a bit of a brawler, tried to take a swing at middle-aged Gene Tunney. The ex-marine blocked his advance and brought up his own left hook which he stopped at the point of the author's chin, quietly but resolutely telling him, 'Don't you *ever* try that again,' before slowly withdrawing his hand.

Jackson, Dempsey, Moore and Tunney were big fellows for their day, and the only lesson they could impart was that getting punched is sore. But what if the tables are turned a bit? What about a big, young, well-conditioned former amateur boxer-cum-writer against a tiny professional? It was a question posed aloud by *Boxing News* senior writer Claude Abrams, who had boxed for over four years in the amateur ranks as a welterweight in the early eighties, before growing into a light heavyweight.

Shortly after the Castro fight, when breakfasting with Naseem while researching an ITV short on the boxer, Abrams provocatively put forward the view that there *must* be a fair degree of hyperbole in all those stories about Naz standing heavyweights on their heads. Naseem invited him to try his luck and Abrams figured that at ten inches taller and over fifty pounds heavier, he would do all right. 'I just couldn't imagine that someone so much lighter and smaller than me could hurt me and I assumed that those tales of him battering all these big professionals were greatly exaggerated,' Abrams said. They agreed on a session of 'body sparring' with the 16 oz pillow gloves, for three two minute rounds – as mild a trial as you could get, or so Abrams thought.

The entire gym turned out to watch, and just before the writer made his way through the ropes, Ingle, who refereed the encounter, whispered to him: 'You know, Naz is a horrible bastard when he's in that ring.'[5] And that, as Abrams remembers it, is exactly what he was. The first punch Naseem landed was a sickening left uppercut to the stomach, just to test the journalist's resolve, and after that Abrams got to watch and feel first hand something of what Naseem's opponents experience in the ring: the constant side to side movement, the punches from angles outside of a normal human being's peripheral vision, the little fellow who seems to anticipate your punches before you do and disappears as you fire, only to reappear with a crunching counter a fraction of a second later.

Abrams's body was aching and he was soon reduced to a crouch. As he put it: 'He chopped me down with body punches until I was at his level and then he let me have it with one or two to the head', at which point the blood started leaking from his nose. 'We had agreed only to go for the body,' Abrams recalls, 'and I had to think, Do I retaliate to the head?, but I realized straight away that if I tried anything like that he could really do me damage.'

Abrams was covering up and doing his best to get out of the way, without much success. After two and a half rounds, Ingle decided it had gone far enough and called time. Hamed wore a look of disgust and disappointment, or as Abrams recalls it, 'He looked like a dog whose just had a piece of steak removed from his bowl before he was able to finish it.'

While Naz continued sparring with the professionals, Abrams left the ring with his ribs, solar plexus and nose aching, full of relief and admiration. 'After that I was totally convinced. Each time he punches you, even if his feet aren't planted, he really hurts you. I was totally amazed by his power. It was quite incredible.'

Afterwards Hamed apologized for going too far, and consoled Abrams by telling him he'd had a hard day on his feet doing some serious shopping at the massive Meadowhall Shopping Centre. Abrams, however, came away with the view that whatever Naseem's mood, he was a fighter who was unable to take it easy once the gloves were on. 'The point is, he becomes a totally different person once he's in the ring. He really doesn't seem to know how to hold back.'

Naseem sees things a bit differently, stressing that he had a point to make that afternoon. 'The main thing that happened before we sparred,' he recalls, 'is that Claude was definitely convinced he was a big strong man and he just couldn't see a guy so small and young upsetting him, so I proved him wrong, and Claude knew from that time onwards that I was going to be great and achieve everything I said I would do.'

Naseem's next fight was not against a light heavyweight journalist, but a world-rated professional super bantamweight. Having finally abandoned the idea of holding out for a shot at a bantamweight title his opponent was the potentially formidable Argentinian, Sergio Liendo. The fight was scheduled for the Forum Centre in Livingston in Scotland on 4 March, with Naseem once again to head the bill.

Liendo, twenty-five, who was rated eighth in the world at super bantamweight by the WBC, came into the fight with a record of 41 wins (20 inside the distance), four losses and four draws, and he had never been stopped. After a fine amateur career he turned professional in 1989 and went undefeated in his first 20 fights, taking the Argentinian title along the way. He went on to win the South American title and then then the WBC international title, lifting it by stopping the unbeaten Zambian Paul Kaoma in April 1993, though he later relinquished it without defence. He had lost only one of his previous 23 fights and had won his last six in a row. Liendo was an awkward, elusive boxer and a fair but by no means devastating puncher.

A week before the fight Naseem was at ringside at the London Docklands Arena to watch Nigel Benn put up the finest performance of his career to knock out the favoured American Gerald McClellan in ten of the most brutal rounds of modern British boxing. The Don King-promoted American arrived with the reputation of being the hardest puncher, pound for pound in the world. He was expected to blow away the smaller, supposedly weaker-chinned Englishman and proceeded to bash

Benn out of the ring in the opening round, wobble him on several other occasions and drop him again in the eighth. But Benn's boxing skills, his heart and his power prevailed and he finished the American off by putting him down and then out in the tenth, to the short-lived delight of 13.1 million ITV viewers (the highest for any sporting event in Britain in 1995).

McClellan underwent an emergency operation to remove a blood clot from his brain, and remained in an induced coma for over a month. He was left blind, partially deaf and crippled, and in a state of what seems like permanent confusion and deep depression – a situation which led to a war of words between Don King, who had publicly promised to pay for his fighter's rehabilitation, and McClellan's sisters, who took care of him after he was flown back to the United States, and claimed that King had reneged on his promises and shortchanged McClellan on his purse money – both accusations vigorously denied.

Naseem visited McClellan's bedside at the Royal London Hospital and was clearly moved by the American's plight. Afterwards he announced he was 'dedicating' his fight with Liendo to the McClellan clan. 'I was very concerned for Gerald and his family,' he said. 'I stayed in London especially so I could pay them my respects. It was a bad blow for him and the whole of the boxing world. I will have to blank all of that out of my mind before Saturday but I do feel sorry for him and his family.'[6]

But while the picture of the stricken McClellan was in his mind for several days before the Liendo fight, he says he cut it completely from his thoughts once he got down to business. 'It was hard in a sense, but I'm a professional, that's the main thing,' he says, 'and when you're a professional you should act like a professional and a champion. I looked at McClellan and it was sad and unfortunate for boxing, but I took it really well. I realize I have so much power for my weight, and this did enter my mind before the fight, but when I entered the ring I blanked it out and the only thing in my mind was to be victorious because when I start to box I've always got a clear head and I don't think about anything else. I like to show people I've got craft and heart, but I don't think about hurting anybody. That's not what a boxer wants to be thinking about before a fight, and I'm aiming to be legend so I can't let anything put me back.'

He also makes it clear he never fears finding himself in the same position as McClellan, because of his all-round superiority over any possible opponent and specifically because his defensive technique means he so seldom gets tagged cleanly. He says he is fully aware of the potential risks of the sport – though he's contemptuous of those trying to get it banned – but does not see himself as being exposed to them.

Brendan Ingle is a trainer who worries a great deal about the risks involved for those he trains, which is why he prefers body sparring and why he emphasizes the evasive techniques he has become known for. Having been the spit bucket man in McClellan's corner that wonderful, terrible night of Nigel Benn's victory, he described it as 'the most fascinating, fantastic, unbelievable fight' he'd ever watched, but said that while it brought home to him the risks of the profession and the agonies he has when his own fighters take their bumps, it was not something that particularly concerned him when Naseem was in the ring. 'I never worry about him and he tells me not to worry either,' he said. 'The only time I'm really confident in the ring is when he's in there with me.'[7]

Despite the raw nerves and controversies stirred by the McClellan fight, Naseem was hardly subdued in his pre-fight boasts. While rounding off his training in Scotland, he remarked: 'I saw half a minute of Liendo on a video and that is all I need to see. He's a stand-up fighter, very strong, but I fancy the job. I can see myself doing something inside three.' And at the weigh-in (where he scaled 8st 9lb 10 oz – 6 ounces less than the Argentinian) he dismissed his opponent as 'a bum' – hardly the kind of remark to pacify the anti-boxing lobby.

Whatever the sensitivities, it had been decided there was to be nothing understated about Naseem's ring entrance, which had been planned several weeks before the tragedy. After the Castro outing, 'Team Naseem' had put their heads together to discuss gimmicks to further enhance the fighter's profile. Brendan mentioned a recent conversation he'd had with one of Naz's female fans. 'She said to me: "You know, he doesn't show a lot of leg," and I thought to meself, women, what are they on about?'[8] Naseem and Brendan's son John knew exactly what she meant and it was then that the now 21-year-old fighter revealed his talent for fashion design, announcing to an amused John and a bemused Brendan that he had 'a great idea for a pair of shorts' and producing a design involving 60 strips of leopardskin material hanging from a waistband with 'Prince' on the front and 'King' on the rear.

One of the St Thomas's Club regulars, Nigel Colton, had a girlfriend fresh out of design school, who had recently opened her own business, so off they went with Naseem's bizarre idea. Joanne Wragg was not convinced at first, but using an old pair of the fighter's size 28 trunks she got down to work a few days before the Liendo fight, and five hours and £50 of material later she was surprised at the effect, noting that the finished version of Naseem's design worked far better than she had anticipated.[9] After that she was commissioned to make new versions of the Flintstone suits for the cornermen, which Naseem also had a hand in designing, and soon others in the stable, like Johnny Nelson, Chris Saunders, Neville Brown and Pele Reid, had also adopted the Hamed patterned trunks.

Coming in for the Liendo fight once again to the beat of 'Here comes the Hot Stepper', Naseem received a rapturous welcome from the 3700-strong capacity crowd. The roar grew louder when he removed his kilt and sunglasses to reveal his hula skirt and then proceeded with his frontflip over the ropes. Even Ingle was won over: 'Women were ringing up from all over the place – "marvellous", you know, "terrific" and "When he does that flip we were just wondering, has he got anything under the shorts?".'[10]

Naseem glided out of his corner jabbing from the orthodox stance, before switching to southpaw. Liendo looked composed and connected with a right to the body and a little later two lefts and a right to Hamed's chin. With his head tucked in tight (and occasionally used as a weapon) the Argentinian made an elusive target and after the first minute he was looking like an opponent to test Hamed, but it was not to last. After switching back to orthodox, Naseem came in, missed with a left hook but found the mark with one of his speciality corkscrew right uppercuts. It was a jolting blow which clearly gained Liendo's respect as he went into a defensive shell, only to be tagged again, this time with a right hook.

Hamed came out from his usual southpaw stance in the second, but soon switched to orthodox after which Liendo managed to land for the fifth time in the fight, with Naseem giving him a gracious nod of acknowledgement. The fight was beginning to look competitive until Naseem steadied his man with a left and followed through with the most devastating punch of his career to date. It was another perfectly timed, measured and executed left hook, thrown with his full body weight behind it and at blurring speed, and landing flush on the side of Liendo's jaw. The visitor's head swivelled 90 degrees to the left, his legs shuddered and dipped and his left glove brushed the canvas. Naseem started a little jig, but when, somehow, Liendo's legs straightened by reflex and before he tumbled, Hamed shot in with a quick, hard right cross to the side of the head.

Liendo wobbled up at the count of six and was quite obviously in no condition to continue, but the Belgian referee, Daniel van de Wiele, seemed oblivious to the seriousness of his plight and after a cursory inspection, allowed Hamed in again to complete the duckshoot. The visitor gazed vacantly at his corner as Hamed exploded another crunching left hook to his head which spreadeagled him on his back.

Van de Wiele, to his limited credit, dispensed with the count and was quick to remove Liendo's gumguard and call the ringside physician, Dr Alastair Howie, into the ring. The Argentinian's eyes opened and he was breathing but he remained prone for three extremely worrying minutes. Given the anti-boxing outcry after the McClellan tragedy, it was not the kind of spectacle the sport needed and the situation was hardly helped by Van de Wiele's attempts at justifying his potentially fatal lapse in judgement. 'It is easy to say I should have stopped it but when I went to him and his eyes were clear, his hands were firm and and when I held his hands there was resistance, his arms and his legs were strong,' he said despite all the visual evidence to the contrary. 'I did not think I should stop it at that stage and the damage was done when Naseem landed that last punch. For a moment when he was lying on the canvas I thought the worst.'

Ingle did well to restrain Naseem's celebrations, and

afterwards the young fighter agreed that Van de Wiele should
have stepped in after the first left hook. 'I just went out and did
my job,' he said, 'but I thought he would have stopped it there
. . . I just hope he's nice and safe and everything's great.'

Liendo eventually rose to his feet and truculently turned down
Frank Warren's impassioned pleas to spend the night in
hospital. The relieved crowd then proceeded to give Naseem the
send-off he deserved, with a throaty rendition of 'Flower of
Scotland', after which he was allowed to give full vent to his self
regard – 'I've proved I'm no flash in the pan. I've told you I am
going to be a legend. I've a God-given gift and I'm going to use
it. Spectacular, superior, extraordinary – those are the words I
like.'

The fight gave Britain its fifth highest sports ratings for 1995,
attracting 9.42 million viewers, well ahead, for instance, of the
FA Cup Final, which had 8.7 million. Unfortunately the ample
press coverage was not altogether favourable, much of it
focusing on the referee's failure to stop the bout when Liendo's
life seemed in danger, rather than on the punches which put him
in that position. But the superlatives came through nevertheless,
and anyone who watched it was not likely to be in much doubt as
to who was best super bantamweight in the world.

Immediately after the fight a Republic of Yemen government
representative, who had attended as part of a Yemeni VIP
delegation, came into the ring to congratulate Naseem. It had
been sixteen months since Naseem's last visit to the Yemen, and
it was time to return the favours. Together with a delegation
which included his father, Brendan Ingle, Johnny Nelson,
Kevin Adamson and Steve Bunce of the *Daily Telegraph*, he
spent nearly three weeks in the country in March and early
April.

In the period between the two visits Naseem had risen from
being a promising young prospect to being a British celebrity,
and the pomp and ceremony of his reception in the Yemen
reflected this. While his agenda was similar to that on his
previous trip, his profile was far higher this time and, once
again, he was a little overwhelmed by his reception. He
discovered that the country's major football teams play for the

Naseem Cup, named after him, and when he attended the final a crowd of 80,000 rose to give him a standing ovation. He could see his face on school exercise books, tissue boxes, postage stamps and posters everwhere, and watch reruns of his old fights on television. Mothers would approach him, saying they had named their sons after him. And this time his sparring exhibitions with light middleweight Kevin Adamson were attended by crowds of up to 20,000 well-wishers.

Everywhere he went he was mobbed by an instant throng who would chant 'Naseem, Naseem, Naseem' or 'Haboob' (the loved one) and invariably the crowd would move forward to get a closer look or perhaps a touch of the great man. Outside his hotel he would be met by hundreds of admirers who would chant slogans like 'Naseem, we love you'. 'I'd never seen anything like it before,' Kevin Adamson recalls. 'We was getting driven around and we had a lot of guards, and we would go into a shop and the streets were empty, there was nobody around. Give it five minutes and you couldn't move. The street was blocked and you had to put the guards outside and they had to clear the streets when you came out of the shops. It was that bad.' Or as Johnny Nelson puts it, 'It was like going to a football match and landing smack bang in the middle of the pitch.'

There was considerable concern about Naseem's security, with fears not only of the crowds getting out of hand, but of an attempt on his life. Particularly in Sana'a (where a few months before, a fresh outbreak of internal military conflict had seen a Scud missile landing in the streets), where a round-the-clock security presence, both overt and covert, was set up. Whenever he was outside Naseem was guarded constantly by the eagle-eyed heavies of the president's personal bodyguard, armed with Kalashnikov rifles, and even when inside the hotel he was watched by three suits, each with a .45 automatic pistol at the ready, while when he drove around he was led by an jeep with a mounted machine gun and a trio of soldiers. 'We were all treated like we were Michael Jackson,' says Nelson, 'army escort wherever we went.'

The delegation also travelled to Malah Rada, his father's old village about three hours' overnight drive from Sana'a – 'to see how my dad grew up'. They arrived in a procession of five cars

early in the morning, expecting a low-key family visit. Instead
they found every citizen of Malah Rada and the surrounding
villages waiting for their arrival, an official holiday having been
declared to honour Naseem. 'That was madness,' Kevin
Adamson recalls. 'When we got to about a mile outside of the
village we was met by the villagers that had come to show us the
way. Everyone was firing guns, there was even machine guns,
and when we got closer to the village we couldn't move. They
had a little reception tent for the villagers to see him, but again it
was mad there, you couldn't get through and there was guns
going off, left, right and centre.'

For Johnny Nelson this aspect of the visit was an object lesson
in the similarities in humanity throughout the world. Sal, Riath
and Nabeel acted as informal interpreters for the rest of the
delegation, who were a little surprised to discover how 'normal'
the villagers were despite the appearance of chaos, guns and
madness. 'You go to see where people's parents come from, and
you find they're just like everyone else deep down inside,' says
Nelson, 'whether they're from the Yemen, Jamaica or Sheffield,
the backgrounds aren't that different. It proves that what got
Naz to where he is is more his mentality and commitment.'

At least in terms of protocol, the highlight was the formal
welcoming ceremony at the presidential residence in Sana'a,
where the President General Ali Abdullah Salah, presented him
with the Order of Merit, First Class medal, the highest civilian
decoration in the country, for his 'outstanding achievements'.
After speaking informally to Naseem, the president addressed
Warren: 'Both the British and Yemeni people can be proud of
Naseem. We want him to be a world champion and with your
guidance he can be.' To which the promoter replied in glowing
but guarded terms: 'It will take an almighty amount of work but
with your support it's possible because I know Naseem wants to
fight in the Yemen for a world title.' To which the Yemenis
responded: 'Insha'Allah' (Allah willing).[11]

For some time in fact the government of the Yemen had been
lobbying quietly but diligently to secure a world title fight there
– preferably Naseem's first title. At a meeting at the Yemeni
embassy in London with the then-Foreign Secretary Douglas
Hurd, the possibility of Naseem fighting in Sana'a was raised

and the issue came up several times during the visit. For instance, the sports minister, Adul-Wahab Rawih, raised the matter with Warren because, he was quoted as saying, 'it is important for the Yemen and for Naseem to win the title here'.[12]

While Warren made serious preliminary investigations into staging a Naseem Hamed–Wilfredo Vazquez fight in Sana'a's 80,000-seat football stadium in July 1995, this option never materialized, and since then there have been no concrete plans for a major fight there. The problems relate partly to security and logistics and the three hour time difference, but more to finance. It was one thing attracting 20,000 spectators to an informal exhibition, but quite another to organize a world title fight where spectators would be expected to fork out amounts way above the average weekly wage packet for a seat. There were also concerns about sponsorship, pending television deals, and a range of other factors, which made the Yemen option a difficult one to organize. Finally, when it turned out Steve Robinson was to be the title opponent, there was no option but to return to Cardiff because of a clause in Robinson's managerial contract. Naseem's management team still talk about him fighting in the Middle East, but are also considering other possibilities among the Gulf States, including the United Arab Emirates.

Nevertheless, the Yemeni connection has continued to be cultivated by both sides, though by the Yemeni government rather more assiduously. Before Naz's world title fight the Yemeni president presented him with a beige top-of-the-range Mercedes (with an 'N8 Nas' numberplate) to add to his growing fleet of vehicles. Afterwards the government presented him with a mansion in Sana'a, while he bought his parents their own mansion there. He is planning to visit the country again in late 1996. 'I love going back there for visits,' he says. 'The people there really love me, and it's great to be loved, but I don't think I would like to live there. I'll always live in Britain and in Sheffield.'

If anything, his reputation has grown in the Yemen since his last visit, to the point where there can be very few of the country's eleven million citizens who do not know a good deal about him. Quite simply, there are no other Yemeni sportsmen or entertainers of any international standing, and never have been. When Naseem lifted the WBO title against Robinson, the fight was screened live by the satellite network Middle East Broadcast Centre (MBC), and, says Yemeni embassy spokesman Mohammed Beshr, there was hardly a household in the country which did not attempt to watch to it, 'and when he won people just poured out onto the streets to celebrate.'

His popularity has also spread throughout the Arab world, mainly through the role played by MBC which sponsors and broadcasts all his fights throughout the region. According to Mustafa Zaru of MBC sport, the network has 200 million viewers in the Middle East, North Africa and Asia, and while they don't have precise figures on viewership for Naseem's fights, they would estimate that most viewers would have watched his victory over Robinson. 'Boxing is not a popular sport there,' Zaru says, 'but Naseem transcends that and is extremely popular and certainly very well known through the Middle East.'

Naseem has been careful to build on this support, stressing more assertively his Arab as well as his specifically Yemeni heritage, and regularly reminding interviewers that he is 'part of the Arab world'. In late October 1995, a month after taking the title, he spent four days in Qatar at the invitation of the government there, expanding Arab links and building on his fame. In addition to public appearances and media interviews, he was officially welcomed by the Emir of Qatar, Sheikh Hamad bin Khalifa al-Thani, who is also Head of State, Prime Minister and the Commander-in-Chief of the military. '[Naseem's] very famous and extremely popular throughout the country,' says Hadia Saad of the Qatar embassy. 'People really look up to him as an Arab hero throughout the Gulf states, because he's a major sports personality and because he's kept his Arab name and identity.'

8

The Road Back to Cardiff

Frank Warren rushed home from the Yemen on 25 March to be in the United States in time for Mike Tyson's release-from-prison celebrations. Naseem extended his trip, and returned a week later. Three days after that Warren announced that Hamed, and all his other fighters, were to join the satellite network BSkyB's boxing programme, as part of a two-year, £50-million-plus deal – by far the biggest in British boxing history and in excess of the package it took for Sky to clinch the Premiership soccer contract.

After fourteen years of doing business with ITV, Warren and his stable were to cut links with the independent terrestrial channel. With immediate effect, Hamed, Bruno, Benn, Steve Robinson and the rest were to have their fights shown exclusively on Sky Sports. A spin-off, not specifically covered by the contract, but certainly one of the motivating factors behind it, was that the best of Don King's fighters – most particularly Mike Tyson – would also be featured on Sky.

At the same time, Warren announced that the opening play of

191

the new deal would be a Hamed title defence against the talented
Mexican southpaw Enrique Angeles, to be held in Shepton
Mallet on 6 May. This fight would 'activate' a package for
Hamed which would make him an instant sterling millionaire,
and, all going to plan, would make him a multi-millionaire by
the end of the year, with his purses increasing dramatically and
his advertising and sponsorship revenues accumulating even
faster. 'Naz is going to be the biggest sporting star of the next
five years,' Warren predicted. 'He is going to become a boxing
legend. That's my commitment to him.'[1]

The immediate reason for Warren's decision was the money
on offer from satellite television and the guarantee of exposure
for more fighters through the screening of 35 shows a year
(which Warren would either promote himself, co-promote with
King, or promote in conjunction with others in his ambit,
including Brendan and Alma Ingle, Alex and Katherine
Morrison and Chris Sanigar in Britain and, from later in 1995,
Rodney Berman in South Africa).

It was clear from the American precedent that satellite and
cable, on a pay-per-view basis for major fights, was the future
and Warren, the man who had been responsible for the arrival of
live boxing on television, saw himself as a promoter with more
foresight than the rest. In fact soon after the announcement he
silenced whispers that this was really a stalking horse for
pay-per-view by openly acknowledging that this was precisely
what he had in mind. As he put it in one interview: 'The
ultimate for me, what I really want to do, is get pay-per-view off
the ground and I'm gonna do that. I did the first WBO fight in
this country, the first IBF fight, now I want to do the first
pay-per-view show.'[2] (This eventually happened a year later
when, at Don King's insistence, the Mike Tyson–Frank Bruno
fight was sold to Sky subscribers at £9.95 a shot.)

The move to Sky provoked ripples of shock, and some
indignation, in British boxing for several weeks. Boxing had
been the most successful of all sports for ITV, with Benn (v.
McClellan), Bruno (v. Marin) and Hamed (v. Liendo) all
making the top five in terms of sports audience ratings for 1995
over all the channels. To put this in perspective only one football
match (the Cup Winners' Cup Final between Arsenal and Real

Zaragoza) made the top five, while no rugby, cricket, tennis, athletics or golf broadcasts even came close.

Suddenly, ITV were virtually boxer-less, and with the BBC already having relegated itself to the margins of the sport, it seemed as though boxing and terrestrial television might have parted ways, a situation which understandably caused some alarm from the British Boxing Board of Control and several of the leading sports pundits, not surprisingly, including those linked to ITV. Reg Gutteridge, for example, called it the 'Snatch of the Day' and warned that it was a 'bonanza for the few'. 'From the die-hard fan's point of view the big names moving to a minority channel is a blow,' he wrote, pointing out that while Chris Eubank fights drew more than ten million viewers on ITV, his last fight on Sky managed only 320,000.[3] The most common concern was that budding stars needed terrestrial television to make their name, and that without this, they would remain unknown to non-boxing fans, thereby further reducing the status and scope of the sport.

Warren fired back that ITV 'couldn't deliver either financially or as a vehicle to develop young talent',[4] and that there was frustration over the failure to secure good fights for regional TV, and more particularly to screen major league Don King fights. In contrast, he argued, the Sky deal had secured the futures of many British boxers and Sky had made a firm financial commitment to the grassroots development of the sport while at the same time giving priority to King's US promotions. Warren specifically rejected the accusation that the deal had lowered Hamed's profile, pointing to the supplementary publicity and income he was receiving from a number of sources including a spate of new advertising deals and the continued requests for stories and interviews from newspapers, magazines, radio stations and the terrestrial television channels.

After the deal was announced, the General Secretary of the British Boxing Board of Control, John Morris, forlornly expressed the hopes that the BBC would re-enter the market and that ITV would find a way of regrouping. 'There are a lot of good fighters who are not with Frank Warren and we hope that ITV will give them their chance,' he said.[5] In fact, by this stage, there weren't too many top British fighters who were not already with Warren or Sky, and most were with both. Warren had continued to expand his promotional stable at an astonishing rate, with the camps of both Hearn and Duff taking some serious haemorrhaging.

Eventually ITV cobbled together a short term deal with former sworn enemies, Duff and Hearn, to promote a good team comprising most of the best of the rest[6] (with the BBC reduced to making occasional forays into the amateur and professional game[7]) but attractive though the new ITV boxing programme was, it had become clear that Sky had taken the pick of the A-team, and early in 1996 ITV effectively opted to downgrade their coverage of boxing and only to screen the sport at prime time nationally when 'blockbuster' fights could be secured, though they retained their contract with Wayne McCullough and said that regional ITV boxing programmes would continue.

Sky, in contrast, having devastated the competition, further upgraded its boxing programme, and it soon became clear from the viewership figures for Bruno and Hamed's fights that the satellite network's faith in the sport, and Frank Warren's faith in Sky, were fully vindicated.

The background to all this came with a deal conducted for Sky by Kelvin MacKenzie, involving the promotion of a number of Hearn fighters, including eight Chris Eubank fights, in one year. It went badly wrong when, after three fights on Sky, Eubank lost his WBO super middleweight title to Steve Collins. It was after this that Sky chose Frank Warren and his expanding stable, while retaining other drawcards such as Lennox Lewis. As the promoter stressed, it was Sky who approached him, not the other way round, and he made it clear he wasn't prepared to negotiate until they put a multimillion-pound package on the table.

Meanwhile, Eubank followed Collins into the Warren fold and then lost the return against Collins even more decisively, after which he retired. This series of setbacks for the former WBO champion, and his replacement by Naseem as the budding star of satellite, prompted the young fighter into a verbal onslaught against a former friend who was now down on his luck and out of the picture.

Although it now seems hard to imagine, there was a time when the two biggest egos in British boxing managed to co-exist in harmony. Eubank invited Naz to his wedding and Hamed had admitted to admiring the older boxer and being grateful for his offers of assistance. But it all broke down when, according to Hamed, Eubank offered to train him, and strove to 'nick' him from Ingle. After Naseem turned him down, he said, Eubank became haughty and distant. 'He even tried to belittle me once when he said: "You can talk when you accumulate the kind of money I make," ' Naseem claimed.[8] 'I told him I was a better fighter than he would ever be and would attract far more viewers than him.' Whether or not this was all a misunderstanding, from then on Naseem was firmly anti-Eubank, and seldom missed an opportunity to mock and insult the other boxer.

One of his favourite stories, first told to *Esquire* magazine in 1994, is that Eubank once phoned him on his mobile to give him a rather bizarre, though perhaps well-meant, word of advice. ' "Naz", he says, "I'm going to tell you something important now. You must listen!" All serious-like he says, "Naz, you must learn to absorb punishment. One day someone is gonna hurt you because it's a brutal trade. You must learn how to soak up punishment like I can." Jeez, can you believe that! I just said, "No, no no Chris – you got it all wrong. I'm not you! I'm the Prince. I'm different. I ain't taking punishment. I want to be doing the hitting – that's why I'm unbeatable and untouchable!" Absorb punishment? You gotta laugh at that one.'[9]

To Eubank's credit, whatever his other shortcomings and bizarre idiosyncrasies, he managed to keep a dignified silence in the face of this two-year barrage of insults. The most he was prepared to offer in return was a slightly barbed compliment: 'I happen to think Hamed can be a great fighter. He has a brilliant talent and considerable ability, but that often isn't enough to be a champion. What really counts is being a man.'[10]

The one-horse town of Shepton Mallet – better known as an agricultural centre and as a stopover point for visitors to the Glastonbury festival – is not where you'd expect a budding superstar to be displayed for his satellite debut, but Naseem had already proved his ability to pull the punters in droves almost wherever he landed (and this was his twelfth town in 18 fights).

With the British light welterweight champion, Ross Hale, from
nearby Bristol heading the 12-fight undercard, it was seen as a
gamble worth taking and with 5500 rowdy punters squeezing
their way into the Royal Bath and West Showground agricultural
hall on a sweltering night on 6 May, it certainly paid off. As one
farmer, who drove 36 miles for the privilege of seeing Naseem
put it, 'You got to realize that, around here, this is the only show
worth seeing, and besides, none of us have Sky yet, so what the
hell.'   .

Once again Warren and Ingle had managed to find a live one
in the tall Mexican fringe contender Enrique Angeles. This
5-foot-7½ southpaw had the kind of give-no-quarter background
typical of so many fighters from his part of the world, good, bad
and indifferent. He grew up on the wrong side of the tracks in
Mexico City where, as one of a family of eight, he learnt to fight
long before his first boxing lesson. His brother Martin started
training at a local gym and Enrique followed him, winning 36 of
his 38 amateur fights before turning professional at the age of
sixteen in 1989.

Most of his early fights were in the intense daytime heat of
Mexico City's Arena Coliseo, where so many of the best Latin
fighters earned their spurs. He won his debut but in 1990 lost a
couple of decisions to older, more experienced fighters. By 1992,
however, he was beginning to rise above the pack, showing a
combination of boxing savvy and power which saw him through
12 wins in a row before he faced the heavy-handed Alejandro
Landeros in an eliminator for the Mexican title. In the second
round Angeles's eyelid split open and the referee ruled it had
been a punch, giving Angeles his only stoppage loss. But he was
soon back on the winning trail knocking off a number of top
Mexican fighters before being granted his return with Landeros
in May 1994, and this time reversing the result by pulverizing
his rival in two rounds. After a couple more impressive victories
he stopped Geronimo Cardoz in six rounds to lift the vacant
Mexican super bantamweight title, but lost it on points to
Enrique Jupiter in his first defence. After that he bounced back
with a two-round stoppage over the useful Pedro Rabago – his
only fight in 1995 prior to arriving in Britain.

At the time of the fight Angeles was still eleven days short of his 22nd birthday but already had a record of 26 wins (15 on stoppages) and four losses and was rated thirteenth in the super bantamweight division by the WBC. He was regarded as a capable and awkward southpaw (the fourth of Hamed's career), with quick hands and a good punch, plenty of heart, and a reliable chin – having never been knocked down. He was also both an aggressive fighter and one who, when the moment required, was adept at counter-punching. All in all, he was anything but the archetypal 'Mexican roadsweeper'.

Naseem had trained with intense focus in the month between his return from the Yemen and fight time, his concentration only broken by advertising commitments.[11] At the weigh-in Angeles came in light at 8st 8lb while Naseem made the 8st 10 limit on the button. But Hamed, who had come away impressed with Angeles's counter-punching and movement after watching a video of his fights, once again showed absolutely no sign of concern. 'I take every fight like a world title fight – it's as if I'm fighting for a world title – but I know I've already won. I only have to turn up. I'm very confident,' he said before parroting his familiar but none-too convincing refrain. 'I may look arrogant but I'm not. I'm a different person altogether outside the ring.'

By fight time a large component of the crowd were happily well–oiled and ready to scream themselves into delirium at the sight of this tiny Northerner who was about to grace their region with his emphatic presence. And when he gave them an entrance that made his previous antics look boringly tasteful by comparison, they roared. An eardrum numbing explosion of fireworks and percussion launched a sound-and-light laser show which gave 'Here comes the Hot Stepper' new meaning. The jiving silhouette of Naseem emerged through a burning sheet covering a door high in the arena, smoke filled the air, the crowd clapped and chanted: 'Prince Naz, Prince Naz, Prince Naz,' as he revealed once again his leopardskin tasselled trunks and frontflipped his way into the ring, followed by a team of bobby soxers, the Union Jack and the Yemeni flag.

Angeles made it clear he was in no way intimidated by all this, and charged straight at Hamed when the bell rang, launching his hooks into the smoky night air. Naseem simply twisted and turned his way out of danger before snapping in a right hand of his own. The Mexican continued throwing haymakers, but Hamed was nowhere to be found. He taunted for more, tapping his chin to suggest a target, before disappearing once again in the face of the onslaught, and reappearing with a crunching combination. Angeles tried again, and this time Naseem leant backwards at an exaggerated angle – a tactic the purists say you should never use because it puts you off balance though Naseem's balance seemed perfect from any angle. In the final minute the Sheffield man got to work, cracking home a pair of huge right hooks, and a few seconds later, a fast, heavy left hook – all of which hit the mark. Angeles emerged with blood seeping from a cut next to his left eye as Naseem fired home several more painful rights which had the Mexican looking wobbly at the bell.

Hamed started the second just where he had left off: with a right from the southpaw stance which sent the visitor staggering, at which point Naz decided it was time for a show before applying the finisher. He walked away a few steps, gazed at Angeles's boots, and then popped in a jolting jab which landed smack on the Mexican's nose. Now it was time for the payoff, and as Angeles trundled forward Hamed connected with a bomb of a right cross from a seemingly impossible angle, followed by a sweeping left hook, just for fun. Clenched leather connected with skin and bone and for the first time in his life Angeles folded. He dragged himself to his knee at the count of six, then thought better of it and sat out referee Larry O'Connell's count. After 3 minutes and 55 seconds of action his shot at the big time had come and gone. Afterwards he would admit he had never been hit so hard before in his life.

As soon as a microphone came near his face Naseem gave his new television audience exactly the kind of thing they loved to hear: 'When I say I'm supreme, people just laugh. Now what they going say when I become world champion? That was a *beautiful* workout. Oh *baby*, I'm feeling *so* good.' This time, however, he was outdone by Frank Warren who shook his head in amazement at the performance of the little gold mine he had acquired. 'He's awesome. He's got so much juice, you've not seen any of it yet. There is so much in reserve. No one's put him under pressure – what's he gonna be like then? This kid is fantastic. He's the best fighter I've ever seen in my time in boxing and I include, you know, all the Tysons.' All the Tysons indeed.

Two weeks later Naseem was back in London where it was announced his next fight would be at the Royal Albert Hall on 1 July – his third outing in the capital, which Naseem announced would soon be his second home. He said he was becoming impatient for a world title shot, and though he was still very comfortable at super bantamweight and would prefer a shot at one of the 8st 10lb world titles, he would be very happy to move up to featherweight to beat Steve Robinson. 'I'm the best boxer in Britain, and the most entertaining,' he boasted and once again he predicted he would win world titles at three, four or five weight divisions, while Brendan Ingle insisted he was capable of going all the way up to middleweight.

A week later Warren came up with an opponent: Colombia's Juan Polo Perez, a former IBF world super flyweight champion who had been a professional for nearly thirteen years during which time he had raked up a record of 36 wins (22 inside the distance), 12 losses and two draws. After a chequered early career, he hit a 14-fight unbeaten streak which included a win over former WBC flyweight champion Prudencio Cardona and a draw with former WBC super flyweight champion Sugar Baby Rojas. He finally lifted the IBF title from Ellyas Pical in 1989, but lost it to Robert Quiroga six months later.

After a brief spell in the bantamweight division, he moved up to super bantam in 1993, and a year later outpointed the former IBF world 8st 10 champion José Sanabria to get his title shot against WBA champion Wilfredo Vazquez in October 1994. Polo Perez boxed out of his skin and seemed a very clear winner, with some independent observers giving Vazquez only the last two rounds, but lost the decision. After that disappointment, Polo Perez was outpointed by twice world featherweight champion Manuel Medina and then in May lost a split decision to the world-rated South African super bantamweight champion Lehlohonolo Ledwaba. While a little past his best at the age of thirty-one, and only rated the twenty-fifth super bantam contender by the WBC, he was still crafty, elusive and tenacious enough to give a big-hitting, highly regarded contender like

Ledwaba a headache after taking the fight at short notice.

What is more, this moustachioed Colombian with a weary but unmarked face, seemed genuinely confident about the job at hand, reasoning that over the past eight months he had been sufficiently lively to 'beat' both Vazquez and Ledwaba (at least in his opinion) and figuring he could do the same with a younger, smaller and less experienced fighter like Hamed. Like so many boxers who have studied videos of Naseem's fights, he thought he saw flaws he could exploit, though he was honest enough to acknowledge the dangers. 'I know he hits hard and is very fast,' he said. 'I've also heard he is a good showman, but what he does outside of the ring is of no interest to me. I'm here to fight and give him a hard time, not just to fill a place on the bill. I will win or lose by knockout. My plan is to make him run for three rounds and finish him in the fourth.' He went on to call Hamed a 'boy' and to predict he would break the youngster's nose.

When the fight was announced Hamed had also predicted a knockout in four rounds, saying that what he had in mind was a display of sufficient brilliance to prove to the world that British fighters really did have the right stuff. After Polo Perez's forecast, however, he rose to the challenge and revised his own to a two-round knockout.

After the fight Hamed explained that his attitude was motivated by his patriotism. 'Perez is a former world champion and everybody said before, "You gonna have to watch it because he beat Vazquez and he's a great fighter and this and that." I looked at him at the press conference and he didn't impress me at all. They all come over to Britain and say they gonna beat me. No way! I'm not having that! I stare them in the eyes and they stare me back. I can't take them coming over and saying, "We gonna beat the British fighters like we done over the years," so basically I told him if he thinks he's gonna stop me in four rounds, I'm gonna stop him in two.'[12]

The Royal Albert Hall was packed with 5000 fans, most of them younger and trendier-looking than the usual boxing crowd. Naseem, who arrived with his cropped hair tinted with a light brown rinse, once again provided a pyrotechnic entry, with the customers reaching out to him in adoration as he boogied his way down the long aisle before dancing on the ring apron and then frontflipping his way into the ring. Perez (at 8st 8¾ lb weighing 1¼ lbs less than Hamed) looked on impassively though his cornermen could not help smiling. Naz viewed his opponent with contempt, moving around the ring throwing combinations in Perez's face with the look of an axeman executioner practising his strokes.

He started more cautiously than usual, pawing with his jab and making regular shifts between southpaw and orthodox, as he probed for openings and weaknesses. All the time he carried his hands by his knees and glided around with his legs spaced widely apart. The Colombian fought behind a peek-a-boo guard, jabbing and missing and occasionally trying tentative right crosses. His only success came in making Hamed miss several times, once with a breezy uppercut which would have ended things if it had landed. Midway through the round Naz suddenly switched from his playful mode and drove Polo Perez into the ropes with a solid left, and when the counter-attack arrived he bent his body backwards at what looked like a right angle and the punch flew harmlessly by. He then taunted his visitor, suggesting a try at his chin, and played with him like a kitten with a grasshopper.

From then on the pattern was that Perez would throw a punch and miss, and Hamed would land with his far harder counter. Eventually Perez connected with a single left jab, which Hamed playfully acknowledged, but that was his sole meaningful contribution to the round. At the end of the opening three minutes Naseem whacked home his corkscrew right uppercut and followed through with a left, before giving a little shrug of satisfaction and bouncing back to his stool.

In the second it was time to fulfil his revised prediction and he fought with a confidence that suggested he could end it whenever he pleased. He fought in flurries, without absorbing anything in return. At one point he came forward with such momentum that Perez was bundled into the ropes, which was certainly the wrong place to be with a puncher of Hamed's speed, accuracy and power. Eventually, after taking a heavy right hook, and several uppercuts Perez freed himself and managed to catch Naseem flush on the chin with a solid right cross, which seemed to have no effect on the rampant

21-year-old other than to increase his determination to end matters.

Showing magnificent dexterity and timing, Naseem avoided a volley of Perez punches and then, as the Colombian moved in, he fired off a devastating southpaw lead left which collided with Perez's mouth and nose and dumped him on his back. The former world champion's conqueror stood over him, with the tassels of Hamed's trunks tickling Polo Perez's nose. Hamed then skipped off to his corner with a delighted little hip shake. The dazed and confused visitor pushed himself back into a sitting position, and wobbled up on toddler legs, his nose broken and his face showing pain and resignation. But referee Mickey Vann ignored his pleading eyes and Hamed moved in for the kill, firing a southpaw right hook which missed, but landing with a big left, and then switching to orthodox and connecting with a right cross. Perez went careering into the ropes and collapsed on his forearms, conscious enough to get up, but wise enough to stay down, despite Hamed's pleas to 'take some more'.

Naseem boasted that he had taken his man out with less than 50 per cent of his power and complained that Polo Perez should have risen to take some more. 'I'm not making a song and dance about it, but believe me, they just can't take the punishment, they can't take the power,' he said. 'The power's extraordinary. I'm blessed by God. What can I say? It's a gift.' He reiterated his desire to get into the ring with one of the super bantamweight champions and to put on a show no one would forget. 'I ain't shouting my mouth off any more. I'm the best and everybody knows it. When I fight they are going to get beat, just like the rest, and in style – early nights all the way. I ain't going for long twelve rounds – make it boring. People like excitement. People want to be entertained. I'm an entertainer, and a banger and a champion too. I'm not bragging or anything, but I'm *too* good.'

Later, Naz indicated that just as had happened against Freddy Cruz in 1994, he had been stung by derogatory references to his maturity. 'He said he was gonna break my nose and silly stuff like that. He got his nose broke and straight after the fight he had to go to hospital. It all happens on them who say it and can't back it up, they gonna get hurt. But if you can say it and you can back it up, then you got no fear. I walk through fear.'[13]

Two weeks after the Polo Perez fight *Boxing News* released the results of a readership poll on 'Who is Britain's number one pound fighter?' Despite not yet having won a world title, Hamed came in first, narrowly beating Nigel Benn, with Lennox Lewis in third place.

The option of showcasing Naseem in the United States has always been a compelling one for the Hamed team, but, for one reason or another, has never materialized, several planned fights and trips there having fallen through. It was originally announced he would be fighting on Mike Tyson's comeback bill on 18 August 1995, but by this stage the Steve Robinson fight had been set for Cardiff and Naseem did no more than make another waving, hand shaking and getting in front of the TV cameras, ringside appearance.

Though he did an interview for *Ring* magazine there – and by the end of the year had been prominently featured by all the major US fight publications – he was a little disappointed with the lack of enraptured interest in the States. All anyone talked about was Tyson and no one was asking him gushing questions or seeking his predictions about what he would do to Marco Antonio Barrera, Wayne McCullough or any of the other North American fighters of his size – though this would come a few months later. 'They only seemed interested in their own boxers,' he complained, 'and to tell you the truth they didn't really know me. If you haven't been on television there, they won't know about you, and until you get that kind of exposure people aren't interested.'

His views on the United States are ambiguous – on the one hand it's a country where his boxing talents will be appreciated to the full once he receives the exposure he deserves, but on the other, it's not a country he has much desire to live in despite its palpable influence on his dress sense, musical taste and even speech patterns. 'I like America in a way, but in another way the people can be kind of shallow,' he says. 'Like, you go to a shopping mall and they have people saying to you, "Have a nice day, sir", "Nice to see you, sir", and they don't have any idea who you are, and have never met you before. I find it a bit insincere actually.'

While he resents the jingoism of much of the American press and their reluctance to recognize and appreciate the talents of all but a handful of fighters from outside the States, he has no doubt that within the next few years he will become one of the chosen few. As soon as he gets significant television exposure there he believes he will become a star of Leonard, Hagler and Hearns proportions – or even bigger. 'I know I will go down well there when they see me fight,' he predicts with a glow of anticipation. 'The Americans will love my style – they'll really appreciate it. You watch Muhammad Ali and Sugar Ray Leonard. The credit they got for winning the way they pleased and putting on a show, was phenomenal, but, you see, they were in America. When you get a British fighter doing it, they don't like the sight of it, but the Americans are going to take to me well because they will like what I do in the ring.'

Despite this view, shared by his entire entourage, his shot at US exposure continued to be like one of those maddening dreams where you can never quite get to where you're supposed to go because something always gets in the way or breaks the narrative. After the Robinson fight he was supposed to go for another US 'networking' visit, but it was never organized in time, and then it was felt that he needed to get back to training for his fight with Arnulfo Castillo, which was then twice postponed because Naz had injured his right hand.

Being specifically a Sports Network, rather than a Don King Promotions fighter means that despite the contract between King and Warren, Hamed will receive less priority from the American promoter than a British fighter contracted specifically to him (like Henry Akinwande) or jointly with Warren (like Bruno and Benn), unless King can get more out of the deal. And from Ingle's side there is a caution about handing over power to anyone else. 'We don't have a professional relationship with Don King – we're just with Frank Warren,' he says, before adding that this is not something he would rule out – depending on the terms – if it gave Hamed the kind of entrée into the US market he will need. 'Whatever suits, you know, whatever's good for his career.'

★

Like all celebrities, particularly those in Britain, Naseem could not avoid press interest in his private life, and like most he has done his best to avoid this focus becoming too specific. Naseem's public pronouncements on the subject usually dwelt primarily on the safe territory of the dangers of womanizing for boxers, something that his religion and, more particularly, Brendan Ingle, had drummed into him from an early age.

Part of the difficulty for Naseem was that the intense exposure to the attentions of considerable numbers of beautiful and 'available' women for any length of time was a relatively new phenomenon for him. Throughout his teenage years he was accustomed to spending every day of the week in the all-male environment of the gym, which meant his contact with girls outside of school hours was more limited than many of his peers. Herol Graham, for instance, says he can't recall Naseem having any serious girlfriends as a teenager. 'Not that I knew of, anyway, and I knew him very well. He might have secretly – I know I did – and there could have been the odd girl around, but not many.'

Even as an adult he continued to live at his parents' home until a few months before his twenty-second birthday, and except for his rented accommodation in Mayfair, his occasional jaunts overseas and his out of town fights, that was where he spent most of his nights. Even today, when he goes to nightclubs and public events he is always surrounded by close friends and family members who act as informal minders. In particular, his brothers Riath and Nabeel do their best to watch his back, though not always with complete success.

Naseem grew up in a household where, on the one hand, his mother and four sisters provided strong and assertive role models, but where, on the other hand, traditional views about women's roles in society and the home tended to prevail. He had to contend with his parents' advice about eventually marrying a Muslim girl, also with Brendan Ingle's frequent admonitions about the potential dangers of women to a boxer's progress and well-being. As with most gyms, the prevailing attitudes to women tended to be rather more predatory than those in the Hamed or Ingle homes, but Brendan did his utmost to ensure that Naseem was regularly reminded of the potential pitfalls of 'chasing' girls, and he saw for himself how this affected many of the best boxers in the gym, including Herol Graham. When you go to the St Thomas's gym it won't take long before you hear Brendan giving a homily on women, lust and sex. 'Ryan Rhodes, come over here, will you,' he says. 'Now tell me what are your two worst vices as a boxer?' And Rhodes dutifully replies: 'Women, and getting up late,' and Brendan will nod, and tell him: 'Right, watch them. Off you go now.'

Ingle will tell you, and his fighters, story after story about young men from his gym whose careers and lives were ruined by sex – the biggest problem in the gym and the biggest motivator in life. He'll tell you of the fighter who loses control of his emotions in the ring because he thinks his girl is not treating him right, the talented prospect who enters the ring with a streaming cold, and gets stopped, because he just can't resist the temptation to get laid behind the pub on the freezing cold night before the fight; the talented 16-year-old who loses focus and direction when he 'puts his girl in the family way', and then does it again a year later; the stablemates who are fighting over one girl, and so on. And then he will preach to them, from the Bible, from his own experience and from common sense.

'It's all been done before,' he says with a note of resignation in his voice. 'King David went with a top general's wife. It was against the religious law, against the state law. He put the top general in the frontline, got him bumped off, and then got his wife. Still happening today. The only thing that hasn't changed is human nature. You get a big breakdown in a marriage – I've seen it so many times in here, and two years later there's another partner and another kid, and then there's three partners involved, so all they're doing is making problems for themselves and for society and I explain this to them.'

Early in his professional career Naseem would often stress he had learnt from the mistakes of other boxers when it came to women and he would predict with confidence: 'You will never read about scandals involving me where women are concerned.' His response to questions on his love life tended to range from assertions of his fortitude – 'There are plenty temptations out there but I don't give in to them' – to coy hints about the implications of his virility – 'I've got female friends, let's put it like that, and it's great to have female friends because at the end of the day I'm only human, just like the rest.'

When asked whether the Prince had himself a Princess, he would deflect the question with his stock rejoinder: 'There is just one woman in my life: my mum' – to which he would sometimes add, 'There used to be two before my grandmother died.' His other frequent recourse was to stress his single-minded approach to his priorities, while making certain that no one should think for a second that he was light on his feet anywhere other than in the ring (not that anyone outside of the Cardiff hecklers ever has): 'Don't get me wrong – I love girls,' he says. 'I'm cool in all them departments, but there are problems in being a household name, and my career comes first and always has.'

But at the same time he acquired, and to some extent cultivated, a reputation as a ladies' man and a flirt, something that most of the boxing writers and social page and 'showbiz' columnists were well aware of. Usually he was happy to be seen and photographed at fights and clubs with various beautiful women, though he would refuse to discuss the details on the record. But having continually placed himself in the public eye, it was not possible to prevent the emergence of sources of information or disinformation about his personal affairs.

Much to Naseem's disgust, he woke up on 14 August 1995 to be confronted with the headline 'GLOVESTRUCK!' in the *Daily Mirror* – a story and picture focussing on, and exaggerating, his relationship with his sometime consort Kadamba Simmons – a beautiful Soho-based model and aspirant actress who had accompanied Naseem to various events, including the Nigel Benn–Gerald McClellan fight. The story went that Naseem had 'wooed' her away from Oasis singer Liam Gallagher, and then 'whisked' her away to Ibiza for a surprise holiday, and that he had helped her get over the 'heartbreak' of her breakup with another boyfriend, Nelle Hooper, the record producer and former lover of Naomi Campbell. All this had prompted her to convert to Islam so that she and Naseem could 'be closer spiritually'. Simmons, then twenty-one, was quoted discussing her relationships with all three men – Hooper, Gallagher and Hamed – and claiming that her life with the young boxer was 'pure' and 'real', that their love was 'unconditional' and that Naz made her 'feel like a woman again'.[14]

The next day, Naseem's family were confronted by the *Sheffield Star*'s take-up on this tale, which came with the banner headline: 'I'm not in love!' In this version Naseem was 'secretly' dating Simmons, and their island holiday was of the 'secret' variety. In response Naseem was quoted as saying: 'It's a load of rubbish. Just paper talk.'[15] The journalist who wrote the *Star* story, Jan Vass, later said Hamed seemed extremely irritated by the whole saga. 'He was very dismissive and annoyed and convinced me it was a lot of old cobblers, but because it was Naseem we ran it anyway,' he said.

Later, however, when approached on the subject by the *Mirror*, he moderated his response. 'Kadamba is a nice girl,' he was quoted as saying, 'but it's not going anywhere. She's not the love of my life and she has overstated the relationship. I'm living my life and she's living hers.' And to this he added the more general point that 'no one would blame me if I was not 100 per cent', stressing that his actions had to be viewed by taking his age into account: 'I think like any other 21-year-old man. I'm only human. God put us here for a purpose and that is to procreate.'[16]

The former *Daily Mirror* columnist responsible for the original story, Kate Thornton, acknowledged that there may have been some hyperbole in her principal source's account, but insisted that the substance was correct. 'Look, Kadamba Simmons is a bit of a publicity seeker but we had proof that Naseem had a relationship with her, took her to Ibiza and later dumped her.' Simmons, on the other hand, told me she was extremely unhappy with the way the stories were used, describing Thornton as a 'nasty journalist' and the *Sheffield Star* story as 'all fantasy and rubbish, absolute fantasy', to which she added, 'Let's face it, 80 per cent of what is written in the papers is complete invention anyway.'

So ended Naseem Hamed's first brush with tabloid muckraking, and, rather surprisingly, after this he became a little less reticent in discussing his personal life and attitudes – speaking, for instance, on what he looks for in a women ('Great personality – funny, you know. Top bod. Great bod, got to be really fit. Good looking')[17] as well as on his reasons for avoiding long-term commitment until he was older.

At the same time he became rather more cautious and even suspicious about casual liaisons. He also became more intensely aware of the way, as he saw it in his chauvinistic frame of reference, Mike Tyson was 'set up' with his rape conviction, and considered this as a vital lesson to be learnt. This came through particularly strongly in a series of interviews he did shortly before winning the WBO world title. 'Being twenty-one is hard – you have to keep women at arm's length,' he was quoted as saying. 'Basically you don't want to fall into the same trap as Mike Tyson. But come on: are you really expected to believe that girl went to his bedroom at two in the morning because she wanted to have a picture of Tyson to give to her dad? If she had come to my hotel bedroom at two in the morning, well – but then I am a bit more on the ball. I have my head screwed on. No girl will ever rip me off or pull any strokes. Women are so devious it's untrue. That's why I cannot commit myself to any girl right now. My commitment is to my sport.'[18]

And in another interview four months after the Kadamba Simmons 'exposé' broke, he referred more specifically to his disappointment and bewilderment about the way he was treated. 'I meet girls, but there's some girls when I meet them, I think to myself, "Well, obviously I've got to keep her at arms length because she might be a bit tricky",' he said. 'I mean you know when you meet girls nowdays, and they can say hello in a public place and basically they can go away and make up some kind of stupid story and sell it to the papers, and obviously you look in the paper and think to yourself, "What is this? Is this with me? How come it's happened to me? Why has it happened to me?" You do get some kind of girls that are tricky and you can get set up in life. Tricky women!'[19]

Right from the start of 1995 the prime aim of the Naseem Hamed project was to get him a shot at a world title – any world title – as soon as it could be arranged. Having reluctantly scotched the original idea – to start with a bantamweight crown – Naseem moved up in weight and Warren put his feelers out to the various holders of world super bantamweight titles. The immediate problem they faced came in their access to the champions and to those behind them, pulling the strings. They needed to cultivate the right channels in the various international control bodies to improve Naseem's world ratings, and also to find a manager of one of the champions who was prepared to take the risk for the biggest purse of their fighter's life. All this proved to be far more difficult than anyone anticipated.

For anyone who has ever counted themselves a serious follower of boxing, the most depressing aspects of the sport – that frequently drive bedrock fans to the point of despair – is the venality and maladministration of the organizations which have appointed themselves the task of controlling the sport at an international level, and the way these alphabet bodies have mutated over the last two decades to the point where one can no longer talk about a 'world' champion as such.

This does not imply a sentimental desire for a return to the sport's 'golden age', whenever that might have been (each generation of boxing writers tends to put it at the time they were children). In fact the good old days were pretty bad old days for many fighters. In the United States organized crime had a lockhold on the sport, to the point where even some of the 'legends' had their mob protectors and sponsors.[20] Fights were regularly fixed and many fighters were given little option but to take a dive or take a hike (and sometimes to take a bullet). Even some of the greats 'threw' fights on occasion.[21] Also, with only one world title for each of the eight divisions (most of the time), some of the finest fighters of all time were frozen out because they were the wrong colour,'[22] because they did not have the right mob or managerial connections or were too good for their own good[23] or because they were not American.[24]

Today, fights are still sometimes fixed, but less frequently, and usually by bribing the referees and judges rather than blackmailing or bribing the boxers. Racism has diminished and there is a far wider international spread of champions and of the sport more generally. The role of organized crime in boxing has been significantly reduced. Fewer boxers are squeezed out of title shots, partly because there are more titles to go around. And mainly because of television, boxers are paid better, even in relative terms, and certainly have a good deal more power than in the pre-Ali days when they were not expected to speak or think for themselves. The medical controls over the sport have also improved.

But where things are undoubtedly much worse is in terms of the value of world titles and the power and spread of the organizations that manufacture them. The world title prospects of top boxers depend more than ever on the relationship their promoters have with the various bosses of the alphabet bodies. Their world ratings can appear to have little to do with who's beaten whom or who is best at each weight, and everything to do with who is paying whom. They can freeze out fighters whose managers or promoters they don't like; they can obstruct unification fights which might result in them losing money; they can create phony titles to spread the largesse further; they can also charge exorbitant fees for the honour of fighting for, promoting and holding their titles. They have devalued the notion of a world champion to the point where it now means very little at all.

While it may also be true that they sometimes help boxers – introducing new safety regulations, pension and hardship funds and providing a semblance of control which might otherwise be absent in some countries (and some would say that by merely existing and continuing to breed new progenies they give more boxers the chance to make money and claim glory) basically they exist to provide jobs, perks and kickbacks for the boys, which is why they continue to proliferate – it's a fine way to print money.

From the start of 1995, Frank Warren began to focus his efforts on getting the WBA champion Wilfredo Vazquez into the ring with Naseem Hamed, partly because he was more attainable than the other champions at that stage, but also because he was a relatively prestigious name fighter, ready to be taken. As Warren put it at the time: 'Vasquez is made for Naz. He'd keep coming forward and that would suit him down to the ground.'

With Naseem not rated as the number one contender by the WBA, Warren's only option was to tempt the champion into a match with a sufficiently lucrative offer. But Vazquez's management, having heard of Hamed's prowess, strung Warren along – expressing interest in the fight but showing a marked reluctance to come to terms. Warren made what was then an unprecedented offer for fighters of that weight (of nearly $500,000) for the fight to take place in Sheffield or Glasgow in late April or May 1995, and at the same time Naseem made it clear he was happy to travel to

Puerto Rico or France if the champion insisted. Vazquez's management, the Acaries brothers of France, eventually responded
that they wanted options on Hamed's future fights, or, alternat-
ively an even higher purse offer. Warren was open to the latter
option and the parties agreed to a tentative date of 15 July, with
the football stadium in Sana'a in the Yemen being cited as a
probable venue.

In the meantime, however, Vazquez was required to make his
mandatory defence against Venezuela's Antonio Cermeno.
Warren did everything in his power to stop this happening, even
offering Cermeno $100,000 to step aside, with the guarantee he
would fight the winner (a large sum for what is a common practice
in the modern fight game). Cermeno's people, seeing the declining Vazquez as a far easier touch, turned him down. Vazquez was
duly outpointed, forcing Warren to start from scratch with the
new champion, while beginning to talk to the managements of the
other champions.

Despite continuing to whip fighters who were rated by one or
more of the alphabet bodies, Hamed was still not granted the
number one slot by any of them – being frozen at the number
three position by both the WBC and the IBF and at number five
by the WBA for several months. This meant that Warren had to
plug away at persuading one of the champions to risk his title
against Naseem voluntarily.

After failing to come to terms with Cermeno's management
(despite the fact that he was promoted by Don King), Warren
tried the WBC champion Hector Acero-Sanchez, but was
effectively turned down. It was only in late July 1995, by which
stage Hamed had made five defences of his WBC International
title, and had beaten seven WBC contenders, that the WBC
granted Hamed the number one position in its rankings. But it
still would have taken several more months to force
Acero-Sanchez into the ring, and by that stage the Hamed–
Robinson fight had already been set.

Warren also opened tentative discussions with Rodney
Berman, promoter of the IBF champion Vuyani Bungu (who
was also regarded as the legitimate world champion by *Boxing
News*) in June 1995. Bungu was a well-respected champion,
having defeated the highly regarded American, Kennedy

McKinney, for the title in 1994, and following that with six defences by early 1996. He also appeared to be genuinely confident he could beat Hamed and there was a war of words between the pair. Berman, seeing it at best as a high risk fight, held out for a purse of £300,000, plus rights to Hamed's next three title defences if he won, and the fight was shelved for the time being.

The only other option at super bantamweight was the WBO title, which Warren was initially reluctant to pursue because of his attitude to the WBO hierarchy and because it was widely regarded as the weakest and least prestigious of the alphabet bodies. This changed in the course of the year as the WBO won brownie points for cleaning up aspects of its act, and, more importantly, when the extremely formidable unbeaten Mexican, Marco Antonio Barrera, outpointed Daniel Jimenez to take the title. Warren had no doubt that Naseem could stop Barrera but because of the Mexican's promotional ties, it was not an easy fight to make despite Naseem being granted the number one contender spot in the WBO super bantamweight rankings early in 1995. It was also felt that it would make more financial sense to build this one up over a year or so, to make it the eventual superfight of the division in late 1996.

Meanwhile Naseem himself was becoming frustrated with Warren's failure to provide him with the chance to get his hands on a title belt, and therefore the option of putting him in with Steve Robinson became increasingly attractive. Originally this was seen as a fight to be held further down the line – after Naseem had picked up one or more of the super bantam titles – but he could not wait any longer. With Robinson under contract to Sports Network it was felt negotiations would be less complicated than with any of the other champions, even though it would inevitably result in one of Warren's major attractions being devalued by defeat. It would also raise questions about the ethics of Warren putting up one of his own world champions whom he clearly expected, and hoped, would be beaten by another of his fighters.

What this meant was that Warren needed to strengthen his ties with the WBO, which he proceeded to do with spectacular results. Suddenly Hamed, a boxer who had never before

ventured into the featherweight division, was made the number
one contender for Robinson's title, meaning that the Welshman
had no option but to fight him or be stripped of his crown (a step
the WBO threatened to take when the Robinson camp
wriggled). The promoter insists he made no representations to
this effect, that the decision to challenge Robinson was made by
Hamed and Ingle alone, and that the move to make Hamed the
mandatory contender was the WBO's alone. It is certainly not
beyond the realms of possibility that the WBO, seeing a chance
to further upgrade its championship stock, took this expedient
decision unilaterally. At the same time, it hardly needs stating
that had Warren not made efforts to improve relations with the
WBO hierarchy, they would have had little interest in accommodating Hamed with such a display of generosity.

Today Warren says that despite the appearance of hypocrisy
on his part, his change in attitude about the WBO is entirely a
consequence of the overhaul in the organization's *modus operandi*
and the removal of various office-bearers he regarded as
particularly loathsome.

But when he talks about the post-1995 WBO, he is
extraordinarily fulsome in his praise, calling the changes a
'revolution', and, with even an larger dose of hyperbole,
portraying the current all-Puerto Rican regime as an angelic
host. 'The new people at the top have cleaned it up and have
nothing but my admiration because what they are doing is right,'
he says, with no hint of a tongue anywhere near a cheek. 'They
cleared away all the old dead wood and they're giving everybody
a fair crack at the whip which means that the boxers, the
managers, the promoters, everyone does well and that's what
I'm happy with. I think the WBO is now coming into second
place among the control bodies.'

Naseem didn't give a toss about any of this. All he wanted was
a title belt to strap around his waist, and when Warren told him
it would be Steve Robinson, he was delighted. He'd been
needling 'Stevo' ever since the Belcastro fight and he'd been
given a rough ride by the Cardiff crowd for the Ramirez fight
and when Robinson fought Pedro Ferradas, and now it was
payback time. He knew the Welshman's style was made for him,
he liked the idea of proving himself against a bigger man and he

loved the idea of humiliating the yahoos who had spat at him, and chanted obscene and sometimes racist slogans. The title, as he saw it, was his from the moment the fight was announced.

9

The Future Delayed

When Naseem woke up in the afternoon of 1 October 1995 he had a smile on his face that pushed the minor aches and stiffness from the night before far to the back of his mind. He was the WORLD champion: the fact that the world of the WBO was a parochial one did not interest him. It was wonderful – marvellous as Old Irish put it – he had arrived.

'I've always wanted to be world champion so bad,' he said. 'Everybody had put faith in me – God, my family, the people behind me, all my supporters – and they'd seen me since I was a little child, growing up, and I'd been telling them it was gonna happen because I knew in my heart that I was going to beat Robinson, and then I went out and did it and it was an absolutely unbelievable feeling becoming a world champion.'

He arrived back in Sheffield to a hero's welcome and to a family who were both ecstatic and, some of them at least, a little overwhelmed by the experience. They had all expected him to beat Robinson, but when the moment arrived it took a while for the fact to sink in – that their little son or sibling had become the

216

most famous Yemeni in the world, the toast of Sheffield, the champion of the *world*. As 15-year-old Saba, Naseem's youngest sister, put it: 'He's been training hard for all of my life, ever since I can remember, not just for this fight but for all his fights, and he just sort of pops up out of nowhere and suddenly he's famous. He's been great, really great.'

Ali Hamed, who had turned eighteen a month before the fight, was the family member with the most intimate feel for the game – being a talented amateur with lofty professional ambitions himself – and he'd been reassuring some of the more nervous members of his clan that Naz would win handsomely. But even he admitted some surprise at how easily it happened, and it brought home to him the speed in which his older brother had gone from being just a normal member of the family to being an international celebrity. 'We never thought he would succeed this well and basically it's been a bit of a shock,' he said. 'Really, his success has gone beyond our wildest imaginations. He's always expected it but not everybody else, in my opinion, and for the rest of the family was, well, because they're not really into the boxing game like I am, so whatever I think, their opinion is like mine. But once it happened – once he knocked Robinson out – it was unbelievable. The feeling was overwhelming. He was just fantastic, and I felt very, very proud of him.'

And for Naseem this was only the start. Each taste of fame and fortune made him hunger for more and more. More victories, more title belts – that was most important – more money, more cars, more houses, more clothes, more women, more recognition, more public adoration, more family love. He couldn't wait.

I caught up with Naseem at the Dorchester Hotel in London a fortnight after his title triumph. He arrived in his brand new Porsche Carrera 4 ('Oh no, *not* the Porsche, not the *Porsche*, he's never even driven it before, let alone in London,' his brother, Riath, complained) – with a couple of days' stubble and obviously exhausted after two weeks of partying, but surprisingly contrite at being over an hour late. By his standards his mood was introspective. He felt like talking quietly.

We were later to discover that during our hour or so together, the life of another Warren fighter, James Murray, was ebbing away while drunken yahoos were throwing chairs, cutlery and bottles at his conqueror, Drew Docherty – the man who had so adeptly avoided Naseem's challenges two years earlier. Fighting for the British bantamweight title in Glasgow, Murray had dropped his rival twice and looked to be headed for victory, but with only 36 seconds to go in the final round, the light-punching Docherty put Murray down for the first time in his career and he never woke up. Afterwards, when the incident reopened the debate about the legality of the sport, Frank Warren said he found it hard to justify an argument in favour of boxing at that moment, though later he was to pledge £400,000 to help improve the safety of boxers, and specifically to raise money for the introduction of compulsory MRI brain scans.

Though we had no knowledge of what was happening at that out-of-control dinner show, we soon got on to the subjects of mortality and immortality, and, more mundanely, of the risks of Naseem's chosen profession. He told me the boxers most in danger of brain damage or worse were those who had not adequately mastered the art of self-defence, and those whose trainers insisted they had real wars in sparring, with plenty of hard head blows to prepare them for the real thing.

'If you take a lot of stick and hammering in the gym in training, it's not going to be very good for you when you box, which is why we spar mainly to the body,' he said, and went on to insist that in any event, in his case, the dangers were minimal. 'I know how to box, how to survive, how to punch. I just know a massive amount about boxing, and I know the risks. You know, in my whole time in this sport – fourteen years – I haven't even had a proper black eye yet so I can't see myself getting hurt. I have mastered the art of boxing.'

But what about his opponents? The men who were on the other end of his punches? Did he feel sorry for them ever? No, he said, a boxer couldn't get into that, and he laughed at the idea – not in a malicious sense, but just that it struck him as absurd that he should ever feel sorry for the consequences of doing his job. 'You can't think compassion,' he said, chuckling some more, 'you can't think sympathy or anything like that for your opponent. Your mind is on something totally different altogether. Your mind is on winning and you have to be so single-minded and straightforward in your thoughts. What you want is there in front of you and you've got to take it, and you got to take it in the time you have, because if you don't you may miss the boat and then it's over.'

And how would he feel if an opponent was seriously injured, or died? Again, that incredulous look. I should know better than to ask – all boxers know the score, especially the professionals, and must be prepared to take the consequences. 'If that happened – if, say I seriously hurt someone – I'd just have to blank it out of my mind and and keep on going. It all comes down to knowing that what is written for a man is written,' he said.

Even in his quieter moments it does not take much for Naseem to get on to his idea of what is written for him. He had so many ideas and plans and he wanted to fulfil them all at once – to 'chill out' in Barbados for a while, travel around the United States, tour the whole of the Middle East 'to meet the main men everywhere', more time to resample the night life of London, a giant shopping spree – new car, dream house in Sheffield, a flat in London, an island in the Caribbean ('you got to have your own island'), more clothes, a kitchen for his mum, the works. Oh, yes, and some hard training for his next fight on 9 December, and make that for another world title, Mr Warren, and then a *big* fight in America, and some more champions to beat – Barrera, Bungu, McCullough, maybe even Oscar de la Hoya one day.

As it turned out, he got the cars (the Porsche and a new top-of-the-range Mercedes from the Yemeni president), the house on the outskirts of Sheffield (a modern mansion purchased from former Sheffield Wednesday manager Trevor Francis), the time out in London and four days in Qatar, and a new girlfriend, but most of the best laid plans of the best fighter in the world fizzled out one by one, and after the highest moment of his life came six months of the lowest – no Caribbean holiday (he had to wait until April 1996 for that one), no US tour, no more title belts (just a lot of hassle about his first one), no new London flat, no island. Instead a broken hand, a postponed fight, a re-injured hand, a cancelled fight, and reams of bad press and negative publicity. To be sure, there were plenty of laughs; it's just that it was meant to be so much better and bigger, so much sooner.

Three days later I met up with him again at the Mayfair apartment block where he was renting a bachelor flat for £950 a week. It's a garishly expensive block with plush carpeting and ostentatious decor, which provides the setting for a slow stream of wealthy, mainly Middle Eastern businessmen who slip in and out, some followed by none-too-elegant local ladies of the night. Once again Naseem was over an hour late, and apologetic for it – he just wanted to get dressed up and buy some tickets for *Grease*. He was in the mood for a night out, so neither of us mentioned James Murray. But he brought down something to show off: his pride and joy, the WBO title belt, which he draped over his shoulders, then around his waist and then handed to me, to get a feel of its weight and splendour.

Trouble was, this particular belt actually belonged to Steve Robinson (Naseem's hadn't arrived yet), and, according to Robinson's manager, Dai Gardiner, Naz was only supposed to have borrowed it overnight for publicity pictures and then return it the day after the fight. Instead, ten days later, the new champion took it with him for a short trip to Qatar, where he had an audience with the Emir and, naturally, took the belt to show him and to parade around during his public appearances there, finally handing it back to Frank Warren after returning home.

Robinson, however, was extremely distressed about his missing token of past glory, as was Dai Gardiner who called the whole thing 'disgusting and unprofessional' and threatened to call the police. Eventually, six weeks after their fight, it was returned to Robinson's solicitors. The incident caused a spate of bad publicity in Sheffield and Wales – the first of several incidents that were to plague the new champion over the next few months.

Immediately after Naseem returned from Qatar, he was inundated with scores of other requests for public appearances, interviews and endorsements and at the same time Brendan was telling him it was time to return to the gym for a 9 December date with an opponent still to be announced. He squeezed in as much as he could before Brendan won the day: making appearances at local sports events; joining Sheffield Wednesday in backing a major anti-racism rally in Manchester, organized by the Trade Union Congress – perhaps his most overtly political public action to date; enthusiastically participating in an anti-graffiti, littering and vandalism drive in the poverty-stricken Brightside area, and helping to raise funds for the Yemeni Community Centre, by giving them twelve Naz-designed, multicoloured tracksuits for auction (at around £2,000 a shot). Together with Joe Bloggs, he also launched his own range of clothes, which, hardly surprisingly, won high praise from the company. 'He has real talent and could make a living as a designer,' said Joe Bloggs managing director Shami Ahmed.

Meanwhile Hamed had to contend with another irritating little controversy. After his victory over Robinson, the General Secretary of the British Boxing Board of Control, John Morris, admonished Naseem for his antics in the ring. A month later the Board finally got it together to publicly congratulate him on winning the title, while at the same time requesting him to stop humiliating the man in front of him. In response Naseem made it quite clear no changes were envisaged. 'I'm not holding back for anything,' he said. 'I've listened to the Boxing Board and spoken to John Morris. Their letter didn't exactly say "Do not do that" or "If you do it again . . ."; it just said try not to do it again. My style's not changing for no man. My style suits me. It's a great formula, a winning formula.'

But though the Board let the matter rest, Naseem's detractors in the media continued to plug away at the issue for several months. There were stories saying he was behaving like a 'prat', criticizing his post-fight gesticulations (which Brendan claimed were really nothing but a 'Yemeni sign'), and most particularly his behaviour in the ring. ITV commentator and *Boxing News* columnist Reg Gutteridge was especially vociferous, expressing strong reservations about Naseem's 'strut, his jungle boy shorts and demeaning an opponent'. And he went on to write: 'Okay, the punters love it, they say. The "Board" have frequently blown in his ear. I know a referee . . . who threatened to "throw you over the ropes if you do it again". That's telling him. Try that intangible thing called class, Naz, it works. You rarely get hit, which suggests you can last the course and keep on winning. You don't need an act and beware the bright lights.'[1]

Henry Cooper, the popular former British, European and Commonwealth heavyweight champion, went even further, announcing that the 'crazy hype' of modern boxing – the interminable sound-light-laser shows and tactics like Naseem's – had made him disillusioned with the sport, and that he was therefore retiring early as BBC Radio's ringside inter-round summarizer. He said he objected most strongly to the way Hamed 'humiliates and taunts his opponents', while acknowledging that 'doubtless he will call me old-fashioned'.

Brendan Ingle replied that the old heavyweight was, indeed, way out of time – the crowds loved the craziness and in any event Cooper should consider himself lucky that he twice had a chance to fight Muhammad Ali, the man who started it all in the early sixties. To which Cooper responded: 'Ali was different. He did it with some wit for a start, and he knew that you knew his antics were just his way of scoring a psychological point. He always did it with a little twinkle in his eye. You could always see his tongue in his cheek, and he meant you to.'[2]

Memory, it seems, has a way of softening the blows and as Cooper acknowledged, boxing has moved on, even if not everyone wants to move with it. Naseem's approach works in an era where television exposure is everything. As *Boxing News* editor, Harry Mullan, put it in his contribution to the debate, 'Hamed, like him or not, is the modern face of the sport.'[3]

The other point made by Naseem's followers is that boxers like Ali and Hamed are allowed a little more leeway because of their exceptional flair and talent. They set themselves up with outrageous claims, and then deliver by making good. As long as they can walk that wire, and continue to pull the punters, the room for complaint is limited.

Beyond the newspaper debating forums, however, there was also a hint of unhappiness that Hamed's arrogance extended outside the ring. There were tales of well-wishers and autograph hunters, journalists and even old would-be friends who had been given the cold shoulder or felt the bite of his sarcasm. But then again he was not always this way. Watching him treating the doorman at his Mayfair apartment with impeccable courtesy and politeness, or allowing an extra half hour to a photographer and then agreeing to pose with him despite being late for a show, or giving an old Arab man, not known to him, ten minutes of his time in his broken Arabic, suggested a very different mentality.

What is clear is that even while he lusts for more and more fame, he has started to realize it has its drawbacks. Wherever he is, people come up to him to slap his back or high-five him, give him unwanted advice, criticize some aspect of his behaviour or his performance, demand his autograph with a pen that doesn't work, ask for their photograph to be taken with their Polaroid and then remark, 'I never realized you were so short,' or give him the 'put it here, old son' routine when they've never met him before.

Sometimes, for instance, when he's out with his girlfriend wanting to be left in peace, he snaps. 'There's times when you like it and times when you don't,' he said two months after winning the title. 'There's times when you want to go out and you don't want to be hassled at all, you don't even want to be spotted, but obviously a lot of people like boxing, so I do get spotted nearly everywhere I go, but I'm holding it down and when people come up I try to treat them in the best way.'[4]

What really gets to him are the casual acquaintances from way back who suck up to celebrity and presume or pretend a friendship which doesn't exist. It is something he has had to put up with ever since he first got his name and picture in the paper as a 12-year-old, and discovered that the classmates who a few years earlier had called him 'chocolate drop' and 'Paki' were treating suddenly him like a long-lost mate. 'I know who my real friends are, though – the people I've known for ages,' he said in one interview. 'You can't just let anybody on the bandwagon but I'm not overly suspicious because of my great sixth sense. I'm a good judge of character.'[5]

His close friends insist that he hasn't changed and that he still treats them in the same way as before. Ryan Rhodes, who has been one of his best chums for thirteen years, says their friendship remains strong despite the fact that he does not see Naz as much as before. 'Before he became world champion he was flashy Naz,' he says, 'and now he's still the same flashy Naz as what he used to be, so in my eyes he hasn't changed. Not to me he hasn't. Not *really*.'

The due date for Naseem's return to the gym finally arrived: 2 October, five weeks before his next fight, set for the London Arena on 9 December. After over a month of searching in vain for an appropriate opponent – IBF super bantamweight champion Vuyani Bungu and former WBA champion Wilfredo Vazquez were at the top of a long list but neither could be persuaded to come to London at that time – Warren settled on the flashy, unbeaten 24-year-old Los Angeles-based Mexican, Arnulfo 'Chico' Castillo, who had won all his 19 professional fights, 11 of them inside the distance.

The view at the St Thomas's Boys' Club gym was that Naz probably wouldn't make it in that afternoon. The whisperings had grown louder – that he wasn't training as hard as before, that he was too taken up with his celebrity lifestyle, that he wasn't approaching his job with the same fire as before. Most of the professionals were more guarded in their opinions, but some of the youngsters were saying that over the past year he had significantly reduced his training load – that he used to work out every single day for six weeks but that by the time of the Robinson fight he had cut this to four weeks, was regularly missing gym sessions, and was no longer working out between fights. In partial mitigation, some of his more loyal gym mates were saying that he no longer needed to train for the same length of time, that his body clicked into the routine faster than before and it took less work for him to reach that unimprovable peak. Others felt he was tempting fate. Brendan Ingle was saying what he had always said: 'The only man who can beat Naz is Naz himself,' but this time there was a hint of resignation in his voice and a slight, knowing smile.

His trainers, Brendan and John, were allowing him a bit of indulgence – after the way he destroyed Robinson they could hardly do otherwise – but some of his erstwhile peers in the gym were less certain. They were not bitter or anything, but if you spent any time there, it was hard to escape the impression that there was a strong collective longing for the old, mad, bad, carefree Naz, or at least for the Naz who just couldn't stay out of the gym.

His own view is that this is all a load of nonsense – that he has not let the public adulation go to his head, and that he does exactly what is needed to get him in perfect condition to go twelve fast rounds and win. 'Success has not changed me in any way,' he insists. 'My feet are firmly on the ground, my goals are there and my mind's set on what I'm going to get. When it comes to training, I'll always be prepared and ready for anything I've got to take, and I take things with two hands and I make sure. When I get to fight I have hit a certain peak because I have always trained hard, and that's why my balance, my timing, my coordination is totally perfect. So there's no slackness whatsoever.'

Naseem confounded the doubters that day by not only arriving, but arriving on time. He had been out of training for five weeks but his weight was still only 9st 3lb – significantly less than most top notch bantamweights when 'resting'. He chatted a bit to his buddies – Ryan, Johnny, Chris Saunders – and pulled on his leopardskin skirt and a Muhammad Ali T-shirt, did a few rounds of shadow boxing for a television company, wrapped and taped his own hands, fitted his 'Prince' gumguard and then proceeded to do eight fast rounds of light sparring with three boxers – a flyweight, a welterweight and a nifty little junior who played Naz to Hamed's Herol Graham. Occasionally he would whack in a few heavy body shots with the adults, but mostly he was concentrating on speed, defence and coordination. He looked fast and sharp and at the end of eight rounds he was still unnervingly fresh. When it was over he did a quick television interview, showered and drove off. Though he was in the gym for barely forty-five minutes, it looked like it would not take too many of these sessions to get him into peak shape again.

Over the next couple of days Naseem stepped it up considerably – more rounds of sparring, working on the heavy bag, the pearl ball and the speed ball. Four days of this, and everything was beginning to flow, but then disaster struck. He was working on the pads with John Ingle and he fired a heavy right cross which landed at the wrong angle. A shock of intense pain went through the hand and up the arm and he knew immediately that something was wrong. It was the same feeling he'd had, in the same hand, as when he outpointed Michael

Wright for the junior ABA title in 1990, though this time the pain was more intense. The X-rays confirmed the worst suspicions: a chip in the metacarpal bones at the back of the hand, and the specialist insisted that the only solution was at least two months' rest for the bones to heal. The Castillo fight therefore had to be postponed until 10 February.

Naseem was devastated by the news, but soon realized that he had no option but to accept it stoically. In early 1994 his fight with Peter Harris had been cancelled after he twisted an ankle, but that was a relatively minor fight and he was back in action less than six weeks later. It represented no more than a hiccup in his career. This time there was far more at stake, not just for Naseem himself, but for Frank Warren, Sky and his sponsors.

Prior to the injury he had been due to follow the 9 December fight with a February date against Vuyani Bungu and there was talk of following this by featuring him on the undercard of the Mike Tyson–Frank Bruno fight on 16 March in Las Vegas. At a mimimum, the injury pushed the Bungu option out of the way for several months and meant that Naseem's hope to win a second world title early in the New Year had been dashed. More generally, it meant that the momentum he had established of regular action and constant challenges, had been broken.

To make matters worse he had to contend with a series of rumours about how the injury occurred. One version had it that it was in a fight in a Sheffield nightclub. Another that it happened in a London snooker hall, and that Naz had to take refuge under a snooker table after being attacked with a cue which he had blocked with his right hand. There was also a view that, in line with an established boxing tradition, 'hand injury' was a euphemism for some other problem or perhaps just for a lack of preparedness. It got to the point where Naseem, Brendan and Frank had to make a specific point of scotching these stories at a press conference called to announce the new date, during which they insisted that it did, indeed, happen in the gym.

The effect of this setback was to send Naseem back to London for a fresh wave of celebrity turns, more nightclubbing, snooker and an intense schedule of newspaper and magazine interviews, television and radio appearances and advertising endorsements, as well as a couple of trips to France and a rap project with the

Lancashire Asian group Khaliphz, in which Naseem's voice can be heard on the backing track of one of their singles. There were also official invitations to visit the United Arab Emirates, Dubai and Saudi Arabia, as well as the Yemen again (where a set of six stamps – two featuring his face and four showing pictures of his fights – had been issued in his honour), but all of these were turned down for the moment.

At the end of 1995 he also came in for his share of awards of various levels of prestige. He travelled to Paris in December for the ninth French Golden Gloves awards ceremony where he was honoured as Outstanding Newcomer, though his French hosts were none too impressed by what was taken as his arrogant and cocky manner. He was also one of the hosts for Sky's Sportstar of the Year awards ceremony, where he won the 'Shooting Star' and 'TV Entertainer of the Year' awards and received a glowing commendation from Sylvester Stallone. The American magazine, *Boxing Illustrated*, made him their 'New Face of the Year' and he won 'Fighter of the Year' awards from the *Boxing News* readers' poll, the Boxing Writers' Club, the Professional Boxers' Association and the British Boxing Board of Control.

But trouble continued to follow him, often not of his own making. In December a new Hamed video was released, *Prince Naseem – The Making of a Legend*, focusing on his amateur days and his first professional fight. Unfortunately, it caused a storm of unwanted publicity because it included a Naz voice-over, taped when he was only sixteen-years old, with a statement some regarded as reflecting anti-Pakistani sentiments: 'I'm looking forward to become known as a British, Arab and a Muslim, but I'm definitely British. You hear my accent. It's like the normal, Yorkshire white kid. When the Pakistanis talk, they always got an accent. Most of the Arabs have got a normal, Yorkshire accent like me.'[6]

Hardly surprisingly this did not go down well among many British Asians, and the comment was seen by some as playing into existing tensions between sections of Yorkshire's Arab and Pakistani communities. *Boxing Monthly* carried several vociferous letters on the issue over two months, most, it must be said, from Pakistanis who defended him. Apparently many of his detractors on this issue did not realize that Naseem was still an unsophisticated teenager when he made the remark – one which seems to reflect more of a desire by a young, first generation Englishman to identify with his country and region, as well as with his parents' origins, rather than any deep ethnic prejudice. Given Naseem's history of anti-racist activity and sentiment, and the way he mixes so easily with lads from a very wide variety of ethnic origins – including Pakistani – in the gym, it would be silly to read anything more into it.

But the debate prompted an obviously shaken Naseem to reply at the *Boxing Monthly* editor's invitation: 'I am sorry if any remark on the video caused offence to anyone, but please understand that what I was attempting to put across is that while I am proud to be both British and Yemeni, my accent belongs to the part of the world I was raised in. I meant no offence to anyone and I certainly have nothing against Pakistanis or any other race. I view myself as a symbol of multi-cultural success. A champion of all people, a true champion of the world.'[7]

Naseem had reached a position by this stage where he was assiduously avoided by many top-notch boxers who had a great deal to lose by fighting him, even when confronted with career-highest purse offers, but at the same time he was constantly courted and challenged by lesser fighters with a great deal to gain, financially speaking. This was particularly the case with British boxers who saw in Naseem the kind of payday that would set them up for life. As Brendan Ingle put it: 'They're the men with the knives and forks and Naz has got the steak.'

Knowing that none of these would-be opponents were anything near his class, and resenting being challenged on his own turf, Naseem loved nothing better than deriding them, telling the press what would happen to them if they ever got their chance – how many rounds he would take them out in and how he would end their careers – and this caused a genuine edge to emerge in some of these intended rivalries. And perhaps none more so than between Naz and the quick, stylish but fragile and light-fisted former WBO featherweight champion, Colin McMillan.

At the time he won his world title from Maurizio Stecca in 1992, 'Sweet C' was viewed by many British observers as a boxer of immense international potential, but four months later he lost the title as a result of a severely dislocated shoulder to Colombia's Ruben Palacio. After a series of operations which put him out of action for thirteen months, he came straight back to challenge the new WBO champion Steve Robinson. He was facing a range of domestic problems, his shoulder was far from being in full working order, but he figured Robinson was a soft target, and instead was outpointed. More surgery and rest followed, and he finally returned in 1995 with a four-fight contract with Frank Warren which was intended to end in a world title shot. But he could not get a world rating, and his position as secretary of the Professional Boxers' Association – the boxers' union – did not seem to endear him to the Boxing Board. McMillan was becoming increasingly frustrated.

Several years earlier, when Naz was at the end of his amateur career, the pair of them had sparred together, and unlike most of the Sheffield teenager's celebrity sparmates, McMillan insists he had Hamed's measure. 'He really didn't give me any problems then. He was not used to men who could match his speed and I was able to make him box to my pattern,' he says. Less realistically, McMillan feels he could do it again if they ever met for real, though he acknowledges that Naseem is a 'really tremendous talent'. But instead he had to face being derided by this fellow exactly eight years younger than himself, who held his old title, and the anger and frustration of this intelligent and gentlemanly boxer led to an 'incident' in the Hanover Grand nightclub in London, which became the subject of a great deal of conjecture. There was talk of a major row, a scuffle, even a brawl. In fact, it was no more than an animated conversation.

As McMillan relates it: 'He had been going around saying that he was going to knock me out and put me in retirement with a final payday. Usually I'm easygoing about that sort of nonsense, but the way he did it made me a bit angry, so I went up to him at the nightclub and confronted him. I said, "You've been saying all these things, so when we gonna get it on?" and he said he was willing to fight me any time, but he wasn't aggressive about it – he was fine. We talked and there was definitely no scuffle. I don't know where that came from.'

Soon after, McMillan received his call-up, but the terms were not to his liking. He turned down what he called the 'derisory

amount' Warren put on the table, claiming it was five times less
than what he was used to receiving from Warren when he was a
world champion. Instead, with his contract having expired,
McMillan decided to leave Warren and go it alone. Naseem,
however, remained eager to get his would-be rival into the ring
and, after beating Said Lawal two months later, he taunted
McMillan again: 'Everybody out there who are listening –
especially the fighters that want to fight me, like "Sweet C" and
stupid people like that in Britain, they'll get knocked out,
sparko!' he announced.

At the start of the new year, Naseem returned to light
training, but as soon as he began to throw the right, the sharp
pain was back and the hand swelled up once again. It was clear
there was still a lot of healing to be done and he had no option
but to return to the Harley Street specialists. This time the
Castillo fight was cancelled, with the prospect of a future
resurrection tentatively raised. At a press conference in London a
dejected Frank Warren announced that three of Hamed's
metacarpal bones had 'fused together' and that Naseem would
face keyhole surgery, though in fact there was no fusion, and the
doctors told Naz that surgery was not an absolute necessity,
suggesting the alternative of intensive physiotherapy plus
cortisone injections and complete rest to reduce the swellings. A
thoroughly dispirited Naseem took the latter option, later joking
that 'operations are too sore'.

Once again Murphy's law had taken its course. After the first
postponement, the revised plans involved following the Castillo
fight with a mandatory defence against Billy Hardy, and then
taking on Bungu for the IBF super bantamweight title, before
moving up to super featherweight to take on WBC champion
Azumah Nelson, with fights against Barrera and Wayne
McCullough tentatively slotted in for later in the year. Don King
was also keen to get a hold on Naseem by promoting him on the
Tyson–Bruno undercard – and Warren was about to announce a
major US television deal with Showtime – but all this was placed
on the backburner and the best they could hope for was a late
March comeback against a softer option opponent, after six
months of enforced inactivity.

For the next month Naseem was banned from the gym and

decided his best option was to get away from it all for a few days by making a trip to Cannes with his girlfriend, but in doing this he came close to being arrested and banned from the flight after yet another 'incident', this one of his own making. Checking in at Manchester airport with his brother, Nabeel, on 23 January, he tried to take two items of hand luggage on to the plane. A British Airways check-in clerk told him only one bag was permitted and that the other bag, which contained his personal stereo system, was over the 20 kg limit. He handed it over to go into the baggage compartment with great reluctance, having seen Brendan's electronic scales damaged after being taken apart by inspectors.

According to the clerk, what followed was a statement made in all seriousness. According to Naseem and Nabeel, it was just an example of the young boxer's off-the-wall sense of fun, which anyone with a humorous bone in their body would have laughed at. What is not in dispute is the content of Naseem's message: 'If my bag doesn't get to where it's supposed to be I'll come back and find you, and sort you out with a shotgun', or words to that effect.

The check-in clerk burst into tears, later saying that no one had ever addressed her in this way in her nine years on the job. When Naseem compounded the damage by refusing to answer standard security questions about the contents of his luggage, she contacted her supervisor, who immediately confiscated his ticket and boarding card, called the airport police and warned Naseem that he might be refused permission to travel. The police, aware of Naseem's reputation, found the tallest, toughest-looking constable on duty, who gave the boxer a 'talking to' in which he was 'advised about his behaviour'. After this Naseem's attitude quickly changed and he apologized to the clerk, explaining that it was all a misunderstanding and that the remark about the shotgun was made entirely in jest. He was eventually allowed to proceed with his journey to Cannes via London.

Naseem's management had to do some quick damage control, claiming he had only realized after the event that the check-in clerk did not share his sense of humour, and that the whole thing had been blown out of proportion. 'It was a complete joke and

everybody in the queue knew that. Naz said one or two things
but the woman checking him in was so dry that she just didn't
laugh,' Nabeel was quoted as saying.[8]

While the remark about the shotgun is certainly consistent
with Naseem's sense of fun, the incident, which was splashed in
all the national newspapers, seemed to confirm for many the
stories about the young celebrity's arrogance and impetuous-
ness. His reputation had suffered and all that he could do was
wait to get into the ring again, when he would be expected to
carry out every threat he issued, carry a shotgun in both hands,
and so on. It was perhaps no coincidence that his next fight was
billed under the James Bond-ish banner, 'Licensed to Thrill'
and featured a picture of a tuxedo'd Naz wielding a hunting rifle.

Finally, at the beginning of February, his hand was deemed to
have responded sufficiently well to the course of cortisone
injections and the intense programme of physiotherapy to allow
him to resume training. The fighter and his management knew
he was chancing it, but the months were passing by, his weight
had risen to a slightly podgy 9st 9lb (the highest in his life,
though still nothing to worry about) and the inaction was
becoming intolerable. He tried the right out on the heavy bag
and then on the pads again, and said he experienced no pain or
psychological barriers when throwing it, though it took another
two weeks before he could throw it with anything close to evil
intent in sparring.

For a number of reasons the option of appearing on the Don
King-promoted Bruno–Tyson bill had fallen through. For one
thing, by this stage, the Tyson fight card had already been set.
Warren and Ingle also hoped to showcase Naseem in the United
States when he was at his absolute best, against a 'name'
opponent. After what would be nearly six months out of the
ring, there were doubts about just how sharp Naseem would be,
and over whether they should take the risk of trying his hand out
on a serious contender. In addition, Warren's contract with Sky
involved Naseem having six fights during 1996 on the satellite
channel – with King's Showtime-televised bills not being
covered by this agreement – and time to fulfil this commitment
was running out.

Most importantly, however, the money on offer from King

and Showtime could not match the £500,000-plus per fight that Warren could deliver in consequence of the Sky contract. Naseem is a Warren and not a King fighter, and the British promoter was not going to give him up 'to America' (for which read Don King) for even a single fight unless a particularly delicious offer came his way. 'Naseem is definitely going to box in America in 1996 – we are going to take him out,' he asserts before pausing to add: 'But you got to remember: while America is a great place for a boxer to get exposure, Naseem is the highest paid featherweight in the world by far, so America's got to come up with something extra-special for us to take him from here where we have guaranteed sell-outs, guaranteed big TV revenue, guaranteed sponsorship and the whole thing that goes with it.'

Instead it was announced that Naseem would fight on the same date as Bruno–Tyson, 16 March, but six hours earlier and in Glasgow. He was far from delighted with this news but did his best to put a brave face on it: 'I like to be the main attraction, although it would have been good to be on the Tyson bill, but there will be loads of people watching me,' he said.

His opponent was the 26-year-old Austria-based Nigerian southpaw, Said Lawal, who quite obviously qualified as little more than a warm body. His number four featherweight ranking with the WBO was a reflection only of that organization's capricious generosity towards its promotional friends. Lawal had certainly never beaten anyone of note and had never even fought outside of Austria as a professional, but, on paper, he seemed like the ideal opponent to test Naz's hand after such a long layoff. He was known as a reasonably skilled boxer and a solid body puncher, but quite clearly did not have the tools to trouble Hamed.

The Lagos-raised Lawal started boxing as a 14-year-old and won 36 of his 40 amateur bouts, before shifting base to Vienna in 1991. He opened his professional account in March 1992 with a points win over the Romanian prospect Stan Mihaly, but it was a year before he would fight again. After that, however, his career got moving and, by September 1994 when he faced Naseem's old victim Freddy Cruz, he had raked up ten wins in a row and held the Austrian title. But Cruz was too crafty and experienced and outboxed him over eight rounds. Nine months and three

victories later they met again and this time Lawal was given a
draw – a hometowner to be sure, but at least an indication of
some improvement. A further move into the outer fringes of the
world scene was suggested by his victory over the Zambian
champion Paul Kaoma for the WBC International featherweight
title, and his successful first defence against the Dominican
bantamweight champion Luis Sosa, both on points over twelve
rounds. His record stood at a flattering seventeen wins (seven
inside the distance), one loss and one draw.

Naseem's approach to this opponent, as to most of those he
had never seen before, was nonchalant. He looked at Lawal's
record, saw that the best he had managed was a draw against
Freddy Cruz, and realized he had little to worry about. As he put
it later: 'I knew I'd win because he couldn't look after Cruz. I
gave that man six rounds of punishment and left him crying like
a woman, so this was always going to go my way.' He also played
a video of his opponent in action, but soon switched it off,
satisfied he had seen enough. 'I watched the guy box for one
minute, like I normally do – put the tape in, watch a couple of
moves, turn it off. That's all I have to see. I saw that he was a
good fighter. He looked very strong and quite tall on tape, and I
saw that he was a southpaw, so I knew what shot to throw and I
knew I was going to knock him out early.'

Though the right hand lead is the classic answer to a
southpaw, Hamed told everyone in the weeks preceding the fight
that he was going to knock Lawal out with the left. 'I'm going to
take him out with a perfect, cracking left hook in the second
minute of the second round,' he predicted. 'For the first round
I'm going to box to the best of my ability and chill a bit, in a
smooth way, take my time, flow around the ring. In the second
I'm throwing an awesome, timing-perfect left hook and – I'm
not saying *if* it connects, I'm saying *when* it connects – I'm
taking him out.'

His training seemed to confirm the preference for the left, and
initially there was a caution about using the damaged right as a
result of this trainers' concern that it would 'go' again. When
Naseem said his hand was 'almost 100 per cent', it was generally
assumed that he meant, 'still not in full working order'. Though
he may have sparred a little less than for some of his fights, he

did more work on the speed ball, in shadow boxing, ground exercises and even skipping, than usual, as well as scores of rounds on the pads, to get his timing and speed back to perfection.

Certainly by the end of his training, both hands seemed to be doing their job with impressive effect. Four days before the fight he showed off his preparedness by handing out a painful body beating to Jon Thaxton and giving heavyweight Clifton Mitchell and cruiserweight Johnny Nelson all the trouble they could handle. That night, Thaxton complained of feeling ill as a result of the blows he had taken. 'He went all out and I could feel every punch,' he said, stressing that Naz was not holding back with the right. 'There was no problem with his hand. I can't see what all this fuss is about. I'm his sparring partner. I wish he had a bad hand – that's one less thing to worry about. He had a bad hand, that healed 100 per cent, so I can't see the problem.' Thaxton insisted that Hamed had actually improved considerably since the Robinson fight. 'He's a better Naz than six months ago. He's getting better all the time,' he said. 'The thing is, he's so accurate. If he looks for a shot he will land it almost every time – 99 times out of 100 he will hit the target. That's the difference between him and other top guys I've sparred with like Billy Schwer and Gary Jacobs. If I make a mistake Naz will hit me six shots before I can recover. I've got a stone on him, so I like to think I give him a good workout, but he's really the bees' knees. He's the man. 'Nuf respect – he's brilliant.'

When the Hamed camp arrived in Glasgow on the Wednesday night, three days before the fight, they expected the usual quiet wind-down after over a month of intensive work, but Naz had other ideas. As Brendan put it: 'Immediately after we arrived he insisted on training and he did fourteen rounds on the pads and skipping and shadow boxing, and then on the Thursday night he did eight rounds of high movement speed work, and his timing and his rhythm were so spot on I thought to myself, "I can't see it going longer than two rounds." '

But while his entourage was convinced that everything was hunky dory, not everyone was taking them at their word. Barry McGuigan, who had examined the hand seven weeks earlier, was one of many to express concern, noting that it 'didn't look great'.

Two days before the fight, McGuigan said he was still not
certain. 'He's had to train with that hand and we know he hasn't
been sparring an awful lot. That suggests he didn't have
confidence in the hand, but he's got so much talent, this kid,
that he could take him out with the other hand. I just think
there's a lot more trouble with the hand than they're suggesting
in the Brendan Ingle camp.'[9]

This kind of comment, as well as press reports suggesting that
Naseem's career was on the line, and that he should lay off for a
year to give his hand a rest, infuriated the young champion, and
added to the frustration that had been building up over the
months. In the changing-room prior to the fight he announced to
Brendan, John and the rest, that his first punch of the fight
would be a lead right, and that if this connected and hurt Lawal,
he would end things then and there. 'What I read before the
fight was unbelievable,' he said afterwards. ' "Naz's career is on
the ropes", and stupid stuff like that. Everybody thought I was
going to make it a left hook, but I wanted to prove that the right
hand was perfect and that there was no problem with it
whatsoever.'

If the intention was to highlight Naseem's prowess, rather
than to ease him back gently with minimal publicity, 16 March
was hardly the ideal date for his return. There are not many
boxers who can upstage The Prince, but Mike Tyson and Frank
Bruno, in combination, in Las Vegas, are certainly two of them.
While Naseem's fight, along with the Scott Welsh–Joe Bugner
show in Berlin,[10] was part of the Sky Sports–Sports Network
package that was tagged on for free as a prelude to the
pay-per-view Tyson–Bruno bill later that night, it was treated by
Sky and by the printed media as very much an afterthought.
Frank Warren, along with most of the sports media's A-team,
were all in Las Vegas, hoping against desperate hope, that Bruno
would do the impossible.

This, however, did not curtail Glasgow's love affair with the
wee lad from south of the border. Paying up to £100 for the
privilege of seeing him in action on a rainy, cold night, they
poured into the Scottish Exhibition and Conference Centre, a
graceless, prefabricated venue equally adept at housing concerts
for ageing rockers or missions for evangelical revivalists, as it is

for accommodating beery, potentially belligerent, fight crowds. By fight time 8,000 had packed the venue for a bill which included a smattering of Scots prospects, but no one of stature other than the Naz-man. A strong Hamed contingent was there too, among them the champion's father, two sisters, three brothers and his girlfriend.

Lawal made his entrance under the Nigerian flag to a chorus of sustained booing, a practice which in recent years has become the standard British fight crowd welcome for foreign fighters. Before the fight he had been saying with apparent confidence that he would be taking Hamed's title belt back to Vienna and the like, but when he stepped through the ropes his eyes had the look of a kudu caught in the headlights.

The crowd began chanting, 'Na-zeem, Na-zeem, Na-zeem' and the letters N-A-S-E-E-M appeared in fireworks above the stands before the Carmen Miranda theme from *The Omen* moaned ominously from the speakers. Then, in a sudden Hamed-like change of pace and direction, the heavy choral tones made way for the thumping beat of Khaliphz's new rap single 'Walk Like a Champion' (which Naz had collaborated on and, three days later, would perform with the group on *Top of the Pops*). The words reverberated: 'Prince is in the house ... Walk like a champion, talk like a champion', and the champion made his way to the ring wearing a new creation, a variation on the leopardskin theme, but this time his long trunks were decorated with six horizontal rows of feathery, white stuff, giving the impression of a kind of sheepskin skirt until the wind lifted the tassles. Naz flipped the ropes, did a little swagger and fist-roll and then brushed past Lawal, giving him a mocking, wide-eyed stare as he went by.

The WBO champion looked hard and trim at 8st 13lb 12oz – the heaviest of his career – as he moved around the ring, grinning approvingly when he was introduced as 'the incredible, the unbelievable Prince Naseem Hamed'. Lawal, two inches taller and 12oz lighter, avoided all eye contact and shuffled about in nervous, jerky movements. Finally the bell rang and Naz strolled out in a squarish southpaw stance, with that familiar contemptuous look on his face, pumping his arms in an almost playful gesture. Then, without warning, three and a half seconds

into the round, he let loose a right hook with the hint of an
uppercut in it, which caught Lawal as he was coming in. The
Nigerian collapsed to the canvas.

He wobbled up at the count of six, a completely vacant look
on his face, his legs barely able to hold his 125lbs. It was quite
clear that the fight should have been stopped then, but Hamed
was allowed one more claw and bite at the wounded buck in
front of him. He measured his man with a right jab, feinted
twice, and then smashed a long, casual-looking right uppercut
which collided with Lawal's nose and mouth at the precise point
his head was coming forward. The impact whiplashed his head
against the back of his shoulders and he collapsed on his face,
rising by instinct but without conviction or even consciousness
at the count of four. At the 35 second mark, the referee waved it
off, giving Hamed the fifth fastest world title knockout in boxing
history.[11]

From the press rows it had been a magnificent half minute –
three punches timed and delivered to absolute perfection and
with such unrealistic force from one so small. For a few seconds
the crowd was stunned, and from the back of the bleachers there
was evident confusion, but when Naseem leapt on to the ropes
and pumped his hands in the air, they realized that their
evening's entertainment was over. For many it was a very brief
bit of pleasure for a fair whack of cash, and before long they
broke into a sustained chorus of boos.

Said Lawal, who was the prime target of this derision, seemed
to have no idea what was going on or where he was and had no
recollecton of the knockdowns or why he was stopped or who
had broken his nose in two places. He asked his corner when he
was fighting, and then wept a little. An hour later, Naseem could
not resist a hint of derision about his unfortunate victim's state.
'I don't think he remembers much. He still thinks he's fighting
later on. I think he was arguing with his corner why he had not
boxed. I seen it myself, him arguing with his corner, but, end of
the day, what can I do about it? I done my job and I couldn't
wait to get out. That was a cool, cool ending you know.'

The crowd eventually tired of booing and began chanting
'Bru-no, Bru-no, Bru-no' in anticipation of the 5 a.m. encounter
which they had alreaday paid £9.95 to watch, but Naseem was

busily gloating at having proved his detractors wrong. 'The right hand is perfect. You see, I don't tell lies. I would have loved to do him in the second round because I predicted it. End of the day, it hit him so hard, that first shot, I timed it so precise, that it put him down, so he was going, he had to go. All I needed to do was plant every shot correctly and hit him in the right place. I waited exactly for the shots I wanted to throw and I threw them and the fight was over, so I can't be more pleased with the way I boxed,' he said before praising his parents, his family, Allah and the people of Scotland for their support.

By the time he had showered, changed and made his way to the low-key press conference at the nearby Moathouse Hotel, he realized that, through no fault of his own, the people of Scotland, or at least the thousands of Glaswegians who had paid to see him in action, were a little put out. 'I apologize to the fans, but it was going to be an early night anyway, so what the hell. I just apologize that it was over *so* early. I'll be back in Scotland definitely and giving an even better performance than that,' he said, before adding, with a typical display of his post-modern sensibilities, 'but them shots were great for television.'

The idea that Frank Warren and the WBO hierarchy had in mind was that Naz's next outing would be a mandatory defence against Daniel Alicea, a Warren-promoted Puerto Rican, with only thirteen fights to his name, who had received the number one WBO ranking mainly by virtue of his nationality and his close connections to the organization's bosses. Five days later Warren announced that Alicea would indeed be Naz's next opponent. Naseem, however, was making it plain that he would be staking a higher claim, now that he proved that everything was in perfect working order. 'By the end of this year I'm looking for four, five world title belts – super bantam to super featherweight. I just want world titles after this. I don't really want to fight people with no titles. I want big fights from now on.' He soon got on to his wish list: Tom Johnson, Marco Antonio Barrera, Azumah Nelson – they'd all get the same treatment as Said Lawal, so would Colin McMillan, Vuyani Bungu and the rest. 'I will stay world champion and I will never get beat. Full stop. In my eyes I ain't getting beat. That is my personal opinion.'

Half an hour later a stretch limo disgorged the Hamed clan at the Marriott, a mile away, for an all-night party where Naseem led the revellers in shouting the odds for their countryman, Frank Bruno, just as he had done from a ringside perch in Newcastle for Nigel Benn's bid to stave off the challenge of Thulane 'Sugarboy' Malinga, a fortnight earlier. When Naz finally retired upstairs at 6 a.m., Bruno, like Benn, was an ex-champion, and the 22-year-old featherweight was indisputably at the pinnacle of the Warren pile, with only Lennox Lewis to rival him for the top place at his country's table. It had been a bad month for British boxing, but, all in all, a good one for Britain's best boxer.

10

Prince Naseem:
the Present and the Future

Most boxing fans, most boxing writers even, like two things in their great fighters: they must be tigers inside the ring and pussycats outside of it.

We have this image of the man who is transformed into something less than human and something more than ourselves when the bell rings; the fighter who comes out snarling, takes two to land one and prevails, who walks through the pain; the man who has the power and ruthlessness to prevail whatever the odds. We revel in these clichés, which are really euphemisms: the kid with the 'killer instinct', the one-punch 'kayo artist', the 'death or glory' merchant, and, with the exception of the occasional 'Sugar Ray', 'Sweetpea' or even 'Butterbean', the *noms de guerre* which tend to stick are those which conjur up images of brutality or animal power: 'The Hitman', 'The Bodysnatcher', 'The Beast',

241

'The Pitbull', 'The Hawk', 'The Sting' and so on.

That is why this sport worships some and ignores others who are far better, and why it particularly resents those who expose the fighters we honour. Gene Tunney would have whipped Jack Dempsey nine times out of ten, even at the Manassa Mauler's best, yet could never be forgiven for twice beating the pants off the 'giant killer'. Ezzard Charles outclassed Archie Moore three times at light heavyweight, then won almost every round against Joe Louis at heavyweight and when way past his best came within a whisker of beating Rocky Marciano, yet the Old Mongoose, the Brown Bomber and the Brockton Blockbuster are the stuff of story books today, while the Cincinnati Man, who was better than them all – pound for pound at least – is forgotten. Jack Johnson was always better than Jim Jeffries, Larry Holmes than George Foreman, and today, we could say the same about Pernell Whitaker and the 'legendary' Julio Cesar Chavez, yet it will always be the punchers, the fighters, the brawlers, we prefer. Muhammad Ali, of course, is the great exception, though it is worth remembering that it was only when he started taking his knocks rather than avoiding them, that the hatred of the white American public turned into sentimental love.

A wonderful variant on the theme is the little leopard who beats up the big tiger (and, therefore, can be excused the indignity of taking anything in return). It is one of the reasons why we love all those stories about Naseem knocking the stuffing out of behemoths. And when applied more generally, this image of the small man dropping some fat-arsed redneck, nimbly stepping over his prone mass, giving a smile and a nod and a wipe of the hands – and saying, 'Now where were we?', is a beguiling one because we would all love to be that fellow once in a while.

The corollary though is that at least the civilized part of us tends to prefer the animal to be caged most of the time. So if our pet warrior goes back to his wife and kids and is described as a doting dad, and gives generously to charity, and helps old ladies across streets, or even if he does no more than tell us he's really somebody completely different outside the ring – Jekyll and Hyde, honest – so much the better; we'll believe him because we want to.

It is also nice to think that when you scratch the surface of any bully, there's a coward waiting to creep out. Therefore the finest fighters can't really be bullies, right? The truth is that most bullies are not cowards and some are blind courageous. And many of the best and bravest boxers are, indeed, bullies, inside and outside the ring.[1] They like to hurt and dominate and it's part of what makes them so good at what they do.

In real life, in the real fight game, the killers inside the ring are seldom angels out of it, and vice versa. Put differently, the best boxers are not very often the best people. Of course, we all know this or that exception out of which we like to make a kind of rule – top notch fighters who wouldn't lift a finger in anger outside the ring – and they do, indeed, exist. But at the same time, certainly from my experience in getting to know many fighters personally, these exceptions arise more rarely than we like to think. Most of the really great fighters are men with a distinct hard edge to them, which is one of the reasons why they got to the top in the first place. So often the opposite image is only maintained because we the fans and writers don't get to know them well enough and perhaps don't really want to.

Think, for example, of Jack Dempsey, the former hobo, who seemed (to the public) to have been tamed outside the square ring, but in fact, had a habit of beating up his women and his friends, hanging out with mobsters, despising black people and a whole lot more. Though he later mellowed, in his prime he was not much better as a human being than Mike Tyson – and even in the supposedly unblinkered 1980s, when we were fed all that non-sense about Tyson really being quite a lovable old thing whose anger was restricted to his opponents – we were inclined to give Tyson the benefit of the doubt until it was too late, and very likely we'll do it again. And in different ways the gap between the image and the reality was almost as wide with, say, Rocky Marciano, Joe Louis, Randolph Turpin, Sugar Ray Leonard and Marvin Hagler.

Again the notable exception may be Muhammad Ali who acquired, to many white Americans, an image of the devil incarnate only to emerge as a flawed but wonderful example of humanity at its finest. But even then, the old Ali admitted the young Ali had once slapped around his own father and his first wife, and despite his Islamic commitment had bonked more women than Warren Beattie and Magic Johnson combined.

We should not be surprised, however, that most of the sport's elite do not match up to Ali's genuine warmth, generosity of spirit and love of people, nor that the demarcation lines between their 'office' and the rest of their lives are not as absolute as they assume. Many boxers are no more able to switch off and on their fury in and out of the ring than the rest of us are in life more generally.

Most boxers enter the game by chance rather than inclination – because there's a gym in their neighbourhood or their father did it – but once there, they have to enter into the amoral logic of the sport. They are trained to score points off other people's heads and bodies, or better still, to hit them hard or often enough to end the fight. And this means hurting people, 'finishing them off', knocking them 'out', being ruthless. Some boxers acquire this 'instinct', but the best usually arrive with it, after which their trainers harness and build it up, or, to use the current jargon, they 'channel' it. However we choose to frame it, cruelty, or at least the temporary absence of mercy, is an essential of greatness.

So we should hardly raise an eyebrow when, to take a recent example, Emmanuel Stewart – one of the finest trainers in the game today – expresses delight with his discovery that his chess playing, book reading, British heavyweight Lennox Lewis, was really quite a lethal street fighter at his Canadian high school, and when he encourages his protégé to rediscover some of that thuggery from his past. That's how it is with boxing. Lewis may still play chess, Tyson may have played with pigeons and read the classics, Bobby Czyz and Nicky Piper may be members of Mensa, Marco Antonio Barrera may be studying to be a lawyer. So what? We judge them on their ability as fighters, and that is all. The rest, if we are to be honest, is garnish.

The point is we should not be surprised when a brilliant young fighter like Naseem Hamed does not quite measure up to his word about being 'a completely different person' outside the ring. You look in his eyes when he's giving an up yours salute to someone after a fight, or when he's cutting down an impudent press conference questioner, and it's the same face of the devil look he has when he's firing blockbusters at Steve Robinson. And when there are reports of the odd 'altercation' here and there, or of an 'incident' at an airport, or when journalists complain he's behaving like a bit of a 'prat', or write snidely about his womanizing or complain that his behaviour here, there and the next place is not what we'd expect from a world champion, we should not assume he's become some kind of fallen angel, or that fame and fortune have soiled him beyond recognition. The capacity for cruelty has always been there, sitting alongside his capacity for self-love and some rather more endearing qualities.

With Naseem we can take some solace in the fact that his 'Mr Hyde' side has always been balanced, if not by a Dr Jekyll dimension, then certainly by other, admirable qualities: his love of his family, his compassion about poverty, his genuine hatred of racism, his ability to show kindness and concern, his spurts of generosity, his occasional bursts of empathy and even altruism, his 'wicked' sense of humour.

All in all, there's a good deal to recommend Naseem Hamed outside the ring. For what it's worth, he may very well be a better, a 'nicer' person than some other boxers, but far more important is that he's a better boxer than most boxers, and maybe all of them, and it is primarily in these terms he should be judged.

From very early in his career, Naseem has been in a position which, for lesser sportsmen, would be invidious. He has been so showered with superlatives by his own people and by the press, that it would seem almost impossible for him to meet up to expectations. Which other boxer – after only 15 fights – has been compared favourably with the likes of Sugar Ray Robinson and Muhammad Ali at their peaks? Which other bantamweight has had his trainer say he's capable of winning world titles all the way up to middleweight? Which other British fighter has said of himself that he would be the only pugilistic legend his country had ever produced? It's quite a tall order, really.

All we can go on is what we've seen so far, which is not quite enough to be able to judge him as a certainty for 'greatness' – not yet anyway. But certainly from what I have seen of him in competition and in the gym – I would have to say that in twenty-five years of following this sport I have never seen a boxer, anywhere in the world, who compares with his level of potential, and that includes the likes of Sugar Ray Leonard and Mike Tyson at the same stages of their careers. But – descending for the moment into the silly game of rating fighters of different weights and eras against each other – that doesn't mean we can be sure he is destined to join the company of the Robinsons, the Alis, the Harry Grebs, Jimmy Wildes, Henry Armstrongs and Ray Leonards. Although Naseem Hamed may already be the best fighter in the world, he can't yet be put above the world's current elite, Pernell Whitaker or Roy Jones, because he has yet to prove it, and because we know from the history of the sport that so much can go wrong.

Donald 'The Cobra' Curry, with his smooth skills and electrifying bursts of power, was almost universally rated as the best boxer, 'pound for pound', in the mid-eighties, until Lloyd Honeyghan and then Mike McCallum exposed in him a certain physical frailty and lack of durability that had previously been concealed. Mike Tyson seemed unstoppable in the late eighties until Buster Douglas revealed his vulnerability when faced with exceptional boxers who were bigger and stronger than himself, as well as his declining commitment to training. George Foreman seemed like an invincible human wrecking ball in the early seventies, until Muhammad Ali and then Jimmy Young outthought him, outboxed him and exposed his lack of stamina.

And though it seems so unlikely right now, it could happen to Naseem Hamed too. At the moment he is such an original, so gifted with natural ability, power, coordination, timing, physical strength, stamina, resilience and determination, that it is barely conceivable that anyone remotely close to his weight could beat him. If there is the hint of a weakness it may come through a declining inclination to work as hard now as he did a couple of years ago, or through his suspect right hand, injured as an amateur and then more seriously as a professional. If it continues to show frailty, it could upset the rhythm and momentum of his career, as happened with that marvellous Australian warrior, Jeff Fenech.

It also has to be conceded that Hamed has yet to face, in

competition at least, anyone else from the sport's top drawer, and there are several styles he has not been confronted with. So far he has beaten several world-rated bantamweights and super bantams (Belcastro, Cruz, Ramirez, Liendo, Polo Perez) and one world-class featherweight (Steve Robinson), and he has done this so emphatically and with such style and brilliance, that one can only surmise he would also dominate better, faster, harder-hitting boxers within this weight range. And from the way he has handled extremely capable big men in the gym, one can safely assume he would have little problem moving up a few more weight divisions. But that's as far as we can take it. So far, betting on Naseem to become, as he likes to put it, a 'legend', is more like trading in a futures market than investing in blue chip stock.

While sticking a while longer on this hypothetical terrain, it is perhaps worth bringing in a little more specificity about the likely or possible options he may come up against. It may be sad that he's relinquished the bantamweight option, but we have to accept that he will never again attempt the 8st 6lb limit. However, if he keeps to his word about dropping down to take one of the 8st 10 lb super bantamweight titles, he will be testing himself within what is currently the finest division in boxing.

A possible option here is the IBF champion, Vuyani Bungu, mainly because of the close relationship Bungu's promoter, Rodney Berman, has with Frank Warren. This 29-year-old South African has a record of 30 wins (18 inside the distance) in 32 fights, with both of his losses being controversial, and has not been beaten in over four years.

After serving a long apprenticeship as the sparring partner to another former IBF champion, Welcome Ncita, he caused a major upset by easily outpointing the previously unbeaten, former Olympic gold medallist, Kennedy McKinney, to take the title, and has since made six defences. Bungu manages to combine being an aggressive pressure fighter and an excellent defensive boxer. He usually has a high workrate and though he is not rated as a power puncher, he has a thumping left jab, is strong for his weight and works particularly well to the body. Having only been dropped once in his career, he has a reliable chin and is always in superb condition – training six days a week, twelve months a year.

While Bungu himself makes brash predictions about giving

Hamed 'the shock of his life' and 'beating him easily', a more considered response comes from his manager-trainer Mzi Mnguni, who has taken three boxers to 'world' titles in the nineties. 'Look, Hamed is obviously a brilliant boxer, but I believe I have spotted flaws which Vuyani would be in a perfect position to expose,' he says. 'He is a fighter who likes to dictate the pace and that is something Bungu would never allow him to do. Vuyani is a much busier fighter and he has the strength to keep the pressure on Hamed so as not to let him get off with his punches, but at the same time, unlike, say, Wayne McCullough, he has a brilliant defence, and he is far faster and more imaginative than Steve Robinson. Also, you can be sure that Vuyani is going to be by far the fitter man, so he will outlast Hamed.'

Hamed does not foresee much problem from the IBF champion. 'From what I've heard he's a good little fighter – nearly complete,' he says in a patronizing tone, 'but really, he's just not in my league at all. Once I get the opportunity, he'll get beat, just like the rest. Three rounds and I'll take him.'

Given Bungu's sound chin and defence it will probably last a while longer than that, but while the South African is certainly one of the better world champions today, he cannot match Hamed in power, strength, speed or versatility. The only form guide between the two is Laureano Ramirez who was flattened in three rounds by a flu-weakened Hamed, but lost a unanimous decision to Bungu. Bungu may well make the fight interesting for a few rounds and will certainly land more often than Steve Robinson, but Naseem should be able to take care of him by the eighth round.

The most intriguing of all the local rivalries in British boxing today is that between Naseem Hamed and Wayne McCullough, who currently holds the WBC bantamweight title. They both arrived at about the same time, took different paths to the top, and both remain undefeated, and seem convinced they can do each other in.

Both sides also blame each other for the failure to secure the fight. McCullough's manager, Mat Tinley, says he offered $1.6 million for the bout on Sky, and was turned down. Frank Warren, however, points out that Tinley insisted the fight take place at bantamweight, which Naseem could no longer make. Warren in turn says he offered McCullough $1.5 million either to fight at super bantamweight, with no titles on the line, or for Naseem's WBO featherweight title with an agreement to make the weight at the super bantam level, and received no response. Tinley responds that this offer was only made after McCullough had signed with ITV, and under the terms of this contract, they could not accept a fight on Sky. Both sides, however, insist the fight will eventually happen, probably in late 1996 or 1997. A possible route is that McCullough rises in weight to take the WBC super bantam title off the ageing Daniel Zaragoza and then Hamed drops in weight.

McCullough, a modest fellow in terms of his sport's vainglorious norms, acknowledges that Hamed's 'awkward' and 'unorthodox' style might make life difficult for him for a while, but stresses that his higher workrate, greater experience and his ability to maintain constant pressure for twelve rounds would prevail. He says that while he would be prepared to meet Hamed anytime if the price was right, Hamed currently needs him more than the other way around because the Englishman is 'unknown' in the United States. Naseem, on the other hand, says that McCullough's 'exile' in Las Vegas has made him a nonentity in Britain where the fight would be sold. And he does not even see it as a competitive contest. After watching McCullough take far too many pit-a-pat punches from Johnny Bredahl, he described his rival as a 'goalkeeper', adding: 'He's not in my class. He's not even fourth division, he's fifth division. He should get his arse down to Ireland so that I can beat him in his own backyard.'

The 25-year-old Ulster Irishman's chief assets are his phenomenal workrate, his stamina, his body punching, his chin and the fact that he is trained by Eddie Futch, who many regard as the best in the business. After 19 straight wins (14 inside the distance), his defence has shown some improvement, but he still takes too many punches, and while he is hitting harder than a year ago, he does not pack anything close to Naseem's power. Although he is currently a champion at two weight divisions below Hamed, he is naturally a bigger man, standing 5-foot-7½ with a walk-around weight of about 9st 12lb.

Despite the intensity of this rivalry, this does not look like being a particularly competitive fight. Frank Warren may be biased, but when he boasts that McCullough 'couldn't hit Naz with a handful of rice, with a wheelbarrow, for chrissake,' he is not far off the mark. Hamed simply hits too hard – and is too hard to hit – and McCullough is far too easy to hit, for this one to go further than five rounds.

Even bigger than the McCullough fight, at least in terms of the American market, would be a 'showdown' with Mexico's unbeaten WBO super bantamweight champion Marco Antonio Barrera. The fight press see this one as the lighter weight super-fight of the decade, and are starting to pump it up. *Ring* magazine, for example, featured a cover story on a Hamed–Barrera 'Dream Match-up' in their February 1996 edition, in which the editor in chief, Steve Farhood, predicted Hamed would stop the unbeaten Mexican in nine rounds, while the magazine's Mexican correspondent, Bruce Williams, picked Barrera in ten or eleven. *Boxing News* ran a cover story on the 'Match Made in Heaven!'

Both Hamed and Barrera say they are keen for this one to take place as soon as possible and Frank Warren is emphatic that it is definitely a fight which will happen – probably in late 1996 or early 1997. 'I'd really like to do it this year,' he says. 'It would be a tremendous fight and a tremendous attraction, and Naz would win.' There are, however, various promotional complications which could delay it further, including the fact that Barrera currently fights on HBO, but public demand and the attitudes of the two fighters will probably ensure it eventually materializes.

Both fighters are extremely confident about the way it will go, though, predictably, Naseem is more vocal about it. Barrera quietly says he is willing to come to London to beat Hamed and Naz says he will fight the Mexican anywhere, arguing that Barrera's style is made for him. 'I really want to get this one on and I'll tell you who will beat him. He will,' he says. 'I've watched him before, the way he comes forward, and what will happen is that he will walk on to my punches, and then I will take him out. I will fight him and beat him and take his belt, because I want to make a habit of collecting these belts.'

Of all the super bantamweights, Barrera would seem to represent the most formidable challenge. He is only a month older than Hamed, but has had almost double the number of fights – a record of 41 fights, 41 wins, 29 inside the distance. The Mexican is a pressure fighter who tends to overwhelm the opposition with a high volume of hard, accurate, fast combinations – with his body attack being particularly formidable – but he does not have Hamed's one-punch knockout power. When he chooses he can jab and move, or counter-punch and his defence is generally sound. He also has an extremely reliable chin. Despite having no problems making the weight, the 5-foot-7 super bantam is bigger than Hamed and has a 72 inch reach, 9 inches longer than Naseem's.

But, as Kennedy McKinney showed early in 1996, Barrera can be outboxed and caught by someone with quick hands and a tight defence, and Hamed is certainly in a different league from McKinney in these departments. Barrera does not appear to have Hamed's strength, being backed up at times by Daniel Jimenez and Agapito Sanchez. He would attempt to put Hamed under intense pressure in the early rounds but would get caught repeatedly by hard, surprise counters and if he tried to concentrate on the body, sooner or later he would get cracked by one of Naseem speciality corkscrew uppercuts. Given the Mexican's ability to take a punch and his all-round proficiency I would expect him to last until about the tenth round, but one way or another it is a fight Hamed would win, probably inside the distance.

There are several other interesting match-ups for Hamed between super bantamweight and super lightweight, which may well be possibilities. Venezuela's Antonio Cermeno, WBA super bantamweight champion, is lanky (5-foot-10), quick and elusive, but lacks the power and probably the chin to survive the distance with Naseem.

But the most likely option is America's Tom Johnson, the IBF featherweight champion for the past 3½ years. He has lost only twice in 45 fights (24 stoppages) and is one of those solid, all-rounders – fine boxer, strong puncher – who has matured late in the day. But though he is bigger than Naseem, he does not have anywhere near Naseem's power, speed, strength or defensive brilliance. Furthermore, Johnson, who says he is confident of upsetting Hamed though has been reluctant to come to terms, appears to be on the decline at the age of 32 and has been dropped heavily in his last two fights. He is also vulnerable to a southpaw like Hamed. All in all, it looks like an easy fight for Hamed – one he would win within three rounds.

Venezuela's Eloy Rojas, the WBA featherweight champion who has lost just once in 35 outings, is a tall (5-foot-8), slick, sharp-hitting counter-puncher who could make life awkward for Naseem until he found his range, but he has shown nothing to suggest he could last twelve rounds, let alone beat, the Englishman.

Each of these champions has been promoted by Don King, which makes the fights easier to arrange, but the more intriguing prospect is for Hamed to move straight up to super featherweight (preferably after taking one of the super bantamweight titles) to tangle with Ghana's great triple world champion, Azumah Nelson, who currently holds the WBC 9st 4lb title, and is also promoted by King, though not under contract to him.

Nelson, thirty-seven, regained his crown last year with a devastating display of controlled punching against Gabriel Ruelas. He sees a defence against Hamed as being the most lucrative match of his career (his asking price is £3 million) and Warren has offered him a three-fight deal culminating in a fight with Hamed late this year. Naseem and Brendan, for their part, are also extremely keen on this match-up, arguing that Naz can match Nelson's power and strength, and that his huge advantages in youth, speed, versatility would make this a relatively easy fight.

Nelson has studied tapes of Hamed, and insists he has found a way of beating him. 'He's good, very good. I like him. He's a showman and I like his style, his confidence, but I will knock him out,' he said in an interview with Claude Abrams of *Boxing News* shortly after regaining his world title.[2] 'He is slick. You have to use your head, make him make mistakes and set him up. With Hamed you have to work the body – that's the way to beat him – and then finish him off. But he can punch. You must be able to take a punch. That's very important.'

Nelson can certainly punch and take a punch, and he is one of the most intelligent boxers in the game, with vast experience after over sixteen years as a professional, and 43 fights, 24 of them for world titles. He is certainly one of the greatest featherweights and super feathers in the sport's history and despite his age he still looks like the best man currently in his division in the world. But as another great, the slippery, inventive southpaw, Pernell Whitaker, showed in easily outpointing him six years ago, Azumah Nelson can be beaten with plenty of movement and speed. Whitaker was considerably bigger than Hamed, but never had anything close to Naseem's punching power, and Naz seems to have all Whitaker's speed and elusiveness and a good deal more besides. It is not hard to picture Hamed boxing rings around the far slower Ghanaian, making him miss frequently and punishing him from the outside, to win a wide points decision or on a late knockout.

Finally, if Naseem is serious about winning world titles at five weight divisions, his ultimate challenge could come against America's Oscar de la Hoya, who at the time of writing was about to challenge Julio Cesar Chavez for his WBC super lightweight title, after having won versions of the super featherweight and lightweight world titles.

To many followers of the sport, and certainly to most in the United States, the idea of a 5-foot-3 British super bantamweight taking on a brilliant 5-foot-10 light welterweight, might seem ludicrous, but stranger things have happened in boxing. There have been several remarkable fighters who have moved through the divisions to whip far bigger world champions,[3] but probably the most remarkable was Henry Armstrong who overwhelmed Petey Sarron to win the world featherweight title in October 1937, then in May 1938 completely outclassed the highly rated Barney Ross to lift the world welterweight title, before dropping down to beat Lou Ambers for the lightweight title in August 1938, and for a while holding all three titles simultaneously as well as defending the welterweight crown nineteen times. He also thoroughly outclassed Ceferino Garcia for the world middleweight title in March 1940, only to be given a draw by a corrupt referee.

Although his style is very different from the mercurial Armstrong's, Naseem is a boxer who also seems to have the ability to be effective at several weight divisions at once. He is a super bantamweight who genuinely seems to be able to hold his own in serious, give-no-quarter sparring sessions with the 6-foot-3, 14-stone Johnny Nelson – himself good enough to fight a draw for the

WBC cruiserweight title. Naseem has the power of a good welterweight, and is so fast and hard to hit cleanly that he is able to nullify the size advantages of far bigger men.

What is more, he seems to relish the challenge of slaying giants. When Pele Reid, the 16 st 5lb former world super heavyweight kickboxing champion, who is currently undefeated as a professional boxer, entered the St Thomas's Boys' Club gym in August 1995, Naseem's immediate response was to size him up. 'The very first thing Hamed said to me when I walked through those doors that day was, "I want to spar with *you*", and I'm sure it will happen sooner or later,' Reid says.

So for Naseem the prospect of a fight with de la Hoya is a realistic one in the medium term, though his management certainly do not see this as a current priority and in any event, it is a fight which would be difficult to make because the two boxers are in rival promotional camps.

'I've watched Oscar de la Hoya box and I think he's a great fighter and I take my hat off to him for all he's achieved,' Hamed concedes, 'but there's definitely a way of beating him. I've seen his strengths, but there are also definite weaknesses which I could exploit and I think I could do it.'

De la Hoya is seven inches taller and is naturally over a stone heavier. He is also an extremely fast, accurate and heavy puncher, who uses every shot in the book and times his blows to perfection. On the other hand he does not have great speed of foot or the best chin in the game and despite his considerable boxing skills, he is far easier to hit than Naseem. It is a fight which, somewhere down the line, could eventually happen, and Hamed would certainly be in with a chance.

At this point it is worth conceding that the further one goes in speculating about Naseem's future career, the more one enters the realm of fantasy. Right now, Naseem is a 21:0 (19) featherweight who owns but one, relatively minor, title belt. Furthermore, because of the politics of the sport, promotional rivalries and the frailties of the fighters themselves, most of these match-ups will probably never happen – and there is ample capacity for disaster along the way. Naseem's hand might let him down, his training schedule might continue to decline, he may crash his Porsche on the M1, he may even get knocked cold by a lucky punch.

It's a tightrope sport, but, right now, nothing Naz has done suggests he will suddenly lose his footing. In mid-1996, at the age of twenty-two, his prospects look brighter than any other British boxer in the 200-year history of the sport. He has already shown signs of being Britain's finest-ever at any weight, and his potential is a very long way from being fulfilled, which is one of the reasons why there is so much excitement surrounding his career.

The other major league drawcards in Britain in the nineties – Lennox Lewis, Frank Bruno, Nigel Benn, Chris Eubank – have been defined almost as much by their vulnerabilities as their strengths. Naseem Hamed, however, retains an aura of invincibility, along with a personality and presence which is a marketing manager's dream. Certainly there is no other sportsman in Britain today who comes to close to him in terms of commercial potential, and this applies not only in Britain, but even more so in the Middle East, and if all goes according to plan, will extend to the United States, parts of Africa and western Europe.

I am sitting having tea with Naseem Hamed in the foyer of the Britannia Hotel in the London Docklands, sharing a plate of ham sandwiches from which he has diligently put aside all traces of ham. Naz has knocked out yet another hopeful, and is starting to focus on the next one. He is talking about the tens of millions he will earn, about all the world champions he will beat and all title belts he will take home.

While we are chatting, Dennis Andries, the still-active, former three times WBC light heavyweight champion, comes over to say hello. 'I presume you're not still going to be fighting in twenty years' time?' I ask as a way of getting the conversation going again after the 42-year-old Andries departs.

Naseem lifts his chin, purses his lips, and gives a knowing smile. 'You *never* know how long I'll be around,' he says. 'I'm very ambitious and there's no knowing what I might do. I would never set a time limit on it. When it is assigned to me to retire, and retire undefeated that is, because I can't see myself ever getting beat, then I will retire. Until that point I'm just going to keep on bringing the world titles back to Sheffield and will become the first great fighter Britain has ever had.' He pauses, gives me an intense look, and reminds me that while no one can predict their future, he does know one thing: 'I will definitely become' – that word once again – 'a legend.'

And what about after that? Where do legends go when they retire? Is there life after boxing for the Prince? 'Oh, most definitely,' he replies indignantly. 'After my boxing career I will probably devote my life, devote myself, to the religion. Obviously!' While he thinks about this for a moment, I try to imagine the Prince as a preacher, but the image doesn't come. Then, a little to my surprise, he deflates a bit and qualifies his assertion. 'I'm not sure, you know. I may go into different kind of things, into acting, there's talk of music. Loads of things have come up on the pipeline.'

Naseem Hamed quickly regroups and once again gives me a look of absolute conviction and certainty, reducing the question of his future, like most fighters, to an intangible called destiny. 'Whatever happens to me after I retire, is written and written from God,' he says. But just to make sure I don't miss the thread he is quick to add: 'I do believe God will give me a great life.'

Notes

Chapter 1   Champion of the Known World

1 Quoted by Matt Jones in 'That's My Boy', *South Wales Echo*, 30
September 1995
2 Interview with Naseem Hamed by Geoffrey Beattie, *Head to Head*,
BBC Radio 5, 3 December 1995

Chapter 2   Roots

1 Quoted from interview in *Natural Born Thriller*, PolyGram Video and
Sports Network, 1995
2 Quoted in *Sheffield Star*, 30 March 1987
3 According to Graham: 'Eubank dropped me the first time we sparred,
I sprang straight up, and after that he never managed to land a glove on
me again.'
4 Quoted in 'The clown prince who dreams of being king of the ring' by
Tanith Carey, *Daily Mirror*, 29 September 1995
5 'Boxing clever with the world at his feet' by Stephen Biscoe, *Yorkshire
Post*, 21 May 1994

Chapter 3   The Professional Amateur

1 *Sheffield Star*, 25 February 1986
2 *Sheffield Star*, 23 December 1986

257

3 *Sheffield Telegraph*, 30 March 1987

4 *Boxing News*, 3 April 1987

5 *Sheffield Star*, 30 March 1987

6 'Boy boxer's amazing deal', *Sheffield Star*, 9 September 1987

7 'Youngster with the ring of confidence' by Jan Turner, *Sheffield Star*, 15 September 1987

8 Ibid.

9 Quoted in 'Prince of Pugilists', *Observer Life* profile by Kolton Lee, 15 January 1995

10 *Boxing News*, 7 April 1989

11 Interview with David Burrows by Daniel Herbert, *Amateur Boxing Scene*, December 1995

12 Interviewed by Gary Newbon for *The Crowning of the Prince*, Sky Sports, 23 December 1995

13 Quoted in 'Now Paul's pure Silk' by Mark Butcher, *Boxing News*, 26 January 1996

14 Quoted in 'The clown prince who dreams of being king of the ring' by Tanith Carey, *Daily Mirror*, 29 September 1995

15 *Boxing News*, 26 January 1990

16 *Sheffield Star*, 2 April 1990

17 Quoted in *Observer Life* profile by Kolton Lee, 15 January 1995

18 *Boxing News*, 1 June 1990

19 Quoted in *Sheffield Telegraph*, 10 July 1990

20 Ibid.

21 Ibid.

22 As David Prior spells out in his book *Ringside with the Amateurs* (Stantonbury Parish Print, Milton Keynes, 1995) the early 1990s were an extremely unsettled period for Britain's amateur boxing administration. In 1990 the full-time ABA executive director, Clive Howe, was suspended and then dismissed from his post, in an action which was later declared an unfair dismissal by an Industrial Tribunal. In September 1991 the *Daily Telegraph* published a story alleging financial mismanagement and unconstitutional behaviour in the ABA. The Sports Council became concerned about the ABA's lack of organization and administrative efficiency and held back part of their grant to the ABA, though they later reversed this move. Then in 1992 one of the ABA's major sponsors, the construction and engineering firm George Wimpey, decided not to renew their sponsorship. The ABA eventually accepted a number of recommendations from the Sports Council, including one reducing London's representation on the council to place it on a par with that of the provincial associations – a move which partially remedied a long-standing complaint of Ingle's.

Chapter 4 The Arabian Knight

1 Quoted in 'Tomorrow belongs to Hamed' by Chris Bryans, *Boxing Monthly*, January 1994

2 Quoted in 'Boxing clever with the world at his feet' by Stephen Biscoe, *Yorkshire Post*, 21 May 1994
3 Quoted in *Sheffield Star*, 23 September 1991
4 Interview with Naseem Hamed by Geoffrey Beattie, *Head to Head*, BBC Radio 5, 3 December 1995
5 *Sheffield Star*, 14 April 1994
6 Quoted by Paul Thompson in 'Naseem's delight!', *Sheffield Star*, 15 April 1992
7 'Hamed springs to victory', *Boxing News*, 1 May 1992
8 *Boxing News*, 8 May 1992
9 Quoted in 'Tomorrow Belongs to Hamed' by Chris Bryans, *Boxing Monthly*, January 1994
10 *Sheffield Star*, 17 August 1992

Chapter 5   Waiting for Mickey

1 *Boxing News*, 18 November 1992
2 *Sheffield Star*, 4 January 1993
3 Ibid.
4 Geoffrey Beattie, Interview with Naseem Hamed, 'Head to Head', BBC Radio 5, 3 December 1995
5 *Boxing News*, 28 January 1994
6 For instance, in early 1996 he agreed to send his aspirant, unbeaten middleweight Ryan Rhodes to work with Henry Wharton, Duff's European super middleweight champion, as a sparring partner for a week, and in 1995 his light welterweight, Jon Thaxton, worked as a sparring partner for Billy Schwer and Gary Jacobs.
7 *Boxing News*, 22 October 1993
8 'Tomorrow Belongs to Hamed', by Chris Bryans, *Boxing Monthly*, January 1994

Chapter 6   Frank Warren and the Big Breakthrough

1 Between 1990 and 1992 Duva promoted 56 'world' title fights, compared with 50 for Cedric Kushner, 42 for Bob Arum (Top Rank) and 31 for the Great Western Forum in Los Angeles. King remained, however, the dominant promoter within the WBC through this period.
2 Interviewed on *The Crowning of the Prince*, Sky Sports, 23 December 1995
3 *The Big Breakfast*, Channel 4, 4 December 1995
4 *Sunday Times*, 15 May 1995
5 Quoted in 'I will not change my style says champ Nas', *Sheffield Star*, 12 May 1994
6 'Prince of Darkness?' by Donald McRae, *Boxing News*, 12 August 1994

7 As before, these included charitable gestures, one of which was a fund-raiser with European Labour MP Roger Barton to raise money for the family of the Leeds boxer, Tony Silkstone, who drowned earlier that year.
8 Quoted in 'Prince in a hurry to claim his crown' by Neil Squires, *Yorkshire Post*, 16 August 1994
9 Quoted in *Sun*, 2 August 1994
10 Quoted in 'The Artist Known As Prince', *ID*, February 1996

Chapter 7   From Glasgow to Sana'a

1 *Sheffield Star*, 4 February 1995
2 *Sheffield Star*, 6 February 1995
3 *Sheffield Star*, 7 February 1995
4 Quoted in, 'High-speed Nas hit by drive ban' by Bill Brotherton, *Sheffield Star*, 4 February 1995
5 Quoted in 'Naseem beats up *Boxing News* man' by Claude Abrams, *Boxing News*, 3 March 1995
6 Quoted in 'Nas dedicates fight' *Sheffield Star*, 11 March 1995
7 Quoted in 'The ascendancy of the man who would be king' by Ricard Edmondson, *Independent*, 4 March 1995
8 Interviewed in the video, *Natural Born Thriller*, Sports Network, August 1995
9 Quoted in *Sheffield Star*, 2 March 1995
10 *Natural Born Thriller* video, Sports Network, August 1995
11 Reported in 'Coronation in the Yemen for people's pretender to the title' by Steve Bunce, *Daily Telegraph*, 4 April 1995 and 'The nation greets a hero' by Charles Smith, *Sheffield Star*, 4 April 1995
12 'Coronation in the Yemen for people's pretender to the title' by Steve Bunce, *Daily Telegraph*, 4 April 1995

Chapter 8   The Road Back to Cardiff

1 Quoted in 'Sky-high Nas!' by Martin Smith, *Sheffield Star*, 6 April 1995
2 Quoted in 'The end of an era' by Glyn Leach, *Boxing Monthly*, May 1995
3 'Pie in the sky for fans seeking a real deal' Reg Gutteridge 'Man About Town' column, *Boxing News*, 12 May 1995
4 'Warren hits back at the "sniping" campaign' by Harry Mullan, *Boxing News*, 26 May 1995
5 'Warren's leap to Sky leaves many fans grounded' by Harry Mullan, *Boxing News*, 14 April 1995
6 These included Wayne McCullough, Eamonn Loughran, Gary Jacobs, Joe Calzaghe, Billy Schwer, Michael Ayers, Adrian Dodson, Johnny

Armour and Paul Weir

7 With European and Commonwealth middleweight champion Richie Woodhall being the prime attraction

8 Quoted in 'Eu have blown it Chris!', *News of the World*, 24 September 1995

9 Quoted in *Esquire* magazine, July 1994

10 *Sun*, 18 November 1994

11 Including one which forced him to interrupt his routine for 16 hours of filming and preparation for a Sky TV advertising campaign in Blackpool, together with Ian Woosnam, Alan Shearer and Ian Botham.

12 From *The Crowning of the Prince*, Sky Sports, 23 December 1995

13 Ibid.

14 'GLOVESTRUCK' by Kate Thornton, *Daily Mirror*, 14 August 1995

15 'I'm not in love!' by Jan Vass, *Sheffield Star*, 15 August 1995

16 'Fighting race hate thugs helped me be No. 1' by Tanith Carey, *Daily Mirror*, 29 September 1995

17 'Sport Interview: Prince Naseem', *Total Sport*, December/January 1995/96

18 'No girl will rip me off – women are so devious it's untrue' by Steven Howard, *Sun*, 29 September 1995

19 Interview with Naseem Hamed by Geoffrey Beattie, *Head to Head*, BBC Radio 5, 3 December 1995

20 For example Jack Dempsey was backed and 'protected' during the twenties by Al Capone, while even his underrated light heavyweight conquerer, Gene Tunney, a good man by the dismal standards of his sport, felt it prudent to purchase the protection of the Philadelphia mobster Maxie 'Boo Boo' Hoff. And they were hardly exceptions. By the fifties it was rare to find a top fighter in some states in the United States without some kind of underworld backing or connection.

21 Joe Gans, Willie Pep, Jack Johnson (against Marvin Hart, if not Jess Willard), Pete Sarron, Jake La Motta, all 'threw' fights for payment, promises or under duress.

22 Three who come to mind from the late nineteenth century and early twentieth century were Peter Jackson (the finest heavyweight of the 1890s, whom John L. Sullivan refused to fight), Sam Langford (a brilliant middleweight who once mauled Jim Jeffries in a sparring session and went the distance with Jack Johnson, but was avoided by champions at three weights) and Harry Willis (an outstanding heavyweight against whom Jack Dempsey drew the colour line).

23 In addition to fighters specifically excluded because of their colour, among the many superb fighters who were denied title shots were Jack 'Chappie' Blackburn (a brilliant lightweight from the 1900s who went 68 fights without defeat against some of the best boxers from lightweight to heavyweight and eventually became Joe Louis's trainer), Mike Gibbons (who lost only three of his 127 fights and was a dominant figure in the welterweight and middleweight divisions in the 1910s), Packey McFarland (an outstanding lightweight who fought

before the First World War, losing only one of his 104 bouts and beating some of the best champions and challengers of his time), and Charlie Burley (one of the finest welterweight and middleweights of the late 1930s and 1940s, who whipped numerous top contenders and champions but never got a tilt at the title).

There were also those who had to pay an unconscionable price for their shot (Jake la Motta, for example, had to throw a fight against Billy Fox), or who waited and waited until they were too far past their best (Zora Folley, who was avoided by Floyd Patterson's manager Cus D'Amato, but eventually got his chance against Muhammad Ali), or those who waited and waited and still succeeded (Archie Moore, for example, who had been a contender for a decade before getting his title shot at the age of at least thirty-six, or Harry Greb, who, for at least six years before winning the world title – by which time he was blind in one eye – was the finest middleweight in the world, and one of the best light heavyweights too).

24 Two of the finest examples were from Britain: Jim Driscoll and Owen Moran – a pair of the greatest featherweights in the history of the sport.

Chapter 9   The Future Delayed

1 'Naz must beware those bright lights' by Reg Gutteridge, *Boxing News*, 5 January 1996

2 Quoted in 'Eloquent 'Enery says goodbye to the circus' by Frank Keating, *Guardian*, 27 January 1996

3 'Unhappy Henry is lost for words' by Harry Mullan, *Boxing News*, 26 January 1996

4 *The Crowning of the Prince*, Sky Sports, 23 December 1995

5 Quoted in 'The Artist Known as Prince' by David Sandhu, *ID* magazine, February 1996

6 *Prince Naseem – The Making of a Legend*, Labyrinth Video, 1995

7 *Boxing Monthly*, February 1996

8 Quoted in 'Hamed in airport "joke" row' by Steve Bunce, *Daily Telegraph*, 24 January 1996

9 Sky Sports, 14 March 1996

10 Held there because the British Boxing Board of Control refused to sanction the fight in Britain, fearing for Bugner's health and the sport's reputation – with some justification, as it turned out

11 By the time Lawal rose from the first knockdown and had been gazed at by Wiso Fernandez the bout was 13.5 seconds old, which, if he had stopped it then, would have given Hamed the fastest knockout by over five seconds, eclipsing the unfortunate record held by his Austrian promotional stablemate, Harald Geier. As it stands, the five fastest on record are the following:
   1 Daniel Jimenez v Harald Geier (19 seconds)
   2 James Warring v James Pritchard (24 seconds)

3 Bernard Hopkins v Steve Frank (24 seconds)
4 Gerald McClellan v Jay Bell (30 seconds)
5 Naseem Hamed v Said Lawal (35 seconds)

Chapter 10   Prince Naseem: The Present and the Future

1 Among the more celebrated bullies (outside the ring) in the game were
   some of the most courageous fighters in the sport's history: Jack
   Dempsey, Sonny Liston, Jake LaMotta, Rubin 'Hurricane' Carter,
   Don Jordan, Mike Tyson, to name a few.
2 'Nelson charts way to sink Naz' by Claude Abrams, *Boxing News*, 5
   January 1996
3 Almost a hundred years ago Bob Fitzsimmons moved up from
   middleweight to stop James Corbett for the world heavyweight title,
   and over five years later, at the age of forty, was still good enough to
   give away 47 lb and carve Jim Jeffries to pieces for seven rounds
   (before being stopped in the eight). He then went on to win the world
   light heavyweight title.
      Sugar Ray Robinson beat five world lightweight champions but
   never got a title shot at that weight. He then won the welterweight and
   middleweight titles and then gave away 17 lb to Joey Maxim in his
   challenge for the world light heavyweight title, winning almost every
   round before collapsing from heat exhaustion at the start of the
   fourteenth.
      Ezzard Charles was the best middleweight and then light heavy-
   weight in the world, but eventually lifted the world heavyweight title
   and defended it eight times, including once against Joe Louis, giving
   away 34 lb but hardly losing a round.
      And over the past decade there have also been several remarkable
   achievements in terms of giving away weight. Michael Spinks, one of
   the finest light heavyweights in boxing history, skipped cruiserweight
   to take the world heavyweight title from the 22 lb heavier Larry
   Holmes and went on to knock out the 6-foot-7, 17-stone Gerry
   Cooney. Sugar Ray Leonard won versions of every world title from
   welterweight to light heavyweight, while Tommy Hearns, who has
   done the same trick, is now attempting to go one better by lifting a
   version of the 'world' cruiserweight title. Roberto Duran reigned for
   seven years as world lightweight champion before moving up to win
   versions of the welterweight, light middleweight and middleweight
   titles. Pernell Whitaker has won every title from lightweight to super
   welterweight.

Appendix 1

Naseem Hamed's Record

Height: 5-foot-3
Fighting weight: 122–6 lb
Walk around weight: 128–32 lb
Chest: 36 in.
Reach: 63 in.
Waist: 29 in.
Thigh: 29 in.
Fist: 10 in.

Amateur Record Highlights
Club: St Thomas's/Unity ABC
Total bouts: 67
Wins: 62 (18 inside the distance)
Losses: 5 (all on points)
Hamed won all 23 bouts in the final two and a half years of his amateur career

Debut: Feb 24 1986 Peter Ironmonger W3 Sheffield

Titles:

1   1987 National Schools Junior A 32 kg champion (w Michael Wright)
2   1989 National Schools Intermediate 42 kg champion (w Scott Dann)
3   1990 NABC Class A 48 kg champion (w RSF 2 Richard Izzard)
4   1990 National Schools Senior 48 kg champion (w RSF 1 Dave Williams)
5   1990 Junior ABA Class B 48 kg champion, (w Michael Wright)
6   1991 Junior ABA Class B 51 kg champion (w Michael Wright)
7   1991 NABC Class C 51 kg champion (w Danny Adams)

International

In 1989 Hamed twice represented England Schools against Wales, winning both bouts; in 1990 he represented an English youth squad against the US Junior Olympic team, outpointing Dan Acevedo at 49 kg at Heathrow on 10 July 1990; in 1991 he was picked to represent England Under 19 in Tunisia but the trip was cancelled because of a shortage of funds.

Defeats:

1   1986 Vince Okenyi 1 3 (never fought him again)
2   1987 Paul Sweeting 1 3 (Hamed beat Sweeting on two subsequent occasions)
3   1987 Vic Brumehead 1 3 (Hamed had previously beaten Brumehead, and beat him again in 1988 and 1989)
4   1988 Jacob Smith 1 3 (Hamed had previously beaten Smith and beat him on two subsequent occasions)
5   1989 Dean Pithie 1 3 (Pithie beat Hamed in Junior ABA semi-final; Hamed had beaten Pithie in National Schoolboys semi-final earlier that year)

Last bout
17 Oct 1991 Michael Brodie KO 1 Manchester

Professional Record
Total bouts 21
Wins 21
KOs/stoppages 19 (8 in 2nd round, 4 in 3rd round, 3 in 4th round 2 in 1st round)

1992

14 Apr	Ricky Beard (8st-2lb)	w	KO	2	Mansfield (8–2)
25 Apr	Shaun Norman (8st 2lb 8oz)	w	RSF	2	Manchester (8–2)
23 May	Andrew Bloomer (8–8)	w	RSF	2	Birmingham (8–2)
14 Jul	Miguel Matthews (8–10)	w	RSF	3	London (8–7–8)
7 Oct	Des Gargano (8–8)	w	RSF	4	Sunderland (8–9)
12 Nov	Peter Buckley (8–10–8)	w	pts	6	Liverpool (8–7–8)

1993

24 Feb	Alan Ley (8–6)	w	KO	2	London (8–5–8)
26 May	Kevin Jenkins (8–6–8)	w	RSF	3	Mansfield (8–7–8)
24 Sep	Chris Clarkson (8–12)	w	KO	2	Dublin (8–10)

1994

29 Jan	Peter Buckley (8–10)	w	RSF	4	Cardiff (8–10)
9 Apr	John Miceli (8–8–8)	w	KO	1	Mansfield (8–10)
11 May	Vincenzo Belcastro (8–4–12)	w	pts	12	Sheffield (8–6)
	(European bantamweight title)				
17 Aug	Antonio Picardi (8–5)	w	RSF	3	Sheffield (8–5–12)
	(European bantamweight title)				
12 Oct	Freddy Cruz (8–9)	w	RSF	6	Sheffield (8–9–8)
	(vacant WBC International super bantamweight title)				
19 Nov	Laureano Ramirez (8–7–12)	w	rtd	3	Cardiff (8–10)
	(WBC International super bantamweight title)				

1995

21 Jan	Armando Castro (8–10)	w	RSF	4	Glasgow (8–9–12)
	(WBC International super bantamweight title)				
4 Mar	Sergio Liendo (8–10)	w	KO	2	Livingston (8–9–10)
	(WBC International super bantamweight title)				
6 May	Enrique Angeles (8–8)	w	KO	2	Shepton Mallet (8–10)

(WBC International super bantamweight title)
1 July   Juan Polo Perez (8–8–12)   w   KO 2   London (8–10)
(WBC International super bantamweight title)
30 Sep Steve Robinson (8–13–12)   w   RSF 8   Cardiff (8–13–4)
(WBO featherweight title)

1996
16 Mar Said Lawal (8–13)   w   KO 1   Glasgow (8–13–12)
(WBO featherweight title)

Appendix 2

Boxing Divisions and Terms

Boxing's Weight Divisions
1 kilogram = 2.20462 lbs
1 stone = 14 pounds
1 pound = 16 ounces

Junior Amateur (in kilograms)

Youth
Class 6:   45 48 51 54 57 60 63.5 67 71 75 81 91 91+
Class 5:   42 45 48 51 54 57 60 63.5 67 71 75 81 91

Schoolboy
Class 4 (senior): 42 45 48 51 57 60 63.5 67 71 75
Class 3 (intermediate): 39 42 45 48 51 54 57 60 63 66 69
Class 2 (junior B): 36 39 42 45 48 51 54 57 60 63 66
Class 1 (junior A): 32 34 36 39 42 45 48 51 54 57

NABC
Class C: 48 51 54 57 60 63.5 67 71 75 81 91
Class B: 45 45 48 51 54 57 60 63.5 67 71 74 77
Class A: 42 45 48 51 54 57 60 63.5 67 71

Senior Amateur
Light fly: 48 kg   (105.82 lb/7st 7lb 13 oz)
Fly: 51 kg   (112.44 lb/8st 0lb 7oz)
Bantam: 54 kg   (119.49 lb/8st 7lb 8 oz)
Feather: 57 kg   (125.66 lb/8st 13lb 11oz)
Light: 60 kg   (132.28 lb/9st 6lb 4oz)
Light welter: 63.5 kg(140 lb/10st)
Welter: 67 kg   (147.71 lb/10st 7lb 11 oz)
Light middle: 71 kg   (156.53 lb/11st 2lb 8oz)
Middle: 75 kg   (165.35 lb/11st 11lb 6oz)
Light heavy: 81 kg   (178.57 lb/12st 10lb 9oz)
Heavy: 91 kg   (200.62 lb/14st 4lb 10 oz)
Super heavy: 91 kg+(over 200.62 lb/14st 4lb 10oz)

Professional
Mini-fly (straw):   105 lb   (7st 7/47.62 kg)
Light fly (junior fly):   108 lb   (7st 10/48.98 kg)
Fly: 112 lb   (8st/50.80 kg)
Super fly (junior bantam):   115 lb   (8st 3/52.16 kg)
Bantam: 118 lb   (8st 6/53.52 kg)
Super bantam (junior feather):   122 lb   (8st 10/55.34 kg)
Feather: 126 lb   (9st/57.15 kg)
Super feather (junior light):   130 lb   (9st 4/58.96 kg)
Light: 135 lb   (9st 9/61.24 kg)
Super light (junior/light welter):   140 lb   (10st/63.50 kg)
Welter: 147 lb   (10st 7/66.68 kg)
Super welter (junior/light middle): 154 lb   (11st/69.85 kg)
Middle: 160 lb   (11st 6/72.57 kg)
Super middle: 168 lb   (12st/76.20 kg)
Light heavy: 175 lb   (12st 7/79.38 kg)
Cruiser (junior heavy):   190 lb   (13st 8/86.18 kg)
Heavy: Open

Acronyms

ABA	Amateur Boxing Association
HBO	Home Box Office
IBF	International Boxing Federation
KO	Knockout
NABC	National Association of Boys' Clubs
NABF	North American Boxing Federation
RSF	Referee Stopped Fight
TKO	Technical Knockout
WBA	World Boxing Association
WBC	World Boxing Council
WBO	World Boxing Organisation

Index

271